Initiating Change in Organizations and Communities

A Macro Practice Model

Initiating Change in Organizations and Communities

A Macro Practice Model

Peter M. Kettner
John M. Daley
Ann Weaver Nichols

Arizona State University

Brooks/Cole Publishing Company
Monterey, California

Brooks/Cole Publishing Company
A Division of Wadsworth, Inc.

Printed in the United States of America
10   9   8   7   6   5   4

Library of Congress Cataloging in Publication Data

Kettner, Peter M., 1936-
　　　Initiating change in organizations and communities.

　　　Includes bibliographies and index.
　　　1. Social work administration—Study and teaching—
United States.   2. Community organization—Management—
Study and teaching—United States.   3. Social work
education.   4. Organizational change.   I. Daley,
John M., 1938-   . II. Nichols, Ann Weaver,
1942-   . III. Title.
HV41.K47   1984   361.3'068   84-12054
0-534-03789-5

Sponsoring Editor: *Claire Verduin*
Editorial Assistant: *Pat Carnahan*
Production Editor: *Carol Rost*
Manuscript Editor: *Pam Howell*
Permissions Editor: *Mary Kay Hancharick*
Interior and Cover Design: *Katherine Minerva*
Art Coordinator: *Judith L. Macdonald*
Interior Illustration: *John Foster*
Typesetting: *Instant Type, Monterey, California*
Cover Printing and Binding: *R. R. Donnelley & Sons Co., Crawfordsville, Indiana*

PREFACE

This book presents an integrated model for initiating and carrying out a change process in human service organizations and in communitywide, human service efforts. We have created this model in response to the rapidly changing and sometimes even turbulent environment present in human services today. Pressures for change come from many directions. Consumers, professionals, politicians, advocates, taxpayers, funding sources, as well as others have widely divergent values and understandings of specific situations. As a result they may expect and even demand widely divergent remedies. The human service professional (administrator, manager, supervisor, direct practitioner, or community worker) is faced with the responsibility of providing effective service while, at the same time, responding to changing needs. We have attempted in this book to provide a model that will help human service professionals achieve these aims.

The model provides an orderly, systematic process for change, incorporates broad participation, and can be applied in either the organizational or community arenas. Implementation of the model requires the joint efforts of many organizations and people but is coordinated and facilitated by a change agent who may be a full-time direct-service practitioner, community worker, supervisor, manager, or administrator. Professional grounding of the change agent in a human service discipline (such as social work, psychology, counseling, or applied sociology) is assumed. Because the model places heavy emphasis on analysis, planning, monitoring, and evaluation, it lends itself well to demands for accountability by consumers and funding sources. In the model, the change episode entails tasks to be accomplished in nine separate and distinct, but nevertheless interrelated, phases.

Chapter overviews and objectives give the reader a frame of reference for the material to be presented. Case studies and questions at the end of each chapter provide an opportunity to apply the material covered. An outline of the tasks associated with each phase summarizes the process at the end of each chapter. Chapter summaries and discussion questions reinforce major points.

ACKNOWLEDGMENTS

Compiling this book has required a rather substantial investment of time and energy by a number of people. We are grateful to the following people who reviewed the book in various stages: Dr. Rino Patti, University of Washington; Dr. Daniel Rubenstein; Dr. Kitach Suh, University of Northern Iowa; and Dr. Patrick Wardell, Pennsylvania State University. To the masters and doctoral students at the Arizona State University School of Social Work who struggled with early drafts of the manuscript and patiently pointed out everything from unclear transitions to typographical errors, we express our appreciation. To Bob Moroney, who generously shared his knowledge and experience in helping us to shape the final product, we express our profound thanks. To our acquisitions editor, Claire Verduin, and to our production editor, Carol Rost, who guided us carefully through the review and publication process, we express our sincere appreciation. We also want to thank the copy editor, Pam Howell, for her thoughtful edit and her contributions to the book. To Laura Orr, Betty Wood, Helen Levy, and Margaret Roark, who always responded in a pleasant and understanding manner to every broken promise that this was absolutely the last draft to be typed, we owe our everlasting gratitude. And finally, to our families, who supported, encouraged, and sometimes did without us through the lengthy writing process, we express our deepest appreciation.

DEDICATION

In every graduating class, in every agency, in every program, some professionals are able to maintain a clear vision about what needs to be done in order to effectively meet the needs of clients, consumers, and community members and are firmly committed to seeing that needed changes eventually are made. Their work is a continual prusuit of excellence, whether in the classroom or in practice. It is they who make teaching a gratifying profession, and it is to them that we dedicate this book.

Peter M. Kettner
John M. Daley
Ann W. Nichols

CONTENTS

Initiating Change in Organizations and Communities

A Macro Practice Model

CHAPTER ONE

The Need for Change

OBJECTIVES

Studying the contents of this chapter should enable the reader to:

DESCRIBE OR EXPLAIN

The need for change in organizations and communities to refine human service delivery systems

Four recent trends in the field of human services that have provided impetus for change

The elements of planned change and criteria for judging when to engage in planned change

The role and responsibilities of human service professionals in initiating change

The risks associated with initiating change

The ethical considerations of the human service professional in initiating change

The pros and cons of alternative strategies for initiating change

The knowledge base that established an analytical framework for organizational and community change

Significant similarities and differences between organizations and communities

1

$\mathbf{O}$n a daily basis, social workers and other human service practitioners face problematical situations: A chronically mentally ill patient is discharged from a state hospital and has limited personal and community resources available to help him adjust and survive. Unemployment-insurance benefits run out for a young family who are evicted from their home and have nowhere to live. An isolated elderly person dies from malnutrition. A minority person identifies acts of discrimination against her child by school personnel. The worker's own agency consistently promotes only males to administrative positions.

In every instance the helping professional must make a decision. Is this a personal problem or a public issue? Should this situation be handled as an individual case or is it a symptom of a larger problem calling for other types of interventions? These are complex questions. The need to immediately alleviate human suffering on a case-by-case basis is clear, and commitment to do so is well established in the helping professions. Yet such alleviations alone do not resolve the larger problems. Individual problems may not be recognized or dealt with as public problems. Discrimination may go on; cultural differences may be ignored; needed services may not be developed; organizations and community service systems may continue business as usual.

Few human service systems are conceptualized and designed in ways that facilitate refinements. In the human services the tendency has been to plan for services rather than to plan for meeting needs. These services then take on a life of their own, and the needs of individuals and special populations may not be recognized or understood. When delivery systems become fixed and inflexible, the emphasis shifts from meeting clients' needs to surviving as an organization and to fitting potential clients into the services offered by the agency. The match between needs and services deteriorates. This process maintains the status quo and discourages program flexibility and experimentation (Moroney, 1977, p. 131). In a field where clients' problems and needs are constantly changing, many agencies resist pressures for change.

TRENDS CHALLENGING THE STATUS QUO

Several trends that have gained momentum in the 1980s are challenging the tendency of human service programs to maintain the status quo. These trends include the increasing focus on the needs of special populations, the decline in the resources available for human service programs, the increasing pressures for accountability in human services, and the introduction of new techniques for both management and direct service personnel.

The Needs of Special Populations

Rutledge (1975, p. 4) identifies discrimination as a persistent problem in our society:

> The denial of opportunity for equal participation in our social economy is one of those intractable and threatening problems. The persistence in our society of inequities based on race, color, national origin, and sex today appear to be due more to systems failure than to policy orientation. It is clear that equal opportunity is the law of the land, but the institutions and social processes of the country, more through inadvertence than through conscious intent, work to deny execution of that policy.

Warner (1977) points out that human service programs often perpetuate racism, sexism, and other forms of discrimination by addressing symptoms rather than causes and by excluding recipients from decision making. "Administrators themselves often decide for recipients what they need and what they receive. The recipients may well perceive such approaches as paternalistic and patronizing, constituting a perpetuation of oppression and powerlessness" (pp. 445–456).

Given the seemingly natural propensity of some service systems to be insensitive to the needs of special populations, individuals and groups have recognized increasingly that it is in their interest to organize for collective action. Collective power is a means for effecting change in the way human service programs are conceptualized, designed, and delivered. Groups have organized around common concerns and needs related to age, race, gender, sexual preference, marital status, handicapping condition, and many other characteristics. Formally organized groups have developed and used political, economic, and legal power to ensure attention to special needs and concerns. Funding requirements, policy guidelines, and legal precedents have established the rights of designated target populations to services.

As a result, human service organizations and programs have begun to be aware of the need for designing or redesigning programs specifically for special populations. Specialized programs designed to meet the needs of newly urbanized Native Americans, battered women, the developmentally disabled, and other special populations have begun to emerge. Devore and

Schlessinger (1981, p. 101) suggest that interventions designed to serve ethnic populations should be examined for their fit with special needs and life styles. Do the interventions recognize the significance of culture in shaping lives? Are they sufficiently flexible to take alternative world views into consideration? Do they guide practitioners in applying knowledge about alternative world views?

Although many specialized programs have been initiated as a result of political, economic, or legal pressures, others have been developed because human service professionals have recognized highly specialized needs. Regardless of the impetus, a heightened sensitivity to and a growing body of knowledge about the needs of special populations have increased awareness of the need for change in human service programs.

Declining Resources

Few human service programs are self-supporting. Most depend heavily on external funding for continued existence. Over the past 20 years, government funding has financed increasingly larger percentages of the cost of programs. Since 1980, however, the federal government has eliminated open-ended funding for programs, has consolidated earmarked funds into block grants, and has steadily reduced the percentage of the federal budget allocated to human service programs. The insecurity that accompanies these unstable and unpredictable funding patterns has become a force for changing arrangements that may otherwise have been considered sacrosanct.

Turem and Born (1983) point out that cutbacks ultimately have an impact on clients, and clients have a right to expect that decision makers will make choices based on what will most protect the clients' interests. The common strategies for dealing with funding reductions—across-the-board cuts and staff reduction through attrition—do not deal with the real questions being raised. More than the size of programs is being challenged. Some fundamental assumptions about social responsibility and about the mission and scope of public social provisions are being called into question. "If human service agencies fail to get across their message that they provide necessary social benefits and if they persist in conducting business as usual in miniature, they may find out that it may soon be too late to prevent their demise" (Turem & Born, 1983, p. 207). Turem and Born identify a number of alternative strategies that require fundamental changes in the way planning, funding, and delivery of services are conceptualized, designed, and implemented. In short, declining resources create situations that require change in human service programs. While serious concerns are being and should continue to be expressed about negative impacts on clients, at the same time opportunities should be seized to streamline, consolidate, and redesign in the interest of improving the quality of life for those served.

Accountability

Accountability, a term that came into popular use in the 1970s in human services, has been defined by Tropp (1974) as a legal obligation to account for the terms of a contracted transaction. These include obligations to the public, the agency, and the client to maximize effectiveness (measurable achievement of positive change as a result of planned intervention) and efficiency (optimum results for the lowest expenditure of resources, including time, money, and energy).

The *public* both funds and sanctions human services. Taxes provide the major share of human services funding. Private and corporate donations provide most of the remaining funds. In only a small percentage of human service programs do consumers pay the full cost of services received and are providers accountable only to their consumers. The public's contribution of tax and voluntary dollars together with its permission for human service programs to operate represent a sanctioning of services. This sanction establishes a trust that the authority and resources provided will be used in a way that maximizes benefits to clients and to the community. Daley (1976) describes a crisis of accountability as resulting from increasing pressure from funding sources for systematic evaluations of professional interventions: "Implicit in these demands by funding sources is at least the possibility that interventions or programs which are unable or unwilling to document the successful accomplishment of desired outcomes may suffer a reduction in their required resources" (p. 241). This oversimplification, however, should not obscure the fact that there are wide-ranging expectations for human service programs. Although all expectations cannot be met, accountability to the public has served an important function. In response to these differing expectations, human service programs have developed statements of intent. These statements provide a basis for accountability to the public.

Statements of intent, crystallized in the form of program goals and objectives, program plans, or contracts for purchase of services, also become the basis for staff accountability to the *agency*. In accepting public funding and sanction, the agency has agreed to provide services within specified limits. By accepting employment within an agency, a staff member either implicitly or explicitly agrees to operate according to the policies and procedures established by the agency. This agreement should never be construed to mean, however, that the human service practitioner imputes infallibility or owes blind obedience to the agency. Quite the contrary. The need for change should be assumed. Human service practitioners carry an ethical responsibility to identify negative impacts on clients and to initiate change. Change, however, can be effected in a variety of professionally responsible ways. Practitioners who choose to ignore either existing policies and procedures or the need for improvements in effectiveness and efficiency fail to fulfill their responsibility to the public, the agency, and the client.

Finally, and most importantly, accountability involves obligations to the *consumer*. Ultimately, this perspective is the one that should guide and direct decision making in human service programs. The consumer is investing time, energy, and sometimes money in the belief that a service or mix of services will improve his or her quality of life. In the marketplace, the consumer clearly expects that a product or service will achieve certain outcomes and meet certain standards of performance. In human services, accountability to a consumer involves attention to both effectiveness and efficiency. Obviously, outcomes for individual clients cannot be guaranteed in human services. Yet if an evaluation of overall worker performance or overall program performance shows no significant improvement in the quality of clients' lives, one must question the skill of the worker or the value of the program or service.

At the same time, it should be recognized that demands from the public and consumers may be made without knowledge of what is realistic or possible. Dialogue and education may be necessary. Regardless of these limitations, accountability and the related issues provided an important impetus for change in human service programs and organizations throughout the past decade.

Expanding Knowledge and Changing Technology

A fourth trend creating pressure for change in human services is expanding knowledge and changing technology. As defined by Brager and Holloway (1978, p. 47), *technology* refers to "the procedures, methodologies, and processes—the 'inventions'—through which an organization accomplishes its goals." They distinguish between social technologies, such as models or methods of practice, and physical technologies, such as scientific breakthroughs in electronics or medicine.

In a review of models and methods of treatment in human services, Parloff (1980, p. 11) discovered that the number of brand names of psychotherapy exceeds 150. "Each new form of psychotherapy poses a new theory or a substantial revision of an existing one" (p. 12). Analysis of research findings increasingly reveals some degree of relationship between outcomes for clients and a range of intervention characteristics (Parloff, 1980; Reid & Hanrahan, 1982). In response to a growing body of research and practice findings, specialized techniques have been developed for working with various problems, clients, cultures, practice models, and other variables. Publication of research and practice findings, then, provides another impetus for change in the ways in which communities and human service agencies respond to needs.

Likewise, new methods for planning, administering, and managing human services have been conceptualized, tested, and refined. This activity adds to the body of human service knowledge and techniques. Patti (1983), for example, provides a list of four distinctive elements of human service administration that, he says, is by no means exhaustive. He includes providing advocacy for client groups and issues, enlisting support and cooperation in the community, building internal consensus, and devising a specialized management-control system (pp. 27–33). Recent texts on human service administration have contributed significantly to a knowledge base for innovation and change in planning, administration, and management practices (Abels & Murphy, 1981; Hasenfeld, 1983; Lewis & Lewis, 1983; Miringoff, 1980; Patti, 1983; Skidmore, 1983; Weiner, 1982).

Turem and Born (1983, p. 208) discuss a range of physical technologies that may be used to increase the efficiency of human service programs. They include the use of word processors and microcomputers to reduce routine recording and reporting, interagency sharing of facilities or equipment to reduce overhead, and refined performance-evaluation processes to permit rewarding of productive workers. As with the knowledge explosion in clinical practice, these new perspectives on management help create an atmosphere in which change can be seen as positive and constructive.

WHAT IS PLANNED CHANGE?

Change—variation or alteration in form, state, quality, or essence—is a constant phenomenon in organizations and communities. If one were to count and to assess the force of all the changes affecting individual and social life, by far the largest number of changes and the most powerful ones would be those that are unplanned. Phenomena such as shifts in the age and ethnic composition of the population, technological advances, fluctuations in the economy, and substantial increases in divorce rates result from seemingly unrelated and uncoordinated decisions and actions by many people. Such change is spontaneous or naturally occurring, part of a developmental process, or the result of interactions of systems.

Planned change, the focus of this text, is distinguished from unplanned change by four characteristics: it is limited in scope, is directed toward enhancing the quality of life of clients, includes a role for consumers, and is guided by a professional practitioner who acts as a change agent. Planned change in our model is an intentional process, a conscious and deliberate intervention to change a specific situation. Sequentially, the change agent considers the possibility of improving the situation, develops a plan to guide the proposed change, and sees that the change is implemented. Usually the change agent, although a central actor in the process, acts in concert with others. This model draws on the ideas of planned or purposive change formulated by social workers and sociologists such as Lippitt, Watson, and Westley (1958), Warren (1971b, 1977b), Rothman, Erlich, and Teresa (1976), and Brager and Holloway (1978).

A planned change effort represents hard work and a substantial investment of time and talent. It requires mobilization of energy and resources that might otherwise be used for ongoing work with different purposes. Before initiating an episode of planned change, the practitioner should assess the situation carefully in order to avoid two pitfalls: unnecessary effort and hopeless effort. Some changes can be implemented through existing channels without the elaborate preparation and planning entailed in our model. Other changes, no matter how desirable, are impossible given the resources actually or potentially available. Chapter 3 provides a detailed process of preparing for change that includes assessment. Planned change should be considered when the practitioner judges that the following criteria are met: the status quo impedes—in some important way—meeting the needs of clients or contributes to social injustice; awareness of the situation exists or can be created so that support can be enlisted for change; change appears feasible; and change in the intended direction would not happen without the effort.

WHO INITIATES CHANGE?

Given the need for ongoing change efforts in human services and the trends supporting change, who is responsible for initiating change? There are differing opinions on the locus of responsibility. One view, widely supported in the literature on human service administration, is that the manager is responsible for recognizing the need for change and initiating it. Patti (1983, p. 36) states: "Conditions and processes within the agency will, from time to time, create problems or suggest the need for improvements that must be addressed by the administrator. Managers are, consequently, central actors in efforts to modify policies, programs, and procedures in agencies." In support of this position, Weiner (1982, p. 8) notes: "It therefore appears that a contemporary approach to human services calls for a dynamic, creative management, which connotes a continuous process of creation, the act of originating or causing to exist orderly processes within a constantly changing environment."

Brager and Holloway (1978, p. 1) make a strong case for the initiation of change by direct service practitioners because direct service workers are closest to consumers and change efforts should be made in response to consumer need. In addition, they contend that many potentially important contributions of workers have tended to be overlooked.

Resnick and Patti (1980, p. 3) support the position that change should be initiated from below for the same reason: change efforts by direct service workers are essential to keep the human services focused on the primacy of client welfare. Also, communication in organizations and communities has become increasingly complex, preventing the flow of information from direct service workers to administrators. Managers may be unaware of the need to refine programs and services if information about problems is screened out at lower levels. Front-line workers should be able to communicate their perceptions of the need for change in programs or services. Finally, change from below improves the work climate and worker satisfaction.

In our view, the responsibility for initiating change in organizations and communities rests with every human service professional at any level who comes in contact with or has knowledge of a situation where the need for change is indicated. All human service professionals should have a positive attitude toward change and a willingness to invest resources in it. Initiating change becomes especially difficult when human service professionals have negative attitudes. Patti (1983) cites a conversation between a consultant and a worker about the installation of a new information system. The worker did not find the reports useful and was asked whether he had discussed his opinion with the director: "Yea, he knows we're not too enthusiastic about the paper work. I've decided just to cut my losses. I save all the forms to do when I'm tired and then just get it out as fast as I can. Frankly, I don't know how accurate it all is, but that's not really my problem" (p. 32). Change requires energy, professional knowledge and skill, and a commitment to cooperation that leaves little room for the view that it's "not really my problem."

This text presents a model for change. The model identifies, defines, and describes activities that take place with the assistance of a change agent—a human service professional who facilitates the successful completion of the change effort. The change agent may come from any level within an organization or any part of a community. The change agent may be a direct service professional, a planner, an administrator, a manager, or a community worker. It is critical that a change agent understand the conceptual framework for the model and the logic of the change processes and their interrelationships; others who participate in the change effort, however, may carry out many of the tasks.

Risks and Costs

Although it is pleasant to envision a system where practitioners, managers, administrators, board members, politicians, advocates, clients, and others welcome change, such is seldom the case. Many fear change, resist it, and attempt to impose sanctions on those who initiate it. Human service professionals contemplating a change effort should consider carefully the potential risks and costs as well as the potential benefits. No change of significance is without risk, and all changes involve some cost.

One risk is the loss of colleague or community support. Direct service professionals are expected to devote most of their time to the provision of services—counseling, teaching, providing health care—and to directly related activities. Change initiatives may be seen by others, including colleagues, as detracting from these primary professional responsibilities. Further, in contrast to administrators, managers, planners, and community workers, direct-service personnel may be perceived as having limited knowledge about organizational and community change. A counselor may be viewed as thoroughly competent as a direct service provider but without credibility as a refiner of organizational policies or programs. The direct service worker runs the risk of being seen as acting improperly when engaged in change efforts, even when engaged in efforts clearly within the worker's expertise and professional arena. Because a worker's reputation may be challenged, it becomes especially important that the change agent adhere scrupulously to ethical and professional guidelines.

Ultimately involvement in change can affect one's professional future and job security. Negative perceptions by superiors can affect promotions and may lead even to loss of a job. We point this consequence out not to discourage initiation of change but rather to encourage careful consideration of the risks and consequences. The positive side is that if the change agent is disciplined and professionally principled in the change episode, many benefits can result that make the risks worth taking. Clients may benefit from the change, worker morale may improve, others may be inspired to initiate change, and the change agent may become respected as a dedicated professional. We believe that adhering to the principles of our proposed model will help minimize risks and promote positive results.

Ethical Considerations

Human service programs and systems should be effective and efficient in responding to the changing needs of diverse client populations. Our proposed model is intended to produce improvements in the quality of life of clients and staff by improving human service programs and networks. Admittedly, the proposed model might be used for other ends, some of which might work to the disadvantage of the clients of human service programs. We anticipate that two factors will provide at least some assurance that change will benefit the consumers. First and most important, the proposed model provides a strong ongoing role for the consumer during the change process. Consumers can (and should) be involved in each phase of the change episode. This involvement ensures that the change agent is accountable to informed clients.

A second factor is the professional values and ethics of the change agent, as well as the values of other participants. The reader may want to review, for example, the Code of Ethics of the National Association of Social Workers. At the heart of the value system of the human service professional—and critical to this model—is the concept of empowerment: self-determination and self-direction for individuals and groups within an interdependent society. A vision of social justice guides change in this model.

The practitioner working for organizational and community change must take a critical and analytical stance toward what exists and must encourage and enable client groups to take such a stance also. Illich (1970) cautions about the difficulty of critical analysis: "We are tempted to shore up and salvage structures rather than question their purpose and truth" (p. 68). The interaction between the clients and the change agent that is integral to this model provides the basis for critical analysis and for generating alternatives. The commitment to social justice and empowerment rather than to order and the status quo provides the direction.

Paulo Freire (1972), the noted Brazilian educator, recognizes both the difficulty of creating empowerment and the persistence of the status quo (p. 36):

> One of the gravest obstacles to the achievement of liberation is that oppressive reality absorbs those within it and thereby acts to submerge men's consciousness. Functionally, oppression is domesticating. To no longer be prey to its force, one must emerge from it and turn upon it. This can be done only by means of the praxis: reflection and action upon the world in order to transform it.

It should be noted that these proposed ends of change—improvements in the quality of life of clients by improving programs and systems—may not address the basic, root conditions (such as poverty, discrimination, and injustice) that cause clients to need human services. Redressing these basic conditions is a legitimate concern of human service professionals but is beyond the scope of this book. Yet modest change objectives that incrementally improve services can ultimately make significant contributions to the quality of life of individuals and groups who receive services as well as those who are involved in the provision of services.

Selecting the Means

The choice of modest change objectives is dictated in part by the recognition that the change agent in the proposed model is assumed to operate with limited resources and therefore must operate within specific limits. Most human service professionals carry responsibilities that require their full time, effort, and energy. Few jobs are structured to allow time for participation in change efforts. For this reason, we propose collaborative and educational strategies for initiating change. These strategic preferences reflect assumptions about the realities involved in initiating change rather than any inherent disinclination to use a conflict strategy. The following assumptions about realities favor collaborative and educational strategies:

1. The change agent usually operates with limited resources, including personnel, money, time, sanctions, and experience with making large changes. Collaborative and educational strategies tend to require fewer resources than do conflict strategies. As the strategies requiring the most modest investment of resources, they should be considered first (Brager & Holloway, 1978, pp. 140–141).

2. Collaborative and educational strategies have fewer potentially negative side effects. Because these strategies are generally acknowledged by other professionals as legitimate, the strategy itself is less likely to become an issue in the change episode. Collaborative and educational strategies are less likely than conflict to arouse opposition to the proposed change. Further, many confrontation strategies have generated effective defensive responses.

3. The change process can move from collaborative and educational strategies to a conflict strategy with fewer costs than would be encountered if conflict preceded collaborative or educational strategies.

4. Specific changes may be achieved more quickly using conflict rather than collaboration or education. However, collaboratively or educationally achieved changes tend to persist. Changes imposed by confrontation may be reversed by those upon whom the changes were imposed (Marris & Rein, 1973, pp. 239–296).

Although we acknowledge these strategic preferences, we find no theoretical or practical reasons that absolutely preclude the use of a conflict strategy. Change proposals regularly encounter opposition based on conflicting interests, values, and perspectives. At times, after careful analysis, the change agent may opt for a conflict strategy, as, for example, when the other strategies have been tried without success or when strong evidence suggests collaboration and education will not get the job done (Brager & Holloway, 1978, pp. 129–133, 140–146).

The change agent might also suggest the use of conflict or confrontation as a specific tactic within a broader collaborative or educational strategy. Conflict tactics, carefully selected and used, can be powerful tools for initiating change activities. As Coleman (1957) points out, one of the most powerful tools available to the less influential members of a community is the threat or use of conflict.

Consideration of conflict strategies is beyond the scope of this book.

Although we have chosen in this book to illustrate successful change efforts and potentially fruitful change opportunities consistent with a rational, participatory, collaborative approach, we acknowledge that in other instances conflict strategies may be required if the desired outcomes are to be achieved. Alinsky (1971), Brager and Specht (1973), and Cox, Erlich, Rothman, and Tropman (1979) address conceptual issues related to the use of conflict or mixed (collaborative and conflict) strategies especially at the community level. Huenefeld (1970), Kahn (1970, 1982), Nader and Ross (1971), and Oppenheimer and Lakey (1964) provide concrete tactics and techniques.

In addition to choosing a strategy, a change agent must decide the degree to which he or she will operate in public or behind the scenes. The proposed change model reflects a firm commitment to openness and honesty. Yet, to be effective, the change agent, acting as an advocate for the proposed change, uses a path more like inwardly spiraling circles moving closer to the desired future state at the center than like a straight line drawn from X (current situation) to Y (desired future situation). The change agent continually is testing participants' commitments to various possible formulations of the change opportunity, to objectives, and to courses of action during numerous private, informal meetings. During these sessions the change agent works behind the scenes, testing perceptions, considering alternatives, and learning from the participants as the process progresses. Yet even in private meetings the communication of the change agent is honest and open. As the change agent encounters differences of values or opinion or opposition to proposed actions, these are acknowledged. Opposition of key parties may indicate termination of the change episode or modification of the process, including a less visible role for the change agent. The key point here is that the visibility of the change agent or the change process should not be confused with the basic honesty and openness of the change agent and the change process. Working quietly should not be confused with deception.

Supports and Resources

The reader may be asking by this point: Should I attempt to change my program or service system? Can I make a difference? What supports and resources do I have for my change efforts? We are optimistic that a skilled, dedicated, disciplined change agent can make a difference in human service programs and systems. Change is both desirable and feasible. The alternative, to choose not to act, may result in continuation of harmful practices, ineffectiveness, inefficiency, or deterioration in the quality of services. These results are not consistent with the ethical commitments of human service practitioners. Although there are limits and risks to involvement in change, supports and resources are also available to assist the change agent.

A major resource and support is derived from the fact that the professions, human service organizations and systems, communities, and our society profess concern for the rights and dignity of individuals and for the effectiveness, efficiency, and responsiveness of human service systems. Within each of these networks, individuals and groups can often be identified who are willing to help build a base for moral, emotional, professional, and financial support. Further, human service professionals are protected from arbitrary retaliation for change efforts by civil-service codes, labor-union contracts, agency personnel policies, and grievance provisions of professional associations.

Initiating change can also bring professional credibility, status, and prestige to those involved in the effort. Policy makers, planners, administrators, managers, and community workers may be supportive of change efforts, especially if the change agent proposes changes that are viewed as improving the quality of life of clients through refinements in organizational or service-system functioning. Thus, although the change effort begins with risks and costs, the change agent can also call on substantial supports and resources. The objectives may be modest and the approach disciplined, but success is a reasonable expectation if the change agent is realistic and selective in choosing opportunities.

A THEORETICAL BASE FOR ORGANIZATIONAL AND COMMUNITY CHANGE

Models vary in the ways in which they relate to theory. Klein (1970) states that a model is "a way of stating theory in relation to specific observations. . . . Models are built from theories around a problem" (p. 9). Pincus and Minahan (1973), however, believe that a model "should be clearly differentiated from any substantive theoretical orientations being utilized" (p. xii). They see theory becoming so intertwined in many practice models that the purpose of practice is often dictated by the theory rather than by a clear notion of the function and purpose of the helping profession. There is, however, widespread agreement that models require theoretical underpinnings to provide a framework for analysis and to develop an understanding of the problem at hand.

The model presented here does not flow from a single theory. Rather, appropriate theoretical frameworks are selected for use in analysis of the change opportunity. Two frameworks—organizational theory and community theory—are considered to be basic to use of the model. Selection and use of either or both will depend on the arena in which the change will take place. In addition, other theoretical frameworks such as social learning theory, human behavior theory, or systems theory may also be used to understand a particular situation. Criteria for selection and use of theoretical frameworks is discussed in Chapter 5. At this point we will attempt to define briefly what is meant by *organizational theory* and *community theory* and to establish a context for their application.

Organizational and management theories have a long history and cover a wide range of perspectives. Weiner (1982, p. 38) divides organizational theory into two categories—traditional and emergent. Traditional theories include bureaucracy, scientific management, administrative management, human relations, systems, structural functionalism, organizational psychology, and sociotechnical systems. These theories provide a base for understanding, from both historical and developmental perspectives, the patterns of thought that have attempted to provide order in organizations while progressively increasing creativity and initiative. Emerging management-science theories, which are rooted in traditional theories, include contingency, decision, cybernetic, communication, game, quantitative, and market. Emerging behavioral-science theories include role, group dynamics, interorganizational relations, and planned change.

From the traditional theorists, change agents in organizations develop an understanding of some basic principles of organizational structure and function. Studying the rationale for hierarchy, authority, formal lines of communication, job descriptions, written job qualifications, clearly defined policies and procedures, and formal procedures for personnel selection, training, and development can help a change agent understand the dynamics of organizational life. Realizing that the functions of the administrator include planning, organizing, staffing, directing, coordinating, reporting, and budgeting can help a change agent understand the nature of administrative responsibility. Examining the theory of human relations can help a change agent understand the importance of employee-oriented management. Comprehending systems theory can help a change agent understand the interdependence among units in an organization and between the organization and its environment.

Among the emerging theories, contingency theory has developed some important themes for understanding and guiding the management of human service organizations. Predominant among these is the notion that the best way to structure an organization and to design work responsibilities, work flow, communication systems, and other organizational components depends on the purpose and function of the organization and the nature of the task. There is no one best way to organize.

Although they are not included in Weiner's classification scheme, we would add the contributions of Drucker (1954, 1964, 1974), which provide a philosophical, theoretical, and conceptual framework for management by objectives. A major goal for human service programs is to move the spotlight from process to outcomes. Drucker's work and the literature on implementation that has followed provide a framework for conceptualizing a management system focused on outcomes.

Defining community theory is perhaps more complex than defining organizational theory. Community theory involves a knowledge of both the history and concepts of community practice as well as a theoretical understanding of the meaning of *community*. For these understandings, we draw primarily on the work of Rothman (1979) and Warren (1978).

Rothman identified three models of community organization—locality development, social planning, social action—and later added a fourth—social reform (Rothman, 1979). These models are induced from descriptions of community work. They are analytically distinct but Rothman stresses that they are usually used in combination in practice. Rothman cites a scholar's description of community organization as "a practice in search of some theory" (p. 25). Despite this limitation, Rothman's models make an important contribution in that they describe alternative perspectives for analysis and intervention in communities.

The model of *locality, or community, development* stresses self-help and the strengthening of an indigenous capacity to deal with community problems and needs. Broad community participation in identifying and solving problems and meeting needs is facilitated by a professional enabler. Community members work cooperatively to reach consensus about community problems and responses to them. Common interests of diverse groups are stressed, using educational strategies and leadership development.

The model of *social planning* involves rational problem solving. Expert professionals guide the process; community influentials have central policy roles; and consumers are relegated to client and recipient roles. Modern social planning can be highly technical. Social planners gather and analyze data and projections, and function as program planners and evaluators. Planners use the rapidly expanding data base related to social concerns and produce studies, reports, and recommendations.

The model of *social action* seeks to restructure power relationships and change basic institutional arrangements. Working with oppressed or disadvantaged populations, the advocate/partisan organizer addresses issues of social, economic, and political inequity and injustice. Confrontation and negotiation are used to resolve issues that have been identified during the process of organizing the groups. Members of the organization are viewed as constituents and employers of the organizer, not clients. To a large degree members control the decision making.

The model of *social reform* resembles the social action model with one important difference: the decision making is done by persons outside the oppressed or disadvantaged group. Such advocacy on behalf of a disadvantaged group has strong historical roots; upper- or middle-class reformers have long sought to improve the conditions for the less fortunate. The social reform model mixes the social planning and social action approaches; it is a sort of genteel middle- or upper-class variant of social action. Decisions made by reformers often are based more on strong ideological positions than on a personal understanding of the situation of the less fortunate population.

To examine further the development of community theory, we turn to Roland L. Warren's sociological insights, which have informed the understandings of two generations of community workers in the United States. *The Community in America* (Warren, 1978) is perhaps the most lucid and influential scholarly analysis of communities and their change processes. Community can be defined as a locality or space, people or members, shared institutions and values, interaction, distribution of power, and a social system (Warren, 1978, pp. 21–51). Using these definitions, one can conceptualize community in much broader and more fluid ways than simply as a geographically defined locality. Collectively the members of a local or national organization such as the United Auto Workers could be perceived as a community. In any given locality health professionals might be defined as a part of the medical community. Those who share values supported by local or national religious groups might be considered a community. These varying definitions provide a range of options in selecting an appropriate arena for initiating change.

Cox (1979) notes that a community can be conceived of as the *context* for community work (a bounded site or place; shared demographic characteristics; shared institutions, values, norms, traditions; and a social system), a *vehicle* or means by which change is effected (an interaction or exchange among people and institutions; a specific distribution of power), and a *problem and target* of change efforts (pp. 224–234). Thus a community is the environment within which conditions, problems, needs, issues, and opportunities exist and within which change efforts occur; the means of change; and the target to be changed.

Understanding alternative concepts of organization and community, drawn from a growing body of research and theory, will provide a change agent with a knowledgeable and informed approach to the change effort. Appropriate theoretical frameworks, together with a thorough knowledge of the system to be changed, provide an analytical basis for understanding the need for change.

WHY A SINGLE MODEL FOR ORGANIZATIONAL AND COMMUNITY CHANGE?

It is becoming increasingly clear that, in discussions of systems change, organizations and communities are interdependent entities. Writers on community change discuss the need for an understanding of the role of organizations in that change (Grosser, 1976; Kramer & Specht, 1975; Warren, 1966). Conversely, those who write about the need for change in human service organizations focus on the need to understand organizations in the context of the larger community (Brager & Holloway, 1978; Resnick & Patti, 1980).

Moe (1966, pp. 361–362) cites some significant differences between organizations and communities. First, the community is a system of systems. Organizations, both formal and informal, are subsystems of a community. Second, the community is not centralized in the same sense as formal organizations. People in a community meet their needs through using a wide variety of institutions, none of which holds a dominant position in relation to others. Third, community as a system is implicit while organizations are explicit. Both goals and means are more clearly identified in organizations.

These differences are significant and should not be overlooked. The formal structure of organizations offers both strengths and weaknesses as does the less clearly defined structure of a community. In organizations, clearly defined purposes, goals, and objectives can be used for initiating change or as a target for change. Organizational structure defines channels and processes for change. As Grosser (1976) points out, "Because behavior in a permanent organization is prescribed by rules rather than by individual preference, predictability and control are facilitated" (p. 137). Division of labor permits a high degree of efficiency when mobilization for change is needed. By the same token the virtues of organizations can become liabilities when they lead to red tape, rigidity, and misdirected action. Perhaps of more consequence is that an organization tends to take on a life of its own and invest most of its energies and resources in maintenance and survival. This goal displacement, as it is often called, obscures social purpose and turns efforts inward toward self-protecting or self-aggrandizing objectives (Resnick & Patti, 1980, p. 3).

Similarly, in community interventions, the advantages of loosely defined structures can become disadvantages. Selecting the community as the unit of intervention has the advantage of setting more fluid, less rigid parameters on definitions of problems or needs. Organizations tend to plan for services, while communities provide contexts in which planning can focus on needs. Moroney (1977) cites a growing awareness on the part of local government managers and planners that a rational planning process is needed in human services. Rational planning allows for consideration of a wide range of options and can stimulate independence from the status quo by focusing on the needs of people rather than on the existing network of human service programs. These considerations are important strengths in community interventions.

However, the lack of formal organization and of a single set of defined goals and objectives is also a limitation. All of the steps of the change process—from identification through evaluation—become more complex, more time consuming, and more expensive as boundaries are expanded. Typically there are fewer clearly defined entry points for community change. Consumer participation may be more difficult to define and limit. The community change process, as a result of the complexity and vagueness of boundaries, may become less efficient.

In spite of the differences between organizations and communities, a single model of professionally assisted, planned change can be applied in both arenas. Both are complex, open systems influenced by the environment, and both involve diverse perspectives. Our model allows for the differences between organizations and communities while drawing together the common elements necessary for conceptualizing and implementing orderly change.

In summary, we see human service systems as operating in a dynamic environment. Remaining relevant to the needs and demands of that environment requires constant change. A series of trends supports the need for ongoing change. Change, in this context, is therefore positive and constructive. We recognize, however, that many people who control, influence, and carry out the functions of human service systems do not share this view of change. Change agents, therefore, take personal and professional risks. However, if the change agent operates in a sound, professional way and follows carefully thought out procedures, the benefits to consumers and ultimately to the system can far outweigh the risks involved. Given the values of human service professionals, initiating change is not simply an option. It is a professional responsibility. These convictions prompted development of the organizational and community change model presented in the following chapters.

SUMMARY OF MAJOR POINTS

1. Human service systems in organizations and communities have not always kept up with the changing needs of their clients.

2. Resolving problems on a case-by-case basis does not lead to recognition of the need for systemwide changes.

3. Four trends are providing impetus for systemwide changes: the increasing focus on the needs of special populations, the decline in the resources available for human service programs, the increasing pressures for accountability, and the introduction of new techniques for both management and direct service personnel.

4. Planned change is an intentional process of altering the status quo within an organization or community.

5. The responsibility for initiating change rests with every human service professional who comes in contact with or has knowledge of a situation where the need for change is indicated.

6. Change agents may risk loss of colleague or community support, loss of prestige, or even loss of their jobs, especially if the proposed change is controversial. Adhering to sound professional practice can help minimize risks and build support.

7. Change is initiated by human service professionals to promote self-determination, self-direction, and social justice for the consumers of services.

8. The model of change presented in this book favors collaborative and educational strategies but does not rule out the selective use of conflict.

9. Organizational theory and community theory provide knowledge for understanding the arenas in which changes take place.

10. The model presented in this book is sufficiently flexible to allow for initiating change in organizations or communities.

DISCUSSION OR SELF-STUDY QUESTIONS

1. Some might argue that the theme of Chapter 1—that change is needed in human service systems—is unfounded. The political philosophies, funding levels, and reporting requirements of various levels of government are constantly changing. If anything, human services need a period of adjustment without pressure for change. Do you agree or disagree? What counterpoints might be raised that would be consistent with the theme of this chapter?

2. How would you respond to a professional person who says, "Sure, I'm committed to initiating needed changes, but you just don't understand my agency. Granted, we could do a lot better in serving minority clients, but the director won't tolerate changes. He believes that what has worked for the past 20 years should work today. If you question him he can make life very difficult for you"? What are the appropriate professional roles and responsibilities of staff members dedicated to serving the needs of clients in such a situation?

3. How does the concept of empowerment for oppressed populations

influence change in human services? In your opinion, can oppressed people gain power over their lives through rational collaborative and educational strategies, or can meaningful redistribution of power come only through conflict?

4. Of what significance are organizational theory and community theory in initiating change? Speculate on some of the things you might do differently in initiating change in organizations and in communities.

SUGGESTED READINGS

Abels, P., & Murphy, M. J. *Administration in the human services.* Englewood Cliffs, N.J.: Prentice-Hall, 1981.

Brager, G., & Holloway, S. *Changing human service organizations: Politics and practice.* New York: Free Press, 1978.

Marris, P., & Rein, M. *Dilemmas of social reform* (2nd ed.). Chicago: Aldine-Atherton, 1973.

Rothman, J. Three models of community organization practice, their mixing and phasing. In F. M. Cox, J. L. Erlich, J. Rothman, & J. Tropman (Eds.), *Strategies of community organization* (3rd ed.). Itasca, Ill.: Peacock, 1979.

Rothman, J., Erlich, J. L., & Teresa, J. G. *Promoting innovation and change in organizations and communities.* New York: Wiley, 1976.

Weiner, M. E. *Human services management: Analysis and application.* Homewood, Ill.: Dorsey Press, 1982.

CHAPTER TWO

A Model for Organizational and Community Change

OBJECTIVES

Studying the contents of this chapter should enable the reader to:

DEFINE THESE KEY CONCEPTS

Antecedent conditions

Preparing for change

Planning

Implementing change

Change residue

Change process

Arenas for practice

Policy

Program

Project

DESCRIBE OR EXPLAIN

A practice model for change in organizations and communities

An episode of change

The nine phases of the change process

The two arenas of practice for change

The three approaches to organizational and community change

$\mathbf{E}$ntering a troublesome situation without the benefit of a practice model is something like trying to build a structure without a plan or blueprint. Progress toward the desired change is haphazard, lacks clear direction, and is inefficient. The well-prepared change agent enters situations with some framework for conceptualizing and assessing what is going on and with some guidelines about how to proceed in intervening for change. Frameworks practitioners use for conceptualizing and assessing situations are derived from theories that explain behavior. Practice models establish guidelines for intervention.

According to Kettner (1975), a model may be defined as "a coherent set of directives, . . . a pattern of symbols, rules, and processes, . . . [and] a statement of what the practitioner is expected to do" (p. 633). Models are designed to coordinate and integrate activities. Models for intervention with individuals and families (crisis intervention, behavior modification, psychosocial casework, and task-centered casework, for example) have been under development for many years. Models for intervention at the organizational or community level are just beginning to emerge.

One human service practice model that is well developed and explicated and that can be broadly applied is the problem-solving model. This model provides a systematic process for change that moves from identifying and analyzing the context or situation to specifying the direction and parameters of change to designing an intervention and controlling its implementation. The concepts and directives of the model are readily applicable to the organizational and community arenas. The process is orderly, and the framework is flexible enough to adapt to different systems and levels of change.

A limitation of the problem-solving model when applied to change in communities and organizations is that it begins with the identification of a problem. This process has proved to be appropriate for work at the direct practice or personal service level, but in some ways it is too narrow and confining for the organizational and community level. In organizations and communities, practitioners must not only solve problems but anticipate needs and plan for services. When used for intervention in organizations and communities, therefore, the problem-solving model must be expanded and adapted. It must become a model designed to initiate organizational and community change, even if a specifically identified problem is not immediately evident. As indicated in Chapter 1, initiation of change is the responsibility of all practitioners and should not be left to managers, administrators, and planners.

The task of the remaining chapters of this text is to propose and elaborate a model for initiating change in organizations and communities. While the process is based on problem solving principles, the model goes beyond the limitations inherent in focusing on problems alone. The remainder of this chapter outlines the features of the model in sufficient detail to provide a comprehensive overview. It begins with a discussion of an *episode* of planned change (the complete cycle of change-related activities within which the model is applied) and continues by presenting the model and discussing its three features: the *process*, the *arenas*, and the *approaches* to planned organizational and community change.

AN EPISODE OF PLANNED CHANGE

The community and organizational planned change process, which moves from identification and analysis of the opportunity for change through stabilization and reassessment of the change, comprises a series of activities. It occurs within a larger cycle, however, which will be referred to as *an episode of planned change*. The five elements of an episode of planned change are considering antecedent conditions, preparing for change, planning, implementing change, and assessing change residue.

Describing mental health social work services, Barker and Briggs (1968, p. 169) define an episode of service as "a cluster of activities that go together to achieve a social work organization's specified goal." Similarly, in organizations and communities, a planned change episode may be defined as a cluster of activities that go together to achieve a set of desired changes. An episode of planned change includes the full series of preplanning, planning, implementation, and follow-up activities. An episode of planned change may be completed in a relatively brief period of time, perhaps a few weeks or months, or it may extend over several years. The five components of an episode of change are described here briefly.

Considering Antecedent Conditions

Antecedent conditions are those circumstances existing prior to or at the inception of a change episode that set the stage for and influence the nature of the change effort. In an organization, antecedent conditions might include administrative style, relationships between administration and staff, morale, or the relationship of the organization to various elements of its environment. In a community, antecedent conditions might include general economic, political, and social conditions; the self-image of the community, or experiences the community has had with similar planned change efforts. Frequently, antecedent conditions include not only past experiences with deliberate attempts to change but also the results, or residue, of past change efforts.

One antecedent condition to be considered by the change agent in each episode of change is the role and location of the change agent in relevant organizational or community structures and processes. Change agents must place themselves within the change situation in relation to their:

- primary responsibilities (Is the potential change effort central to the change agent's job, is it tangential, or is it unrelated?)
- own power, influence, and authority (Can the change agent require completion of specific tasks, or must the change agent function essentially in a consulting or advisory role? What resources, including sanction to proceed, time, and information, are available for the change episode?)
- position in the organization or community in relation to other participants in the change effort (Is the change agent close to or distant from other participants; similar in perspective, values, and needs? Does the change agent have access to information? Will the change agent have the opportunity to participate in various change activities?)

Change agents recognize the impact of their position on the manner in which they pursue the change tasks. Based on a clear understanding of roles and relationships, change agents apply the proposed change model in a manner appropriate to the context of a specific change episode.

Preparing for Change

A specific set of tasks must be accomplished to prepare for the change effort. These tasks include considering antecedent conditions, identifying possible sources of relevant information, identifying the systems to be involved, obtaining sanction to intervene, and deciding to engage in a planned change effort. Each of these tasks is treated in detail in Chapter 3.

Planning

Planning activities are carried out in the first five phases of the change process. These phases are described and analyzed in Chapters 4 through 8 and consist of identifying the change opportunity, analyzing the change opportunity, setting goals and objectives, designing and structuring the change effort, and resource planning.

Implementing Change

Implementing change entails activating the intervention based on the planning activities. It consists of the following phases of the planned change process, which are described and analyzed in Chapters 9 through 12: implementing the change effort, monitoring the change effort, evaluating the change effort, and reassessing and stabilizing the situation.

Assessing Change Residue

Change residue refers to the aftereffects of organizational or community changes. Change residue may be intended or unintended, desired or not desired, tangible or intangible, specific or vague and elusive. Often planned change efforts are flawed by preoccupation with the change process to the exclusion of consideration of the results. The process may fail to lead to full implementation of the planned changes. Change efforts nearly always have some unintended consequences or unforeseen results. Thus assessing the change residue is a final and vital component of an episode of planned change.

Assessing the residue of change brings the episode full circle. The cycle is complete. The residue or results of each change episode become part of the antecedent conditions for subsequent episodes. Thus, the way in which earlier change efforts were conducted and their results will influence when, how, and if new planned change efforts will be initiated. Change residue will be further discussed in the chapter dealing with the final stage of the planned change process, Chapter 12.

Placing the organizational and community planned change model within the larger context of an episode of planned change enables the practitioner to examine the full scope of activities and factors relevant to intervention. It provides a comprehensive and holistic view of a change effort. The focus of the remainder of the text is on the nature and specific application of the planned change model.

DEFINING THE CHANGE MODEL

The model proposed here for organizational and community change includes three components: the change process; arenas for practice; and approaches, or types of interventive effort anticipated.

The change process involves nine steps, or phases:

Phase I   Identifying the change opportunity
Phase II   Analyzing the change opportunity
Phase III   Setting goals and objectives
Phase IV   Designing and structuring the change effort
Phase V   Resource planning
Phase VI   Implementing the change effort
Phase VII   Monitoring the change effort
Phase VIII   Evaluating the change effort
Phase IX   Reassessing and stabilizing the situation

Arenas for practice are organizations and communities. *Approaches*, or types of interventive effort, are the creation or modification of policy, the creation or modification of a program, or the initiation of a project. Each of these components is described briefly in this chapter.

NINE PHASES OF THE PROCESS

As indicated earlier, the process of organizational and community change is based on the problem-solving model but attempts to go beyond the limitation of first identifying a problem. For purposes of discussion, this process is presented in an orderly sequence of nine phases, as if they were strictly sequential. In practice, change efforts are never so straightforward and neat. Aspects of several phases may be undertaken simultaneously, as when exploration related to resource planning (for example, researching conditions for foundation grants) goes on while analysis of the problem is still under way. Information acquired in the monitoring phase might lead to modification of earlier efforts in designing and structuring. Phases are interrelated and dynamic, not static. A diagram with spirals and loops might be a more accurate representation of the actual process than is a straight line.

A full description and analysis of each phase of the change process constitute the major portion of this book (Chapters 4 through 12). At this point, brief descriptions of the phases provide an overview.

Phase I: Identifying the Change Opportunity

A change effort may be initiated in response to a condition, a problem, a need, or an issue. The first phase is a systematic definition of the nature of the change opportunity. In this phase the relevant actors identify the change opportunity, the initiators of change, the people likely to benefit from change, the target of change, and the people likely to be involved in planning and implementing the change. The change agent then initiates dialogue among relevant actors to clarify values and explore differing views.

Characteristics of the change opportunity—such as its complexity, intensity, incidence and prevalence, control, urgency, and duration—are identified, and data are collected to provide an information base that can be analyzed in the next phase.

Data contributing to awareness of and interest in the change opportunity come from multiple sources. Formal needs assessments conducted by community groups or human service organizations give impetus to change efforts. Public commentary on a newly recognized phenomenon in the community (for example, the limited or nonexistent resources for battered women) often stimulates action. And statistical data (for example, the number of women in the community who have been victims of physical abuse) help guide the planned change effort. Identification of the change opportunity defines the need for change and begins to suggest directions for intervention.

Figure 2-1 depicts the nine-phase change process. This is an artificial depiction for the purpose of conceptualizing the process and some of the

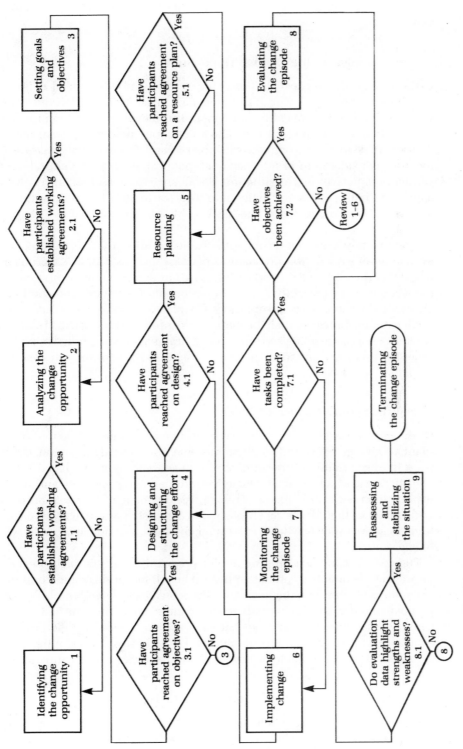

FIGURE 2-1. Nine phases of the process of organizational and community change

decision points. In practice, the process will seldom work in such a linear way.

Phase II: Analyzing the Change Opportunity

In the analysis phase, the definition of the condition, problem, need, or issue, and the data gathered during the identification phase are further studied. The purpose of analysis is to clarify, understand, and explain the dynamics and causes of the change opportunity. The practitioner looks for patterns in the data and makes linkages with theories and research findings. This phase also includes consideration of interpersonal, political, economic, cultural, and gender perspectives on the situation. The change agent and others involved assess alternative courses of action and their feasibility. The final product is an analytic statement that is the basis for developing appropriate change strategies.

Analysis may lead to a reconceptualization of the situation. Complaints from inner-city residents and business people that prostitution is a problem might initially suggest the need for intensive law enforcement. An analysis of the situation may reveal that many of the prostitutes are minors who have arrived in the community as runaways. Their lack of resources or of access to services contributes to their becoming prostitutes. The need to plan for shelters, crisis counseling services, and job training or educational opportunities for runaway youth might become evident as a result of an analysis of the situation.

Phase III: Setting Goals and Objectives

By detailing desired future states, goals and objectives give direction to the planned change effort and facilitate movement from study to action. Goals state the broad aims of the intervention. Each goal typically has a set of objectives associated with it. Objectives are derived from goals and make explicit the results anticipated. They express specific, measurable outputs and outcomes that can be accomplished in a limited time—usually a year or less. Objectives specify what is to happen, by when, and how the results will be measured.

The goals of an outreach program for pregnant teenagers might include improving the quality of prenatal physical health for mothers and children. One *outcome* objective might be to reduce by 50% the number of teenage pregnant women who show evidence of malnutrition at the time of delivery. One *process* objective might be that each pregnant teen identified by the school system be visited by an outreach worker within a week of identification for a discussion of available resources for prenatal care and treatment.

Phase IV: Designing and Structuring the Change Effort

Designing and structuring activities determine the organizational or structural arrangements that will facilitate achieving change objectives. During this phase, decisions are made about the focus and content of the policy, program, or project to be initiated. Details of the delivery of services and definitions of all service components are developed during this phase. Formal relationships and lines of accountability are specified. This phase entails choosing strategies, describing jobs, and elaborating work plans.

An organization may decide to establish job training for displaced homemakers. Designing and structuring activities include defining the kinds of services the program will offer, establishing how clients will enter and go through the program, developing staffing patterns, specifying roles and responsibilities, and establishing formal relationships and communication lines among staff members.

Phase V: Resource Planning

Resource planning entails analyzing the resources needed and determining the allocation of those resources. Anticipated costs of all kinds are identified. Resources, including funding and in-kind donations, are also identified. Expected resources are matched to the anticipated costs. Adjustments in expected resource levels or anticipated costs or both are frequently made, perhaps affecting which problem will be addressed, what the objectives will be, and what methods will be used. Finally, a budget is developed that ties resources to specific program objectives. Resource planning completes the preparatory phases of the planned change process.

If a policy is proposed at the state level to initiate mandatory counseling for custody cases, decisions must be made regarding location of the counseling services, sources and levels of funding, number of staff, qualifications and salary levels, office space, furniture and supplies, telephone costs, travel costs, and many other resource considerations. Planning for these considerations is accomplished in the resource planning phase.

Phase VI: Implementing the Change Effort

In the implementation phase, the change is put into effect. A coordinated sequence of activities is initiated that will put the plans into operation, put the structure into place, and carry out the objectives. The change agent works for compliance and performance, recognizing that adaptations and adjustments may be needed. Implementation may be carried out by entirely different people from those involved in the initial planning, so clarity about goals, objectives, responsibilities, roles, and resources is crucial. Technical tasks in this phase include initiating the plan of action, orienting the implementers, maintaining flow and integration, ensuring communication and interaction among the participants, and keeping activities on schedule. Interpersonal tasks include addressing resistance to change, promoting conflict resolution through problem solving, and ensuring compliance with the plan.

In the case of a project to develop a training program for people who will understand and work with Hispanic elderly, implementation would entail a series of activities. It would begin with meetings of consultants and teachers, the development and testing of resource materials, and the reworking or revising of proposed materials and activities not judged helpful or effective. The change agent would facilitate production of lesson plans and teaching manuals and would put the training into effect.

Phase VII: Monitoring the Change Effort

In this phase, the change agent keeps track of progress. Objectives and work plans will have specified dates for completion and criteria for successful accomplishment. The monitoring process checks to ensure that activities are completed on time and that results are as anticipated. A data collection system is instituted to provide the data and information needed to conduct monitoring activities. When monitoring reveals barriers or delays in progress toward expected outcomes, adjustments are made in some part of the implementation plan.

A family counseling program may plan to establish ten discussion groups designed to increase parenting skills. The coordinator reviews statistical reports after two meetings and finds that eight groups have the targeted number of participants (12 to 16) but two have only 6 each. Monitoring alerts the coordinator to the need to take action by combining the groups, canceling them, or recruiting more members, so that valuable resources will be used effectively.

Phase VIII: Evaluating the Change Effort

The purpose of evaluation is to provide information to make the change episode effective and efficient. While monitoring keeps track of the completion of activities and outcomes, evaluation places a value on their usefulness. Evaluation responds to the questions "Is the process effective?" and "Is the change effort making a difference in the situation it was designed to address?" Evaluation needs to be oriented to the clients. Evaluation in this model is an ongoing process that provides information that can be used to shape the direction of the change effort while it is under way.

The evaluation of a job training and placement program would address several aspects of the intervention. Participants and employers might assess the effectiveness of the training by analyzing skills needed and whether they were learned. Data on the dropout rate and reasons for it could provide a basis for decision making in the episode. Finally, the evaluation plan might include tracking graduates to see how many were successfully placed and how long they held their jobs.

Phase IX: Reassessing and Stabilizing the Situation

This phase entails overall review of the process and final adjustments in the change effort. It concludes the process of change. Every component of the planned change is examined, using information generated during monitoring and evaluation. As in other phases of the change process, the recommendations and opinions of consumers are sought. In this phase, practitioners try to stabilize identified strengths and correct weaknesses in the effort. Activities are identified that will lead to maintenance of the system as planned. Information and judgments about how the change process succeeded and failed may provide the basis for future planned change episodes.

A project to equip all public-transportation vehicles with devices to make them accessible to the handicapped might conclude with a final report detailing the results (number of buses and vans equipped, increase in riders, and other measures of accomplishment). The report might also include a recommendation for review of the routes to further enhance disabled citizens' access to public facilities.

TWO ARENAS

The second element of planned change is the arena of practice. Planned change in the human services occurs in the organization and in the community. The phases of the change process are the same in both arenas, and in either arena the approach to change may be through policies, programs, or projects.

Organization

In their classic work on formal organizations, Blau and Scott (1962) define an organization as a social unit comprising a number of persons "that has been established for the explicit purpose of achieving certain goals." Their discussion further suggests that a degree of planning is implicit in all formal organizations (p. 5):

> The goals to be achieved, the rules the members of the organization are expected to follow, and the status structure that defines the relations between them (the organizational chart) have not spontaneously emerged in the course of social interaction but have been consciously designed a priori— to anticipate and guide interaction and activities.

Human service organizations offer a wide range of programs and services, from mental health clinics to child welfare services to senior citizen centers, which provide socialization, treatment, or other services for groups and individuals. Most human service organizations (or social agencies) owe their existence to the concern of some individuals about a social problem. Interested legislators or citizens create an organization for a specific purpose, and planned change is a way to assure that the intended purpose is being accomplished.

Planned change may occur within, among, or through organizations. An example of a policy change approach within an organization is the revision of eligibility and fee criteria at a family counseling agency. The establishment of a well-baby clinic in an existing medical facility illustrates the initiation of a new program designed to change existing practices. When foster care agencies initiate a short-term outreach effort, such as a one-time attempt to increase the number of foster homes available for children with special needs, they are utilizing a project approach for planned change, working through an organization.

Community

Community is a more elusive concept than organization. Warren's seminal book, *The Community in America*, defines community as "that combination of social units and systems that perform the major social functions having locality relevance" (Warren, 1978, p. 9). The emphasis in his text is on communities as geographic entities that provide five basic functions for their members: production, distribution, consumption; socialization; social control; social participation; and mutual support.

For the purpose of this text, as well as in everyday life, *community* is used more broadly to refer to groups of people, institutions, or organizations that interact and share a common identity. Planned change may be implemented in geographic communities (a city), in functional communities (health-care professionals), and in communities based on shared values, interests, or characteristics (the Navajo community, the professional social work community, or the military veteran community). In human services, community often refers to a political subdivision such as a state, county, city, or township. Whether geographically or otherwise defined, communities are characterized by boundaries, sizable populations, and a considerable amount of diversity.

In distinguishing between communities and organizations, Moe (1966, pp. 361–362) notes that the community includes many organizations within its boundaries; the community is not structurally and functionally centralized in the same sense as a formal organization; and the community as a social system is a natural occurrence as compared to the planned nature of a formal organization. Communities and organizations are, however, interacting and interdependent entities. Organizations exist within and are given sanction by communities, and planned change in a community is typically implemented through organizations.

Communities utilize policy, program, and project approaches in planned change efforts. An example of a policy approach in the community arena is the development of guidelines for school desegregation. The establishment of a community mental health program is an example of a program approach. A communitywide coalition of agencies engaging in a short-term refugee relocation effort illustrates a project approach to planned change.

THREE APPROACHES

The third dimension of the organizational and community planned change model is the approach. An approach is the medium through which the change will be effected. Approach options include change through creation or modification of a policy, through a new or modified program, or through a

TABLE 2-1. Definitions of approaches to change

Approach	Definition of Focus
Social policy	"A social policy is a statement of social goal and strategy or a settled course of action dealing with the relations of people with each other, the mutual relations of people with their government, the relations of governments with each other including legal enactments, judicial decisions, administrative decisions, and more" (C. Schottland, quoted in Gil, 1973, p. 5). "Social policy [is defined] as planning for social externalities, redistribution, and the equitable distribution of social benefits, especially social services" (Rein, 1970, p. 5).
Organizational policy	"Policy refers to the formal strategies and decision rules by which objectives are to be reached. Policies are guides through which organizational members are directed toward objectives" (Filley, House, & Kerr, 1976, p. 303).
Program	"Program . . . implies a prearranged set of activities which specify the means to achieve a goal. In the public sector (health, education, welfare, and government), a program is formulated in order to provide services which accomplish defined human service objectives" (Delbecq, Vandeven, & Gustafson, 1975, pp. 1–2). "A program represents a conceptual synthesis of both an objective and a set of concrete actions directed towards its attainment" (Gates, 1980, p. 8). "Programming involves the detailed spelling out of implementing actions to carry out broad policies related to a goal" (Perlman & Gurin, 1972, p. 3).
Project	"The usual distinction between a 'program' and a 'project' is that a project is a single operating activity while a program comprises many such activities bearing the same general title" (Williams, 1976, pp. 272–273). "In organizations faced with a dynamic and changing environment, it may be desirable to structure some activities with considerable flexibility. Such structures could be highly adaptive and temporary, existing only for the life of an activity. This describes project structures or task forces" (Robbins, 1980, p. 273). "Segments of programs are often called projects" (Kahn, 1969, p. 215).

project. Table 2-1 lists several definitions from the literature that will suggest the boundaries of each approach. The remainder of this section presents definitions and describes the relationships of the three approaches and discusses the distinctive aspects of each approach.

Definitions and Interrelatedness of the Approaches

The *policy* approach is intended to be comprehensive and long range in nature. Policy in the community arena frequently is made by elected public officials. In the organizational arena policy is made by boards of directors. Frequently the authority to establish agency policy around day-to-day intra-organizational concerns is delegated to the agency director.

Policies set forth guidelines, frameworks, boundaries, and conditions within which programs are developed or administered. They are generally formulated as statements of principle or guidelines regarding the directions in which subsequent actions should proceed. Policy is usually implemented through programs or projects.

Title XX of the Social Security Act, passed in 1974, is an example of a policy. The law established five national program goals:

I. Achieving or maintaining economic self-support to prevent, reduce, or eliminate dependence
II. Achieving or maintaining self-sufficiency, including reduction or prevention of dependence
III. Preventing or remedying neglect, abuse, or exploitation of children and adults unable to protect their own interests, or preserving, rehabilitating, or reuniting families
IV. Preventing or reducing inappropriate institutional care by providing for community-based care, home-based care, or other forms of less intensive care
V. Securing referral or admission for institutional care when other forms of care are not appropriate or providing services to individuals in institutions.

Title XX also required each state and the District of Columbia to prepare a Comprehensive Annual Social Services Program Plan. This policy, passed at the federal level, required implementation through state and local programs and projects.

The second approach to initiating change is through the development or modification of a *program*. Programs are relatively permanent structures designed to meet ongoing client needs. Programs carry out policies that are intended to meet community or organizational goals.

In responding to the goals established by Title XX of the Social Security Act, states established, redesigned,or continued child welfare programs such as protective services for children. Within these programs, objectives were established regarding the identification and investigation of neglected or abused children and their families and the provision of services for them. These programs were designed in a manner consistent with the policies established by Title XX.

The third approach to initiating change is the *project* approach. A project can be carried out at the national, state, local, or agency level. Projects are typically highly flexible and short-term—often a year or less. The focus of projects tends to be narrow and specialized. Projects are typically responses to nonregular, if not unique, situations, needs, problems, or issues.

As child protection received increased emphasis and funding as a result of the passage of Title XX, many program administrators recognized a lack of knowledge and skill among their staff members, especially in highly sensitive areas such as sexual abuse and exploitation. Specialized training projects were designed and implemented to increase understanding of these problems and to develop skills for working with abusing or exploiting families. These projects were brief and allowed for flexibility in implementation by varying training methods, content, location, and other factors.

The three approaches to initiating organizational and community change are distinct and are discussed separately in the following sections. Yet they are also interdependent and interrelated. In some instances, their relationship can be diagramed as a hierarchy, with policy setting the parameters and direction, programs controlling the implementation, and projects dealing with special needs. This relationship is illustrated in Figure 2-2.

Yet such a neat hierarchical scheme is misleading. It should be understood that other interrelationships are possible. Projects operate within the context of a set of policies just as programs do. Policy can be implemented solely through programs or solely through projects. Also, projects can be the basis for subsequent initiation of programs or for policy changes.

An additional dimension is encountered when the community and organizational arenas are introduced. Policy initiated at the federal level may require the development of state policies, which, in turn, may require new agency policies. New agency policies may create new programs, which, in turn, may lead to the development of policies for specialized projects. In short, many interrelationships are possible.

The multidimensional change model presented in this text recognizes elements of interdependence and interaction between and among the three approaches. Although policy, program, and project approaches can (and do) occur in relative isolation from each other, we suggest that an integrated model—a holistic approach—will in the long run produce effective and efficient human services.

In many instances, a given human service intervention may involve two or three approaches in order to meet the full range of needs. A neighbor calls authorities to report an incident of suspected child abuse. After an investigation, the public social service agency refers the family for counseling. During counseling, the father's unemployment is identified as a contributing factor to the family disturbance, and he is offered an opportunity to participate in a retraining project for workers whose industries are closing down. The child, who is also experiencing difficulty in school, is tested and diagnosed as having learning disabilities. He enters a tutorial program at his school.

In this example, it was a *policy* (statutes relating to reporting suspected child abuse) that initiated referral to a specific family treatment *program*.

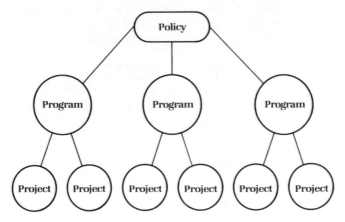

FIGURE 2-2. Interrelationship of policy, program, and project

While there, the father was enrolled in an employment retraining *project* and the child was diagnosed as eligible for a special education *program* provided under another public *policy* mandating equal educational opportunities for all children. Thus, an integrated model promotes accountability and effective and efficient use of resources.

Table 2-2 highlights selected similarities and differences of the policy, program, and project approaches to organizational and community change.

Policy Approach

The term *policy* as used here refers to formally adopted sets of decisions, parameters, and guidelines that define and determine the nature and direction of activity. Social policies define goals and strategies for dealing with social needs and the distribution of social benefits. Organizational policies direct action toward the achievement of objectives. Policy change or devel-

TABLE 2-2. Variables that differentiate policy, program, and project approach

Variable	Policy Approach	Program Approach	Project Approach
Function	To provide long-term guidance; establish guidelines and parameters	To meet permanent or anticipated steady, on-going need	To remedy unique situations or to use when standing structures and processes are inadequate
Time	Long, frequently indefinite and unspecified	Indefinite or ongoing services anticipated; time may or may not be specified	Short, usually one year or less; time usually specified
Objectives	Often remain at general level of specificity	Specific and related to both process and outcomes	Highly specific and outcome oriented
Target population	Very broad definition of categories of people	Client population usually defined, sometimes including eligibility criteria	Highly specific population
Geographical or system boundaries	Can be international, national, regional, statewide, local, agencywide, or agency subunit in scope	Can be international, national, regional, statewide, or local in scope	Can be international, national, regional, statewide, or local in scope

opment is undertaken in response to a condition, problem, need, issue, or situation in society, a community, or an organization.

The *function* of policy is to provide a context for resource allocation, delivery of service, or procedural change. Policies are generally expected to endure for long periods of time—even indefinitely—to provide stability and consistency to decision making and program development. Because of the long *time* period, as well as necessary political processes involved in securing support for proposed policies, the policy approach typically sets forth conceptual goals and broad mandates rather than specific *objectives*. The five Title XX goals illustrate the broad nature of policy goals.

The *population* covered in the policy approach usually consists of large groups and categories of people, defined by shared characteristics such as age, income status, or gender. *Geographical or system boundaries* may be international, national, regional, local, agencywide, or agency subunit in scope. The *content* of policy is focused on problems or needs of some segment

TABLE 2-2. Continued

Variable	Policy Approach	Program Approach	Project Approach
Content	Broad changes in social, economic, or organizational areas predicted or intended	Definite parameters set for service provision; expected results usually identified	Highly specific results expected and identified
Planning locus	May be planned at agency, local, regional, state, or national level	May be planned at agency, local, regional, state, or national level	Usually planned by persons close to the problem or opportunity who will closely monitor implementation
Implementation	Implementers can be separated by great distances with limited control exercised by planners	Implementers usually at delivery level, geographically or administratively removed from planners and administrators	Implementers usually in direct or close contact with project planners and administrators
Evaluation	Results usually measured in organizational or program changes or social-indicator changes for broad populations; cost/benefit analysis	Results and process both measured and evaluated	Result and process both measured and evaluated; outcomes or changes to specific situation and/or populations determine success

of society or organization, so broad changes in social indicators or service-delivery patterns may be anticipated as a result of the development of policy planning.

The *locus* of the policy approach to planned change is with groups or individuals authorized to make decisions or oversee the allocation of resources at the agency, community, state, or national level. *Implementation* can be far removed from planning, geographically or administratively or both. As a consequence, there may be confusion on the part of the implementers about the intent of a given policy or its feasibility. Unexpected consequences are often the rule, not the exception, and are difficult to remedy unless there is a close tie between the policy setting and the program development processes.

Policy *evaluation* examines data on changes in organizational practices, impact of programs, or broad social indicators. The focus of policy evaluation is on the impact on population groups in the area of social functioning addressed by the policy. Cost/benefit analysis is an important tool in policy evaluation.

Program Approach

The term *program* as used here refers to a range of services within a specifically defined category; they usually continue over a number of years and are sometimes permanent and are designed to meet a specifically identified and defined set of objectives and needs.

Program change or development is usually an ongoing *function*, when there is an expectation that a continuing service will be needed to resolve a particular problem or meet a particular need and that a time-limited approach would not be adequate. For this reason, programs are typically planned for an indefinite *time* and are terminated only by special action of a decision-making body. Program *objectives* are clearly defined and specify both the process of program implementation and outcomes in measurable terms.

Clients who are to be served by a particular program are usually defined, and these definitions may vary from the general (for example, all children who have experienced abuse, neglect, or exploitation) to the highly specific (for example, all juveniles between the ages of 13 and 17 who have been arrested for their first offense). Likewise, the *geographical or system boundaries* of a program can range from a narrowly defined community or neighborhood to international programs such as those provided by the Red Cross. The *content* of a program is a particular service or range of services to be provided, with expected results identified. Funding is usually limited to the provision of those services specified in the program description.

The *locus* of program planning can be at the agency, community, state, or national levels, depending on the jurisdiction of the program planners. Even when change is initiated at a local level, however, *implementation* eventually becomes the responsibility of direct service practitioners who may be several administrative levels removed from the change agents or instigators. The quality of preparation and the communication between planners and implementers can be factors in program success. Program *evaluation* is usually focused on both service processes and client outcomes or client satisfaction. Evaluation findings may be used to make decisions about program continuation or refinement.

Project Approach

The term *project* as used here refers to the development of specific sets of short-term, result-oriented activities providing support or direct services in response to unique conditions, problems, needs, or issues, in a community or organization. Projects are selected as the preferred structure when there is no expectation that the need identified requires permanent services or when experimentation is called for.

The *function* of project development is to respond to unique needs, issues, or conditions in organizations or communities. Projects supplement long-range, comprehensive change efforts; they are incremental and flexible and provide rapid feedback for adjustment in subsequent change efforts. The *time* for the project approach is specific—typically one year, more or less, for implementation after the planning period. *Objectives* for projects are time-limited and highly specific in terms of expected outcomes.

Projects are the most precisely targeted of the change approaches, with a highly specific *population* defined. They may be used in a wide range of *systems or geographical* areas, although they tend to focus on a specific component of an agency or a highly defined and limited community. The *content* is clearly defined, with explicit expectations with respect to results.

The *locus* of project planning tends to be with agency or community personnel or others who are close to the problem to be addressed. *Implementation* is carried out within close geographical and administrative proximity to planning. *Evaluation* of projects includes process measures but relies mainly on outcome measures directly related to accomplishment of the objectives.

THE RATIONALE FOR PLANNED CHANGE

What is gained by a planned, analytical, and disciplined manner of initiating organizational or community change? Basing human service interventions on a clear definition of the change opportunity, an analysis of the situation, the specification of desired outcomes, the development of planned acquisition and allocation of resources, the selection of methods of action, and the assessment of results will increase the probability that the intended results will be achieved. Participation of those affected by the change effort is built into the process to make it responsive and democratic.

The proposed model for initiating organizational and community change focuses on a dynamic interaction. It is based on interplay between the needs and the expectations of a community or a specific client/consumer population on the one hand and the performance of the agency and its services on the other. Because of the nature, scope, and complexity of human needs and services, and the systemic nature of the human service "industry," a change model cannot focus exclusively on the internal functioning of the service agency or on one-to-one direct client services. It must begin with an identification and analysis of conditions, problems, needs, or issues, and proceed systematically forward to develop interventions that will make a difference in an intended direction. This text advocates the use of a rational change model because it promotes a positive approach to initiation of change, maximizes resources for the benefit of clients, and generally leads to enhanced accountability, predictability, and responsiveness to human problems.

SUMMARY OF MAJOR POINTS

1. A practice model gives guidelines for planned change in organizations and communities.

2. The process of organizational and community change occurs within a larger cycle called an episode of planned change. The five elements of an episode of planned change are considering antecedent conditions, preparing for change, planning, implementing change, and assessing change residue.

3. The model for organizational and community change has three components: the process, the arena for practice, and the approach.

4. The process of planned change entails nine phases: identifying the change opportunity; analyzing the change opportunity; setting goals and objectives; designing and structuring the change effort; resource planning; implementing the change effort; monitoring the change effort; evaluating the change effort; and reassessing and stabilizing the situation.

5. Planned change occurs in two different arenas: the organization and the community.

6. Community and organizational changes utilize three approaches— policy, program, and project. The policy approach is comprehensive and long range and is concerned with the establishment of guidelines for the direction of action. The program approach is systematic and is concerned with service delivery to meet ongoing client needs. The project approach is specific and short and concerns an immediate or specialized community or organizational need.

7. The use of a planned change model in the organizational and community arenas makes coherence between intentions and outcomes likely and generally leads to enhanced accountability, predictability, and responsiveness to problems.

DISCUSSION OR SELF-STUDY QUESTIONS

1. The direct service workers in a child welfare program have been expressing concern that decisions that have an important impact on services to clients are being made at higher levels in the organization. Workers have not been consulted prior to these decisions. They would like to have a voice in developing new policies and procedures that affect service delivery. One

worker suggests that a delegation should approach a sympathetic supervisor to raise their concern. Do you agree? If a delegation goes, what should they do before the meeting?

2. A Presidential commission has reported that the U.S. educational system is failing to prepare students well for technical careers in science and math. Responsibility for delivery of education rests with the community. What kind of approach might you suggest to address this problem, and why?

SUGGESTED READINGS

Filley, A. C., House, R. J., & Kerr, S. *Managerial process and organizational behavior.* Glenview, Ill.: Scott, Foresman, 1976.

Kettner, P. M. A framework for comparing practice models. *Social Service Review,* 1975, *49,* 629–642.

Perlman, R., & Gurin, A. *Community organization and social planning.* New York: Wiley, 1972.

CHAPTER THREE

Preparing for the Change Episode

Initiating change can be an expensive undertaking in time and energy, social costs, and money. A decision to become involved represents a commitment to use resources wisely and efficiently. It is therefore incumbent on the change agent and other involved parties to think through, in a systematic way, some of the issues and considerations surrounding the possible change episode. As noted earlier, an episode of community or organizational change may be considered analytically to consist of five components: considering antecedent conditions, preparing for change, planning, implementing change, and assessing change residue. This chapter explores antecedent conditions and preparation for change.

THE PROCESS OF PREPARATION

Preparation activities develop a frame of reference for the planning and implementation phases that follow. Specific tasks must be completed to increase the probability that subsequent change activities will be effective—that is, will lead to intended and desired results. Five essential preparation tasks will be discussed: considering antecedent conditions; gathering preliminary information on needs, results, approaches, and resources; identifying the participants; obtaining sanction to intervene; and deciding to continue the change process. Although these tasks will be discussed separately, in practice the professional change agent often accomplishes several tasks at the same time. For example, the change agent in an organization may at an early stage discuss with the agency executive the nature of the problem, the results the executive expects from a change episode, and who should be involved. The change agent may also ask the executive to establish a planning committee. Thus, in a single interview with the executive, the organizational change agent performs several preparation tasks. Similarly, a community change agent might carry out more than one task in a single interview with a community leader, resource allocator, or consumer of services.

Preparation for change is a continuing process leading to the planning phase. Participants explore potential change opportunities, using new information to develop new insights, expectations, and commitments. A continuous weighing of the strengths and weaknesses of each option is a basic feature of preparation, just as it might be in comparison shopping for a home or an automobile.

Some preparation tasks are similar to tasks found early in the planning phase itself. Identification of the antecedent conditions and consideration of preliminary information are similar to elements of the first three steps of the planning phase (identifying and analyzing the change opportunity and setting goals and objectives). Identifying participants and obtaining sanctions to act are similar to the interactive (interpersonal and political) tasks in all phases of the change process. The products of preparation are initial drafts of shared insights, expectations, and commitments. If the process continues, these initial insights, expectations, and commitments will be evaluated and revised periodically.

The change process as described here requires completing specific preparation tasks. Failure to do so may lead to inappropriate or ineffective change activities. Failure to identify the outcomes expected from the change effort may result in unrealistic expectations. For example, in considering a new program designed to train physically disabled adults for employment, some may expect radical changes in laws, buildings, and transportation, while others expect only minor modifications to existing programs. Early identification of at least general outcomes can help achieve consensus about the direction of the change effort. Preparation activities also develop a set of shared expectations about the change process itself. Who should take which roles and responsibilities? Should deliberate, professionally assisted change be pursued? Which strategies will most likely produce the desired changes? Potential resources must also be considered. In addition, during the preparation phase the people and interests involved develop initial commitments to the change efforts to follow.

Finally, one possible, but frequently overlooked, key decision of the preparation phase is not to continue the change process. Under certain circumstances further activities are inappropriate. At other times, even though change is needed, it is not possible. Time, expertise, sanction to act, and other resources may not be available, possibly precluding a change effort (Kahn, 1969, pp. 1–59, 328–340). Therefore, preparation for change has serious implications for the subsequent process.

PREPARATION TASKS

Considering Antecedent Conditions

Antecedent conditions provide the context within which a change episode will take place. Consideration and assessment of those conditions are thus logical first tasks in preparing for change. Past experiences, relationships, and interpersonal, intergroup, and interorganizational dynamics all influence the way in which a change episode will be perceived and accepted. Levels of trust, motivation and morale, and perceptions of the impact of change can determine success or failure.

A new and well-funded training program was planned in a large state agency. The planning effort began with an assessment of training needs. To the dismay of planners, responses were highly negative. The general theme of the responses was "I have already completed too many of these forms and nothing has ever happened. Why don't you put more effort into actual training and less into surveys?" Failure to assess antecedent conditions resulted in a setback for the planning and implementation of the program.

Considering antecedent conditions involves developing answers to a series of questions: Who will be affected by a change? What impact will a change have on these individuals, groups, and organizations? How will a change proposal be perceived by those affected? What prior experiences have participants had with change efforts? Who is likely to support and who to oppose a change and why? Careful involvement of all the people affected can help change agents answer these questions and decide whether antecedent conditions support a change. A political candidate routinely considers these factors during early decision making about whether to run for office because of the need for popular support. More often than not these factors are overlooked in initiating organizational and community change.

Gathering Preliminary Information on Needs, Results, Approaches, and Resources

During preparation for change, the change agent identifies sources of information that may be of use in this episode. As sources are identified, each is evaluated for its relevance. Some information is discarded, some is used with caution, and some is judged to be relatively useful and is pursued. In many ways, preliminary consideration of relevant information involves a quick preview of some of the early phases of the change process. Such information can help the change agent identify and analyze the need for change, expected outcomes, approaches to change, and potential funding sources.

Information on the need for change. Preliminary data collection and analysis, using at least the knowledge and information of key participants, will help begin to crystalize the need for change. People and interests involved may be potential or actual consumers of services, citizens, influential people in the community, direct service personnel, administrators, organizers, or planners. These persons often act through voluntary associations, service or planning agencies, political structures, or other formal organizations. They may be stimulated to act because of personal experiences or for less direct reasons, including altruism.

Key participants use preliminary information as the basis for agreements about the nature of the change opportunity and the probable results of the episode. Frequently this shared appreciation is couched in the most general terms ("to help sexually abused children," "to assist handicapped persons to become economically independent," or "to increase the number of minority mental health professionals"). The lack of specificity may allow participants with diverse views to agree at least to begin the change process.

Key participants will have formed perceptions of the need for change based on their individual, and perhaps collective, sources of information. Participants bring with them values, beliefs, facts, and experiences. The change agent facilitates the process by providing information to the participants. This shared information contributes to the formation of a consensus about the nature of the opportunity.

Early data and information should include at least a chronology of events or critical incidents leading up to the need for change. Frequently, viewing the present in the context of the past can shed light on possible reasons for the current situation and can influence the direction of the change effort. Examining the history of a situation involves looking at information about how long the condition, problem, need, or issue has existed, how it has changed over time, its dynamics, and possible causal or contributing factors. This information helps explain the development of the need for change. Many organizational and community change efforts are undertaken in response to situations that have evolved over an extended period of time. Often systems affected by the situation have made some gradual accommodations to it. The change agent needs to be aware of historical roots and the concomitant adjustments in order to understand sources of resistance and targets for change.

An example may illustrate historical dynamics and the process of accommodation. Parents are concerned about the quality of education in an elementary school, which they see as having deteriorated over the last eight years. The teachers have become accustomed to a permissive administrative style, with no overall school goals or planning. While the parent/teacher council was active, there were still field trips, a classroom volunteer program, and other enrichment activities, but about five years ago the council ceased functioning. A strike had closed all the schools for several months, and the district withdrew support funds for parent/teacher councils. Because of the absence of parental involvement and administrative oversight, each classroom became an independent unit. School grounds were littered, there were few special events, and there was poor coordination of classes. Although teachers deplored the absence of school spirit and the low morale among staff, they liked the freedom they had to do whatever they wanted with their classes. They were not accountable to anyone, and they did not have to coordinate their efforts with those of other staff members. Neighbors complained about the rowdiness of the children waiting for school buses and wanted the school district to place a guard on duty to establish control.

Knowledge of the history is useful in understanding the dynamics of the situation and identifying appropriate responses. It helps avoid interventions based merely on symptoms ("rowdy children"). It suggests areas for change (administrative performance and style, parental involvement, and teacher participation in school planning). Developing a list of critical incidents can facilitate the analysis of the history. Table 3-1 presents such a list.

TABLE 3-1. Critical incidents list

September	1977	Mr. O. begins his tenure as principal of Elm Elementary School.
Fall	1979	Schools are closed because of teachers' strike.
April	1980	Parent/teacher councils lose school-board subsidies under the new budget.
June	1980	Mr. O. disbands the parent/teacher council at Elm School.
February	1981	The school board receives first complaints about the littered schoolyard at Elm School.
May	1981	A delegation of parents visits Mr. O. to discuss the lack of field trips and special activities.
September	1981	Mr. O. announces that because there are no helping parents, the school bulletin will not be published this year.
October	1981	The principal and the school board receive complaints about noise and disorder at bus stops in front of Elm School.
January	1982	An attempt by a small group of parents and teachers to reestablish the parent/teacher council fails because of low turnout.
September	1982	The principal is visited by representatives of the neighborhood homeowners' association urging that he request children not to cross their yards and leave litter on their way to school.
March	1983	The school board and the principal receive a letter of concern from the neighborhood homeowners' association about the appearance of Elm School grounds and the behavior of children before and after school.
November	1984	A Girl Scout troop meeting at Elm School makes posters and tries to initiate a "Keep Our School Beautiful" campaign.
March	1985	The neighborhood homeowners' association presents signed petitions to the school board requesting guards or monitors at the school bus stops to maintain order. The association threatens newspaper publicity about their complaints and the lack of action by the board.
April	1985	Parents and a few teachers meet to discuss how to improve conditions at Elm School.

In examining the history, the change agent should explore how long the situation has been regarded as a problem and who perceives it as needing change. Some situations have existed for many years without being regarded as potential targets for planned human service intervention. Only in the past decade have programs for displaced homemakers been developed, although divorced women have long needed to find careers and to assure an adequate income for themselves and their dependents. Heroin and other hard drugs were used in poor neighborhoods in cities for many years, but not until drug use became prevalent in the suburbs was it perceived as an area for substantial human service programming. Questions to be asked include: Did the behavior change? How? When? What caused the change in perception? How was the condition previously handled? Can information, education, or training counteract established traditions? Will new structures and processes be needed to effect change, or can existing structures be used?

The need to identify, collect, and consider information in a preliminary way must be balanced against the costs of developing this information. Lindblom (1970, pp. 291–301) describes administrators' use of limited information. Administrators typically cannot afford to collect complete information. Similarly, other change agents must operate within the limits of time and other resources. They usually work with incomplete information and information that is not of the best quality, especially during preparation for the change episode. The existing data may be old, may cover slightly different populations, may touch only tangentially on the change opportunity at hand, or may have other limitations.

Creativity and flexibility are essential characteristics of the change agent when there is no opportunity to develop new data and existing data must suffice. One technique frequently available and appropriate is to use multiple sources of preliminary data. By combining data that individually suffer from known or suspected limits, the change agent can have more confidence in common points than would be possible using any one source (Webb, Campbell, Schwartz, Sechrest, & Grove, 1981). Thus, creative use of existing data is often required, and tradeoffs in the quality or quantity (or both) of information are often necessary. The change agent seeks the best information available or capable of being developed with the resources at hand.

Using this information, the change agent and other key participants attempt to develop a preliminary formulation of the situation in an attempt to discover the degree of consensus or disagreement. Broad definitions are appropriate and useful in order that possible participants and directions for change not be prematurely eliminated.

Information on expected results.   Defining the results desired entails consideration of participants' expectations of the ends of a possible change episode. What, exactly, are the expected results? The professional change agent must help key participants make their expectations explicit. For a single episode, is the agency director hoping to initiate a change that will improve the quality of services? Is a funding source attempting to maintain the same level of services with reduced funding? What does the change agent expect? What do potential beneficiaries of the change expect? At times, key participants may have implicit and inconsistent or even conflicting expectations for the results of an episode of change.

Clearly, when dealing with diverse people and interests, the change agent may not be able to reconcile expectations or even find it necessary to do so. The change agent must, however, be sensitive to varying expectations and avoid encouraging unrealistic expectations. It may be possible to reconcile some expectations and accommodate others by using broad definitions at this early stage of the change process and by emphasizing commonalities and similarities rather than differences. Some differences must simply be accepted as inevitable, and possible reconciliation must be deferred to a later time. At this early stage, it is sufficient if the participants move incrementally toward a definition of the expected results of the change episode.

The results expected, however, must be both desirable and feasible. Desirability refers to agreement by participants that some future state is preferred to the present state. Feasibility refers to agreement that it is in fact possible to achieve the desired future state. Thus, participants must have a common understanding of both the current situation and the desired future situation. Absolute, irreconcilable disagreement about the results expected may suggest that deliberate change as defined here is not possible and should not be pursued. Other interventions (for example, contest strategies such as negotiation or arbitration) may have to be pursued. The change agent considers these various factors when deciding whether deliberate change is indicated.

A product of the preparation stage of the change process should be a written statement of general outcome expectations that encompasses as wide a range of perspectives as possible yet avoids skirting any major areas of disagreement. Stating alternative perspectives on expected outcomes is acceptable if agreements cannot be reached and if key proponents wish to continue to participate in the effort (as they should if any change is to be effected).

Information on approaches and resources.   A final commitment to a policy, program, or project approach (or some combination) need not be made until the design and structure phase is reached. Again, however, early consideration can help determine the degree of consensus among key participants and can help guide data collection and analysis. A cursory assessment of the situation helps clarify thinking in this area.

For example, the legal or policy base for current practices should be assessed for its soundness and scope. Poorly conceptualized and defined policies can lead to ineffective implementation and dissatisfied consumers. If laws or other policies are poorly designed or are nonexistent, a policy approach should be considered as at least a part of the change effort. If the policy foundation is sound but the implementation phase is poorly designed or carried out, program or project approaches should be considered. A program approach is appropriate for the modification of an existing program or the creation of a new one. A project approach is appropriate when creativity, innovation, and flexibility are important. Discussion of possible approaches in the preparation stage helps clarify these issues and establishes a basis for further study, analysis, and dialogue.

Likewise, discussion of potential funding sources is important in the preparation stage. Existing agency budgets (either individually or combined in some way), client fees, new public funding, grants, contracts, and other sources should be considered. The pros and cons of generating private sources of support rather than public funding should be discussed. The major consideration, however, should be feasibility. What might such an undertaking cost, and is it likely that some funding sources will be willing to underwrite the costs? If the change does not seem fiscally feasible at this point, the change agent should consider continuing the change effort through to the design and structure phase in order to develop a proposal that can be used as a basis for the pursuit of funding.

Identifying the Participants

A third preparation task involves the initial identification of individuals, groups, organizations, and interests who will participate in the change process. In this section, these participants are described and their functions and relationships are discussed. Frequently problems develop in the change process when the right persons or interests are not involved. Needed information, resources, or cooperation may be withheld if individuals, groups, and organizations representing various interests have not participated. For example, problems can easily arise when plans for change are developed by one group with the expectation that an entirely different group will implement the change.

During preparation for the change episode the change agent should list the actual and potential participants. This list will be revised periodically during the planned change process, as some participants are added and others withdraw for various reasons. Nevertheless, identifying the participants at this early point helps the change agent to consider in a disciplined, structured manner who will be or should be involved, in what capacity, when, and why. This listing prevents resistance by key participants because of their being left out early in the process through oversight. Drawing up such a list is a participatory process. The change agent has primary responsibility for ensuring that this vital task is completed. Other participants assist by suggesting others for the preliminary list and by responding to this working document periodically during the change episode.

The participants include the change agent system, the initiator system, the client system, the target system, and the action system (Lippitt, Watson, & Westley, 1958; Pincus & Minahan, 1973). A relatively simple episode of community change will identify the possible participants.

In a rural community, a teacher observed migrant farm workers' children having difficulty concentrating on their schoolwork. These children reported they were too hungry to work; they had not eaten since the previous day. The teacher discussed this problem with the public health nurse, who visited the migrant camp on a local farm.

Migrants were living under extremely primitive conditions. They lacked food, warm clothing, and adequate shelter. Several families lived in a small hut, which lacked electricity and running water. The nurse provided some information to the mothers of the migrant families and discussed the situation with the local health planner. The planner remembered that earlier he was approached by a labor organizer who had described similar conditions. The planner accompanied the county health officer on a visit to the migrant camp, verifying the observations of the nurse and the organizer. They approached the owner of the farm, who agreed the migrants' living conditions were not what he'd like them to be, but stated he was doing the best he could for the migrants while trying to stay solvent in a highly competitive agricultural business.

The planner suggested that perhaps outside resources might be available if the farm owner would invest his time and resources in a concerted effort to meet the needs of the migrants. With some reluctance, the farm owner agreed to cooperate in an effort to improve the migrants' conditions as long as he was not (as he suspected) singled out from the other owners as a target for the labor organizer's efforts to unionize the migrants. The health planning agency appointed a special task force to explore the migrants' needs and status and to recommend ways to improve their living conditions.

Participants in the change effort are defined and discussed here using this simple episode to illustrate their functions and the relationships between and among them.

The *change agent system* is both the professional engaged in a planned change process and the change agent's sanctioning institution (Lippitt, Watson, & Westley, 1958, pp. 10–12; Pincus & Minahan, 1973, p. 54). In the migrant illustration, the change agent system consists of the health planner and the health planning agency, which sanctions the special task force. The change agent may be a policy maker, planner, administrator, or direct service professional. What is important in the definition is that the change agent engages in deliberate, professionally assisted change. Typically, the change agent is employed by a human service organization and derives sanction at least in part from this employing institution. At times, however, the change agent is given sanction by a group or community, as when a neighborhood group gives legitimacy to a change agent acting in a voluntary capacity to assist the group. In some situations the change agent may even seek to change his or her employing institution, with or without its sanction. The public health nurse might decide that it is necessary to change public health department policies that work against the interests of the migrant children even if the department opposes the changes. Obviously, decisions to take on one's own agency should be thoroughly considered, as the implications are quite serious. Nevertheless such situations do occur.

The *initiator system* is composed of those people who bring a condition, problem, need, or issue to the attention of the change agent system and request action. Multiple initiators are common. The initiator system may or may not be the expected beneficiary of the change episode. Their function is to raise the question and to ask for action. In the migrant example, the schoolteacher and the public health nurse are the initiator system.

The *client system* is that set of individuals, groups, organizations, or communities who are the expected beneficiaries of the planned change. Again, multiple beneficiaries are common (Lippitt et al., 1958, pp. 12–14). The client system does not have to ask for help or engage the change agent's services in order for the change episode to benefit it. This broad definition of the client system facilitates conceptualizing a wide spectrum of beneficiaries and thereby helps to build a broad support base.

A useful distinction can be drawn between primary and secondary beneficiaries. *Primary* beneficiaries are individuals, groups, organizations, or communities whose quality of life is directly and tangibly improved as a result of the planned change. Primary beneficiaries are those most easily identified as having gained from the change. *Secondary* beneficiaries are those individuals, groups, organizations, or communities whose quality of life is less directly and tangibly improved as the result of planned change but whose status nevertheless is improved as a result of the change. Using the migrant situation to illustrate, a change episode that results in improved sanitation and nutrition for the migrant families might benefit the children and their families directly (primary beneficiaries). The local school and the community in general would also benefit but less directly, making them secondary beneficiaries. In the local school, teachers and children might function better if the migrant children's nutrition and general health improved, and the community in general would benefit from less potential for communicable disease epidemics and better general economic conditions based on healthier and more productive farm workers. Some of these potential components of the client system might not ask the change agent for help. Nevertheless, each can be seen as benefiting from the change. A major contribution of our inclusive definition of *client* is that each beneficiary can be appealed to on the basis of enlightened self-interest to support the planned change effort (Alinsky, 1971, pp. 53–59; Blau, 1964; Daley, 1971, pp. 54–71).

The *target system* is defined as those individuals, groups, organizations, or communities the change effort needs to change or influence in order to achieve the objectives (Lippitt et al., 1958, pp. 21–50, 185–216; Pincus & Minahan, 1973, p. 58). Target system components may be the change agent or the sanctioning institution itself as well as initiators or clients. The target system may change through time. For example, in the migrant situation, if a personal hygiene approach is proposed by the schoolteacher, public health nurse, or public health officer, the target system may initially be the children and their families. In time, if a public sanitation approach is proposed by the health planner, the target system may become the owner of the farm. At another point, the target system may be the school system, with efforts directed toward initiating a breakfast or lunch program at no cost to children of migrants. The target system must be kept flexible. New targets can be expected to be added and old ones dropped as the change process develops.

Finally, the *action system* includes individuals, groups, organizations, and communities who attempt to accomplish the tasks and objectives of the change process, including implementing the planned changes. The change agent facilitates and coordinates the activities of the action system to ensure all are working toward the same desired results. There are two kinds of action systems: the planning system and the implementing system.

The *planning system* is defined as those actors who provide legitimate and needed input into the planning phase of the change process—up to the implementation phase. This system may include initiator, change agent, client, and target systems. Obviously the planning system can become complex and can pose special management problems for the change agent if not carefully and sensitively organized and utilized. Planners develop the framework or blueprints for action. They often constitute a study committee or task force. They define and analyze the change opportunity, set objectives for the change, explore alternative ways to achieve the objectives, and structure resources around a specific approach. In the migrant illustration, the planning system might include the health planner (the change agent), the health planning agency (the sanctioning institution), the schoolteacher, the labor organizer, the public health nurse, and the county health officer (the initiator system), the migrant families (the client system and the target system), and the farm owner (the target system and, perhaps, the client system). Other potential planners might be influential people in the community (for community legitimacy) and health professionals (for professional expertise).

The *implementing system* has responsibility for or has a legitimate and necessary role in implementation of the planned changes. In many, if not most, instances, the planners are different from the implementers. This fact can have significant implications for the process presented in the remainder of this book. In the migrant illustration, implementers might include various health professionals, school personnel, the farm owner, and the migrant families themselves. Often the primary beneficiaries (the migrant families) are not considered implementers, but they, in fact, have a significant role to play.

Overlapping roles are possible and often desirable for participants in an episode of planned change. Overlapping roles provide vital continuity during the episode. For example, several advantages can result if the change agent consciously builds in specific overlapping roles for the planners and implementers. The probability is increased that the plans developed will be implemented. During the early planning activities, the involvement of implementers ensures that their perspectives, concerns, and questions about implementation will be considered. During implementation, involvement of planners ensures that their ideas and commitments will be represented. This proposed arrangement will make less likely a pattern frequently observed in human service systems: plans made by one set of actors are not implemented or are implemented ineffectively by another set of actors. In these cases, the implementers do not understand the proposed change or do not agree with the changes. As a consequence they do not support the implementation plan (Pressman & Wildavsky, 1979). Similarly, including targets in planning and implementation tends to increase the probability that planning recommendations will be implemented effectively. Returning to the migrant illustration, involvement of the migrant families and the farm owner (along with influential people in the community and health professionals) in the planning increases their commitment to carry out the recommendations of the special task force. Failure to involve any of these interests during the planning might sow the seeds of subsequent problems with implementation.

A general depiction of the relationships of the participants is suggested in Figure 3-1.

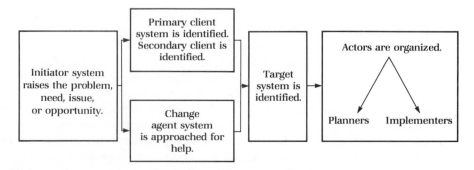

FIGURE 3-1. Relationships of participants in planned change

Obtaining Sanction to Intervene

A fourth major preparation task is obtaining sanction to intervene. Sanction may be derived from a number of sources including laws and regulations, court decisions, administrative authority, citizens, political leaders, influential people in the community, and experts among the participants. Frequently, multiple sources combine to provide the sanction.

Although formal sanctions and mandates play an important role in legitimizing change efforts and are routinely obtained by the change agent, equally important informal sanctions frequently are overlooked.

Change agents (and attempts at planned change) historically have experienced serious problems when various groups have contended they have been inappropriately excluded from or given limited participation in decisions affecting their lives. Blacks, Hispanics, Native Americans, the poor, the handicapped, women, students, and the elderly all have mounted successful campaigns either to withhold sanction from planning and implementation efforts or to obtain increased participation in the planned change process. Within an organization, where administrative sanction is crucial, change efforts have been challenged because appropriate sanction either was not obtained or was not communicated to relevant parties.

A crucial component in gaining legitimacy for the change effort is therefore the participation of the right people, groups, and organizations in the change process (Altschuler, 1970; Arnstein, 1969; Goodman, 1971; Lloyd & Daley, 1971). Professionals (direct service personnel, administrators, resource allocation planners), politicians, citizens, consumers, and influential people seek input appropriate to their status. The composition of the group of participants significantly influences how the planned change tasks are defined and the outcomes of the change process. Involvement of key people and interests is necessary for the process to be effective at all (Blau, 1964; Daley, 1971; Mott, 1968; Weissman, 1970).

Participants should have relevant expertise, power, and interests; in particular, the change agent should recognize that consumers have specific and unique expertise as consumers. The participation mixture can be expected to vary during the phases of the change process. For example, consumers might be heavily involved during problem or need identification, and service providers might be involved during program design. A short illustrative list of variables to be considered in choosing the participants would include: consumer/provider status, expertise, age, sex, race, power, socioeconomic status, and area of residence. Kahn (1969) characterizes these variables according to competing sets of values, preferences, and interests.

The concept of *representativeness* is significant in a discussion of participation (Alexander, 1976; Alexander & McCann, 1956). If indirect participation (through representatives) is used, the nature of the representative relationships and process needs to be consciously analyzed by the change agent. If, for example, a Black representative is the method of involvement chosen by the change agent to involve Blacks, do the represented persons, groups, or organizations recognize this representative as legitimate? Was this person chosen by the group represented? Does this person see those represented as a constituency? Is there adequate interaction between the representative and those represented? These and other questions must be satisfactorily resolved if representatives are to participate in the planned change process.

For both ideological and practical reasons, therefore, participation of diverse interests and perspectives is essential. Yet this prescription is easier stated than accomplished. Engagement of diverse interests and perspectives in the change process is a complex and at times frustrating task of the change agent. In one sense the change agent may be viewed as balancing the benefits for participants in the process against the costs of participation. On a practical level, participation of diverse interests and perspectives takes time and other resources. Participation of diverse elements may make the change process complex. Motivating participants is an ongoing and often frustrating task of the change agent (Alinsky, 1971, pp. 53–59; Brager & Holloway, 1978, pp. 82–92; Rothman et al., 1976, pp. 22–57; Tropman, Johnson, & Tropman, 1979). Yet investments of time and other resources in encouraging participation are justified ideologically and, on a practical level, can contribute to a realistic and acceptable product of the change process. These ongoing investments are made with full recognition of the costs of the participatory process.

Deciding to Continue the Change Process

Successful completion of preparation requires that a formal decision be made to continue the change process. Again, the change agent facilitates the process whereby this decision is made. A working consensus about the nature of the change opportunity is necessary at this point among key people and interests. Some may end or modify their participation because they disagree with the working consensus or with the results expected from the change episode.

As noted earlier, one possible, but frequently overlooked, decision is not to continue the change process. For various reasons, in some situations the process should be terminated at this time. Perhaps sanctions are lacking, a problem resolves itself, or resources are not available to meet the need in question. In each of these situations, it might be wise to terminate change efforts. Perhaps no further action is feasible at this point.

If, however, the decision is made to engage in the formal organizational or community change process, the products of the preparation tasks are useful as preliminary documents. In sum, the successful completion of the preparation tasks sets the stage for the change activities that follow. Although modifications are expected, a foundation for an effective and efficient, deliberate, professionally assisted change process has been established.

Case Study

A student intern was placed in a family service agency in Claridge, a city of about 100,000 people. As part of a classroom assignment she wrote a paper on crisis services for rape victims. Because of her heightened sensitivity to this issue, she began to ask questions and collect information about the availability of services in Claridge. She found that the problem was handled exclusively by the police. Counseling services were provided by existing agencies only if sought out by the victim. Little expertise was available in the community on understanding the nature of the trauma or providing appropriate and timely services.

After discussions with her executive director and several police officers, she was given sanction to hold some preliminary discussion sessions with key people to decide whether further action was appropriate. When she approached the president of the Chamber of Commerce, she learned that he opposed any effort to offer rape counseling services. He felt that identifying such a need might give the city a bad reputation and frighten newcomers and consumers away.

In spite of lack of support from this sector, the student decided to pursue preliminary discussions. She arranged a meeting to include the executive director and one family counselor from her agency, two police officers, two former rape victims, a community council planner, a minister, a health clinic administrator, a school principal, and a city-council member. Her agenda for the first meeting was to discuss antecedent conditions; to explore the history, definitions, and analysis of the problem; to discuss expected outcomes; to identify individuals and groups who might be involved; to consider obtaining sanction; to identify representatives of varying interests and expertise; and to decide whether to continue.

Case Study Discussion Questions

1. What community perspectives should be considered in the discussion of antecedent conditions?
2. What type of critical incidents might the change agent look for in explaining the history of this problem? What readily available data might be used?
3. How might initial perceptions about expected outcomes differ among the participants?
4. What individuals, groups, or organizations do you feel should be represented in each of the following systems: initiator, change agent, client (primary beneficiaries and secondary beneficiaries), target, and action (planning subsystem and implementing subsystem)?

SUMMARY OF MAJOR POINTS

1. Preparation for deliberate change is a vital set of activities that contribute to effective change by setting the stage for subsequent activities.

2. Preparation tasks include considering antecedent conditions; gathering preliminary information on needs, results, approaches, and resources; identifying the participants; obtaining sanction to intervene through participation of key people and interests; and, finally, deciding whether to continue the change process.

3. The change agent should identify the membership of various systems and subsystems participating in the planned change process.

4. Change systems include: change agent system, initiator system, client system (including primary and secondary beneficiaries), target system, and action system (including planning system and implementing system).

5. The source of sanction for intervention should be identified, and those with specific interests and expertise should be represented in the change effort.

6. After completing the preparation tasks, participants should make a decision about whether or not to continue with the change process.

DISCUSSION OR SELF-STUDY QUESTIONS

1. What is the purpose of preparation activities? What tasks must be accomplished during this period?

2. Identify a need for change in an organization or community with which you are familiar. List individuals, groups, and organizations who are potential participants in the various systems and subsystems discussed in this chapter. Note overlapping roles. How does this analytical exercise in identifying the composition of change systems help you as the change agent to facilitate a deliberate change process?

3. If a student group wishes to initiate change in a private high school, what individuals, organizations, policies, or other factors would form the basis for a sanctioning system? How would this sanctioning system be different from the system in a public high school?

4. How might the student group described in the previous question achieve representativeness with a widely diverse and sizable student body?

SUGGESTED READINGS

Alexander, C. A., & McCann, C. The concept of representativeness. *Social Work,* 1956, *1,* 48–52.

Brager, G., & Holloway, S. *Changing human service organizations: Politics and practice.* New York: Free Press, 1978.

Kahn, A. J. *Theory and practice of social planning.* New York: Russell Sage Foundation, 1969.

Lippitt, R., Watson, J., & Westley, B. *The dynamics of planned change.* New York: Harcourt Brace Jovanovich, 1958.

CHAPTER FOUR

Identifying the
Change Opportunity

OBJECTIVES

Studying the contents of this chapter should enable the reader to:

DEFINE THESE KEY CONCEPTS

> *Change opportunity*
> *Condition*
> *Problem*
> *Need*
> *Issue*
> *Boundary*
> *Participants involved in change*
> *Input into the definition of the change opportunity*
> *Incidence and prevalence*
> *Needs assessment*
> *Complexity*
> *Intensity*
> *Urgency*
> *Duration*
> *Control*
> *Barriers*
> *Costs of nonresolution*
> *Project, program, and policy approaches*

DESCRIBE OR EXPLAIN

> *How to conceptualize a need for change*
> *How to establish boundaries for the change effort*
> *How to identify participants involved in a change effort*
> *How to collect the data needed to understand the situation*
> *How to identify varying perspectives in defining a problem*
> *How to set up a change situation for analysis*
> *How to select the preliminary approach that best fits the situation*

$\textbf{A}$ quick overview of the change process might lead the beginning practitioner to conclude that the identification of the problem, need, issue, or opportunity is a relatively simple and minor consideration in comparison to the rest of the process. To the practitioner, problems often seem quite obvious, and there tends to be a feeling of urgency to move to intervention. In the initiation of planned change, however, identification and analysis of potential change situations are critical tasks that determine, to a great extent, the direction of intervention. Identification of a problem, need, issue, or opportunity is based on values, and the perceptions of the change opportunity held by those involved are seldom in total agreement. Premature movement into intervention carries the risks of unproductive activity, splintering of the support base, and failure to make an impact on the areas of concern.

Given high unemployment in a community, one group may identify the problem as racial discrimination, another group may see it as a need for retraining people with obsolete skills, another as a lack of tax incentives to lure industry, and still another as the inflexibility of the workplace. All may be at least partially correct, but failure to respect each group's views and to involve each group at this early stage can lead to a prematurely narrow definition of the problem and possible alienation of a support group. All groups, of course, will probably not be satisfied with the way in which problems, needs, issues, or opportunities are eventually defined. The decision about a final definition, however, should come through careful assessment and debate during the phases of identifying and analyzing the change opportunity.

Identification of a change opportunity encompasses far more than the simple designation of content. It includes three basic activities: conceptualizing the change opportunity (framing a definition, delineating the boundaries, specifying membership of change systems, and utilizing input from various sources); documenting the need for change (establishing parameters and collecting data); and exploring subjective factors (assessing characteristics of the change opportunity, identifying barriers to change, and considering change approaches).

CONCEPTUALIZING THE CHANGE OPPORTUNITY

Framing a Definition

Identifying the change opportunity need not be a lengthy or drawn-out process. Too often professionals from all fields are accused of studying problems indefinitely without acting to resolve them. Rather than length of study time, the principal focus here is clarity of perception of the situation. The way in which the problem, need, issue, or opportunity is conceptualized at this stage will influence the way in which the change process is carried out. As the possibility of engaging in deliberate change is pursued, it becomes increasingly important to be precise in the use of terminology. The following section defines terms commonly used to conceptualize factors that lead to an episode of change: social condition, problem, need, issue, and opportunity.

Organizational and community change opportunities come in many forms. A single incident of a young child being frightened by a stranger loitering around a playground can initiate a problem-solving episode by a group of concerned parents, while a disaster such as a flood or tornado may necessitate planning and intervention at a community or state level. It is therefore necessary to clarify at an early point in the change episode whether the focus is on a condition, a problem, a need, an issue or an opportunity.

Social condition. Analysis of a problem or need begins with a consideration of social conditions. A social condition is defined as "a steady state of organization of persons, things, events, and relationships existing in reality" (Northwood, 1964, p. 201). A condition is simply what is or exists, as conceptualized, defined, and enumerated by those who compile data on that particular area. An assessment of social conditions is an attempt to look at the facts, not at values or judgments. Social conditions are any set of social circumstances: economic or employment status, housing, health.

Social problem. When a social condition becomes a focus of concern it begins to be defined as a social problem. A social problem is simply a social condition that has been recognized, identified as a negative one, and labeled. Northwood (1964) defines a social problem as "social conditions that cause discomfort to members of a group or threaten the continuance of the group in its steady state of organization" (p. 202). Meier (1964) states, "The idea of a social problem carries a certain quantitative implication. Only when a certain number of similar situations become troublesome to a community or endanger the safety and well being of others is the phrase social problem likely to be applied" (pp. 168–169).

Problems are defined within the context of value systems, however, so one person's problem is another's condition. Etzioni (1976) makes this point well with the following illustration: "Most of us would agree that drug abuse is a social problem, whereas driving a car hardly qualifies. Yet, in 1968, . . . accidental poisoning by drugs . . . caused 1692 deaths in the United States, whereas, in 1970, automobile accidents killed about 55,000 Americans" (p. 1). He goes on to describe how drugs damage the health of thousands, while automobiles injure millions. In addition, automobiles pollute, use up natural resources, and require highways, which destroy nature and neighborhoods. A given condition may or may not be perceived as a social problem depending on the number of people affected and the community or societal values that are challenged by the condition (Etzioni, 1976, pp. 3–27). The perception of a social condition as a problem may also be based on whether the benefits are worth the cost of dealing with it.

The change agent involved in community or organizational change must, therefore, take differing values into consideration. If the episode is to be built around a problem, the change agent must know who says it is a problem and from what perspective this statement is made. Often, for example, ethnic minority populations do not make use of social services. Agency staff may consider this a problem of public relations, while the minority community may consider it a problem of insensitivity to their needs, aspirations, and culture. The lack of women and minorities at upper levels of management and administration in an organization may not be considered a problem at all by some, while from another perspective their absence implies serious race and sex discrimination. On any single issue opinions typically range from perceiving the individual as the cause of his or her own problems to perceiving the individual as a victim of social, economic, and political structures and processes (Etzioni, 1976, pp. 3–27).

Problems require study and analysis, including a study of etiology and characteristics. "Prevention of a problem through rational planning," says Cohen (1964), "is predicated on knowing the cause of the problem" (p. 366). In an analysis of poverty, for example, Lourie (1964) describes causes as economic, social, and personal (p. 8). Economic causes include recessions, technological changes, variations in productivity, market variations, and irregular or seasonal demand for labor. Social causes for poverty might include the poor health or death of a wage earner; discrimination because of race, sex, or other reasons; the lack of programs for social or educational preparation; or the lack of public transportation. Personal factors might be an individual's physical or mental inability to perform the tasks required for employment. Examination of the characteristics of a problem reveals information about dynamics, incidence and prevalence, geographical location, victim population, and other such data, which can be helpful in the planned change process.

Need.   Northwood (1964) distinguishes the concepts of need and problem: "A need usually refers to a lack of something, which lack contributes to the discomfort of members of the group. A problem usually refers to the presence of something, which presence contributes to the discomfort of members of the group" (p. 202). A need, therefore, can be defined as a lack or deficit in relation to a set of standards.

The critical issue in defining need is who is setting the standards. If standards are set by experts, such as income or housing standards, normative need is established. If they are set by those surveyed, such as respondents' perception of the need for health care, perceived need is established. If the intent is to determine how many people are seeking help from existing programs, expressed need is established. And if standards are set by comparing deficits and resources in one community to those in another, relative need is established.

Moroney (1976) discusses these four types of need (pp. 136–137). *Normative need* refers to the establishment of standards through the use of professional judgment and expertise. When these standards are applied to actual conditions, those falling short of a minimally acceptable standard are defined as being in need. Obviously, for a variety of reasons minimally acceptable standards change over time.

Perceived need is defined as what people view their needs to be. Expressions of perceived need can provide important information useful in designing service systems that are responsive to what potential consumers see themselves as needing rather than to what experts believe they should have.

Expressed need is based on the number of people who seek a service and is basically a demand function. Waiting lists, for example, are one indicator of the number of people having an expressed need for a service. Expressed need indicates how many people perceive themselves as being sufficiently in need to ask for help.

Relative need is defined as the gap between services in different geographical areas, weighted to account for the differences in population and social pathology. Relative need is concerned with equity of services and is often a consideration when comparing rural need to urban need, for example. Although two areas could be objectively defined as being in need, if one has significantly more services than the other, the relative need of the latter would be greater.

Although these are four distinct ways of evaluating need, they are not exclusive but interdependent. Each provides relevant information to the change agent and contributes to a thorough understanding of the problem.

When building an episode of organizational or community change around a need, the change agent should be aware of the relationship between needs and problems. The existence of a need indicates that a group of people is experiencing some lack or deficit. The assumption (which must be studied and tested) is that meeting the need will solve or at least alleviate part of the problem on which the change effort is focused. For example, a high percentage of respondents might state that they need day care and public transportation. Whether or not provision of day care and transportation will lower unemployment can be determined only by further study and analysis of the problem. As Gates (1980) points out, one must look behind the need to determine why the need has been identified and defined. He proposes that, instead of stating that people need to know how to read, one should look at the specific conditions that will be improved if this need is met: "Their mobility is improved because they are able to read maps and street signs; their safety is enhanced because they are able to read the word 'poison'; their employability is enhanced because they are able to read blueprints" (p. 120).

Issue.   Another factor that can stimulate a change episode is an issue. An issue is a point around which there is disagreement by two or more parties. If disagreement does not exist, there is no issue (Daley & Kettner, 1981). A change episode can be built around an issue such as neighborhood preservation and revitalization. If the city wishes to expand its civic center or extend a freeway through a neighborhood, pro and con positions will be developed. Some within the neighborhood will anticipate increased value to their property or business and will support the renewal efforts. Others will see the destruction of relationships and the community as they have known it and will oppose the development. Regardless of varying perceptions of problems and needs in such a situation, the existence of an issue presents an opportunity to develop outcomes of the change episode that optimize the values of the participants.

Opportunity.   Much of the social work and human service literature focuses on social conditions, problems, needs, or issues. While this focus may lead to well-conceptualized change efforts, it tends to play down the positive perspective of social change. Conceptualizing a potential organizational or community change episode as an opportunity may broaden thinking about the change process and encourage awareness of those nonproblematic situations in which the status quo is sufficiently open or disrupted to allow for change. A community or organizational situation may be viewed in relatively positive terms but may still be improvable. A future problem may be prevented. In order to avoid the cumbersome repetition of the terms *condition, problem, need,* and *issue,* and to stress the positive aspects of change, the term *opportunity* will be used throughout the remainder of the book to encompass a variety of factors that may lead to a change episode. Where appropriate, however, the terms *condition, problem, need,* or *issue* will continue to be used as defined here.

Delineating the Boundaries

As identification of the change opportunity begins, a boundary decision must be made—a judgment about how widely or narrowly to view the opportunity and what organizational or community systems to include. What components of the situation should be included? Many social problems, needs, issues, and opportunities are manifested in several institutional systems and are associated with multiple causal factors. Edwards and Sharkansky (1978, p. 100) comment on the challenge of distilling conceptions of problems from symptoms and determining where analysis should be centered:

> It is sometimes difficult to decide whether there is a single large problem or many separate problems independently causing the observed symptoms. Does poverty result from one overall problem such as racial discrimination,

or is it caused by several problems like inadequate welfare payments for members of broken families, and low earnings and lack of employment opportunities for the unskilled? If poverty is considered the result of discrimination, then it is tempting to focus on the passage of civil rights legislation. However, policies such as occupational training, social security adjustments, guarantees of jobs, or adjustments in the minimum wage may be more appropriate to meet each of several discrete problems.

Delineating boundaries consists of making judgments about which organizational or community systems and subsystems are to be considered and which excluded. In some situations, one might take a map or an organizational chart and actually draw lines around those systems to be included in the change effort. In others, however, where policies, attitudes, or values may be the target of change, delineating boundaries is a conceptual task. The time, money, and human resources available will also affect the size and scope of the change effort and should be taken into account. The following set of questions might guide the practitioner and others involved in the identification of the change opportunity as they delineate boundaries:

1. Is this change opportunity to be approached from an organizational, local, regional, or national perspective?
2. Is it to be considered fundamentally a psychological/personal, intergroup, or societal/institutional issue?
3. Which are the critical variables (or factors that appear to have the greatest relevance) in the situation?
4. Which organizational or community systems and subsystems would be specific targets for change?

At the outset, it is usually wise to keep boundaries open and fluid so that the change agent does not close out important considerations because of preconceptions or assumptions. However, since part of the purpose of identification of the change opportunity is to develop a definition of the situation in order to take appropriate action, as the identification and analysis phases progress, the boundaries will narrow and become defined. Eventually, boundaries will be delineated that exclude all but the major factors believed to have an impact on the situation.

Specifying Membership of Change Systems

As clarity about the focus of the change effort begins to emerge, the change agent moves to specify the participants. Initial identification was begun during the preparation for change. Specification requires answers to a series of questions about the change opportunity. Who is asking for help? Who are the expected beneficiaries—both primary and secondary? Who might be targets of change? Who favors the change? Who is opposed to the change? For the change episode to be successful, who will need to favor it (or at least not oppose it)?

The *initiator system* is composed of individuals or groups who initially bring the situation to the attention of the change agent and ask for help. The initiators may or may not be the primary beneficiaries of the intervention but are clearly concerned about improving the situation as they see it. A citizens' committee studying violence in the schools might ask a change agent to become involved in an effort to reduce the violence. Although not necessarily the primary beneficiary of intervention, the initiator plays an important role in the change process by asking that something be changed. Identification of concerned individuals and groups as well as their sanctioning organizations, if appropriate, is important for the change agent. Although motives for initiation of a planning episode are often obvious, at other times they are less clear, and an understanding of why people get involved and what they expect is helpful.

The *client system* is made up of those individuals, groups, organizations, or communities that are the expected beneficiaries of the episode. *Primary clients* benefit directly, while *secondary clients* benefit indirectly. Several authors have defined clients as those who ask for help and are the expected beneficiaries of the intervention (Compton & Galaway, 1979, p. 84; Pincus & Minahan, 1973, p. 63). Although this definition of *client* is useful in direct practice with individuals, groups, or families, initiating change in organizations and communities introduces the need for additional and specific information about those involved. Separating initiators from clients recognizes that those who ask for intervention are not always the same as those who are expected to be the primary beneficiaries. It also recognizes that, in some instances, for whatever reason, those who would be primary beneficiaries may never ask for intervention. One problem in dealing with the frail elderly, for example, is that many suffer serious deprivation but do not ask for help.

The separation of initiators from clients, however, introduces the need for caution in making assumptions about clients. Although, from the perspective of some, certain individuals and groups may appear to be the expected beneficiaries of a change episode, ultimately the decision to initiate change must rest with those who are defined as being clients, except in extreme circumstances. Change should not be imposed by those outside the situation. This requirement can pose serious ethical and value dilemmas. If, for example, the migrant families discussed in the illustration in Chapter 3 were opposed to any intervention to solve the health problems of their children for fear of losing their jobs, their concerns would certainly have to be respected and dealt with. At the same time, the health of the migrant children could not be ignored. This type of situation calls for careful weighing of concerns on both sides and, perhaps, a need for preliminary activity such as ensuring protection for jobs prior to requesting the migrants' sanction for intervention. Ultimately, in most situations, before a change effort can proceed the clients must agree that help is needed and wanted to deal with the situation or condition.

However, in some situations, intervention is appropriate even without the sanction of the primary beneficiaries, as, for example, when the beneficiaries are persons with diminished capacity because of age or mental ability, such as young children or chronically mentally ill persons. Or, as another example, the primary beneficiaries may lack the information to make a decision, and sufficient time may not be available to give them the information. Perhaps a particular school district plans to quietly shut down several programs serving handicapped children, and there is not time to inform, educate, and mobilize the primary beneficiaries. Intervention must take place quickly or the opportunity to save the programs will be lost. In situations like these the change agent is sometimes faced with difficult ethical dilemmas. To take risks without the consent of those who may suffer the consequences is a serious matter. Acting on behalf of clients without the clients' approval challenges the clients' right to make their own choices. This basic right cannot be abridged without serious cause.

Before acting without the consent of a client, the change agent balances the probable benefits and costs to the client against the costs associated with not acting. The change agent acts without the client's consent only if the client would be seriously disadvantaged by a failure to act. If no substantial harm is likely to result because of inaction, the change agent is ethically bound to seek sanctions from the client, from an appropriate agency (service agency or court), or from the guardian of an incapacitated client. We stress that in most situations the change agent is ethically obligated to assist the client to understand the alternatives available and to make his or her own informed decision. The resources invested by the change agent in working with the client to achieve informed consent may be considerable but are valued as supporting a basic professional tenet—the client's right to self-determination.

The concept of secondary, or indirect, beneficiaries of the change episode is important because it offers the potential of substantially expanding the base of support for the change effort. Many of the areas of concern to human service professionals are not areas that tend to be politically popular. Poverty, disease, hunger, and unemployment are not always perceived as conditions deserving sympathy, support, or investment of community resources. Broadening the concept of *client* to include many constituencies increases the possibility of a strong base of support for intervention. Secondary beneficiaries differ from primary beneficiaries in an important way. Although the support and involvement of secondary beneficiaries should be solicited in change efforts, secondary beneficiaries do not exercise the same type of power over a change episode that is extended to primary beneficiaries. Secondary beneficiaries usually play a less important role in making decisions about the change episode.

The *target system* is defined as those individuals, groups, organizations, or communities that need to be changed in order to achieve the objectives of the change episode. Precision of definition is important here. Lack of precision in defining the target can set up almost insurmountable odds and can lead to defeat. For example, initiators, in their anger and frustration over past practices or events, often attempt to focus on the school system, the foster-care system, or the welfare system. Specific organizational or community elements, individuals, policies, or program designs are more likely to yield to change. Alinsky (1971, p. 130) promotes the tactic of identifying individuals in the system, holding them accountable, and refusing to allow for a passing of responsibility onto an impersonal bureaucratic system. Although Alinsky's model was designed for conflict and social action, the tactic of identifying a highly specific target can be equally effective in other change efforts. However, oversimplification or too narrow a definition of the target can be as unproductive as being too general and vague. Often the top administrator of an organization becomes the target of a change effort when problems exist in many parts of the organization. Replacement of the top administrator, without addressing the other problems, is unlikely to bring about the desired changes.

Action system members include those individuals, groups, organizations, and communities that participate in the change effort. In many ways the action system is more complex and difficult to define than the other change episode systems. Although it is helpful to have as broad a base of support as possible for the change effort, it is equally important to ensure that roles and responsibilities are clearly defined. The action system could include all individuals, groups, organizations, and communities defined as being in the initiator system, client system, change agent system, planning system, implementing system, and even target system. The role of the change agent is to orchestrate the efforts of the actors. This role requires, as a minimum, clear definition of roles and responsibilities. Who will take the lead on what tasks? What role will each actor have? How can links be established between planners and implementers? These and other questions must be answered.

Utilizing Input from Various Sources

As the composition of the various change episode systems is considered, many interested parties with a variety of perspectives on the situation are expressing points of view on the change opportunity. Which perspective is correct? Whose definition of the situation does the change agent accept?

Initiators can certainly make a strong case for adopting their definition since they were the first to raise the situation for consideration and to ask for intervention. The clients also have an important interest in the way the change opportunity is defined and pursued. Likewise those individuals and organizations identified as targets or members of the other change episode systems have a legitimate concern about the definition of the focal situation. And, finally, the change agent has a stake in the way in which the change opportunity is defined. Identification of the change opportunity requires input from all these diverse participants to ensure that no source of information has been overlooked, no perspective on the situation ignored.

A critical consideration is the extent to which clients influence the definition. Client input can be conceptualized as falling on a continuum between a diagnostic model and a client-definition model. The diagnostic model, popular for many years in social work literature (Hamilton, 1940), called for exhaustive study of the situation by the professional. Using the results of this study and a body of established knowledge and theory, the professional prepares a diagnostic statement about the problem. Others involved may have full, partial, or no knowledge of the conclusions drawn by the professional. They may agree or disagree with the problem as defined and they may influence the professional to alter the definition, but the ultimate decision on how the problem is defined belongs to the professional.

At the other end of the continuum, a client-definition model identifies the change opportunity as what the clients define it to be. The rationale behind this approach is that the diagnostic model leads too often to double-agenda casework, where the client is interested in pursuing one set of problems while the professional focuses on another. Total commitment to the client's agenda removes barriers between the professional and the client and increases the effort and energy a client is willing to invest in resolution of the problem.

In most instances neither extreme is appropriate for planned change in organizations and communities. There is general agreement in the problem solving literature that all participants should have input into the definition and analysis of the problem but that final decisions about the definition are made through negotiation between the client system and the change agent system (Compton & Galaway, 1979, p. 331; Pincus & Minahan, 1973, p. 165; Reid, 1972, p. 67). Several authors have proposed ways to resolve differences of opinion among participants in the change process. Although they make their proposals in reference to designing the change effort and to establishing objectives, the processes they suggest can also be used in defining the change opportunity.

Recognizing the importance of values in planning and the setting of goals, Davidoff and Reiner (1973) propose that planners accept or reject alternatives on the basis of the client's values: "If a planner is to be permitted to reject alternatives it must be because he has some knowledge or skill that provides a rational basis for such acts of rejection. This basis can be provided only by the values of clients" (p. 22). In another article, however, Davidoff (1965) presents his concept of advocacy planning, which gives primary importance to the planner's values: "Values are inescapable elements of any rational decision-making process, and the values held by the planner should be made clear" (p. 331). Since planning cannot be done from a position of value neutrality, the planner not only should explicate values underlying his or her prescriptions but should be an advocate for them. Under this model, multiple sets of plans representing varying perspectives are submitted, and planners actively support acceptance of their own plans.

As an alternative to either strict adherence to client values or advocacy for the planner's values, Friedmann (1973) proposes transactive planning. In response to what he perceives as a widening gulf in communication between planners and their clients, he proposes a style of planning designed to narrow that gulf. The heart of transactive planning is dialogue. Dialogue means not simply formal communication between the two parties, planner and client, but rather an intensive interaction that gives each party a genuine and authentic idea of the other's perspective. Through this transactive process, each party learns from the other. The client emerges with a clear understanding of the planner's perspective, and the planner with a genuine appreciation for the values of the client.

In summary, in community and organizational change efforts, the change agent rejects extremes where either the definition and values of the change agent or the definition of the clients is totally accepted and imposed on the change process. In the process of defining the change opportunity, the change agent will often draw on Friedmann's transactive techniques, focusing on a mutual exchange of perspectives. Both clients and change agent thus share responsibility for extensive and intensive dialogue in defining the situation. To the extent that time and resources permit, each should attempt to become immersed in the perspective of the other in the interest of discovering a mutual definition of the change opportunity. Once consensus is achieved, the role of the change agent is clearly that of advocate for the mutually derived position. At this point attempts at objectivity or neutrality serve no purpose.

DOCUMENTING THE NEED FOR CHANGE

Once a change opportunity has been clearly defined, the boundaries clarified, and the participants identified, an analysis of the change opportunity should be made; ways of making this analysis are covered in the next chapter. In order to prepare for analysis and further clarify the nature of the change opportunity, data and information to be used in analysis are collected and compiled. Documenting the need for change requires collection of data that indicate the number of people affected by the problem, need, or issue. Such data can be collected through the use of various needs assessment procedures.

Establishing Parameters

Before resources are invested in change, efforts should be devoted to generating data that support the contention that change is needed. Preliminary examination of the incidence and prevalence of the problem or need will help to define the extent to which the condition is a private or a public matter. *Incidence* refers to the actual occurrence of a phenomenon during a specific period. An example might be that there were 217 high school dropouts in Smithville during the 1981–1982 academic year. *Prevalence* refers to the number of cases or instances of a phenomenon existing in a community or group at a given time. An example might be that 25 Smithville high school students are pregnant at the time of graduation, 1982. Precisely what incidence and prevalence data should be collected depends on the definition of the problem, need, or issue. If no attempt is to be made in a given episode of change to collect original data, a review of existing data should be undertaken to identify the populations affected and to establish incidence and prevalence rates.

Collecting Data

Systematic data-collection techniques in human services are discussed in the needs-assessment literature. It should be pointed out, however, that needs assessment typically covers both the identification phase and the analysis phase of the change process. Data collected in the identification and definition phase must be analyzed and prepared for use. Data analysis will be covered in the following chapter.

Many resource books are available on needs assessment techniques, and no attempt will be made here to cover that material in detail. Rather, the present discussion provides brief descriptions of a variety of techniques and refers the reader to original sources for further study (Armentrout, 1976; Warheit, Bell, & Schwab, 1977).

Warheit et al. (1977) identify four primary sources of data, each reflecting a distinct perspective on need: the participatory strategies, social indicators, community surveys, and data derived from social service agencies.

Participatory strategies rely on people knowledgeable about a condition, problem, need, or issue to generate estimates about such factors as size, scope, complexity, and intensity. The *key-informant* approach relies on information from those people who are presumed to be experts on a given subject—acknowledged or elected community leaders, human service professionals, clergy, educators, and others whose professional and community roles enable them to have knowledge of the situation. A *community-forum* approach attempts to bring together a wide variety of people from the community who have an interest in the situation—consumers, taxpayers, service providers, professionals, and others. Through discussion and exchange using a variety of group techniques, consensus on major problems or needs is expected to emerge. Experience with participatory strategies has shown that participation is generally weak, especially among the poor, minorities, clients, and other groups (Gates, 1980, pp. 131–132). Participatory strategies should, therefore, include special efforts to involve these populations.

Social indicators are broad statistical reflections of the conditions, problems, and needs of a population within a given geographical boundary. Statistical indicators generated by the Bureau of the Census, the Federal Bureau of Investigation, or the U.S. Department of Labor are commonly used as one basis for the assessment of need at the local, state, or national level. Government document sections of university and public libraries provide social indicator data on a variety of subjects for a range of political jurisdictions. Social indicators often provide a helpful supplement to data collected in project and program approaches, and they are a primary source of data for policy change efforts. For example, population statistics are often used as a basis for resource allocation when policy change is planned and implemented. Although social indicators do provide a broad overview of a condition or problem these data alone usually cannot be used to identify the precise number of people in a given area who have a particular problem or need. Additional needs assessment techniques often must be used in specific change situations.

Community surveys are designed to collect data directly from individuals in the community. If questions about validity, reliability, and sampling are answered satisfactorily, such surveys are the most accurate source of data for a particular community. Community surveys are conducted for the purpose of enumerating need—providing a basis for estimating the needs of a total population.

A major consideration in conducting community surveys is cost. Gates (1980, pp. 131–132) illustrates the problem of cost graphically with a simple example. To examine the relationships among five simple variables (race, income, sex, age, and need for dental care), there are 320 possible different sets of responses. If ten of each profile will yield reliable results and if the sampling design will distribute respondents evenly (both highly unlikely assumptions), then minimum sample size will be 3200 respondents. Gates goes on to point out that if a telephone survey were conducted by volunteers at the extremely nominal cost of $3 per respondent, the survey will cost $10,000. Thus, community surveys should be conducted only when data cannot be collected from other sources and only when resources are available to produce reliable findings. If an organizational change is intended and the target population is small enough, a survey may be a feasible option.

Users of survey results should be aware that findings may be generalizable to a total population only to a limited extent. Research has demonstrated that special care must be exercised in conducting surveys among ethnic minority and other special populations (Montero & Levine, 1977). The potential for distorting questions, responses, and findings increases as the cultural, social, political, economic, gender, and value gulf between survey creator and respondents widens.

The fourth source described by Warheit et al. (1977) is data derived from social service agencies, or the *rates-under-treatment* approach. Like other data sources, this approach has its strengths and weaknesses. Most social service agencies routinely collect data about clients who come to them for services. These data are then aggregated in monthly, quarterly, and annual reports, which often become the basis for determining community needs. Advantages of this approach are that the data are relatively easy and inexpensive to obtain and that the number of people receiving services plus those on the waiting list do provide a reasonably accurate assessment of one type of need—expressed need. Disadvantages of this source are, first, that data-collection and reporting systems vary from agency to agency and standardized definitions are not used by all agencies. Thus there is no assurance that data aggregated across communities represent discrete and clearly defined categories of need. Second, because clients often receive services from more than one agency, there can be no assurance of an unduplicated count. A third problem is generalizing rates-under-treatment data to an entire community. People who seek out and use services may have characteristics that differ significantly from those of the rest of the community. For example, race has been established as a factor in inhibiting the use of both health services and social services (Gillespie & Marten, 1978; Hickey, 1979).

In its analysis of factors to consider when selecting a technique of needs assessment, the Research Group (Armentrout, 1976, p. 11) proposes the following considerations:

1. The use of existing methodologies
2. The use of existing staff
3. The extent to which a technique complements another technique
4. The flexibility of a technique
5. The cost
6. The amount of time required
7. The staff required
8. The validity of the results

An additional factor to be considered in the assessment of need is classification. A classification system, called a *taxonomy*, will aid the change agent in identifying the size and scope of populations in need of services. Used at the community level, for example, a service taxonomy divides the service system into categories such as employment services, health services, and housing services. Figure 4-1 depicts the total service system.

Within each service category, three populations should be identified. Population I includes all those people (in the area surveyed) who are in need of and are receiving services. Population II includes all those people in need of but not receiving services. Population III includes the population at risk—that is, those people who, without intervention, are likely to eventually fall into Populations I or II. Figure 4-2 shows the taxonomy divided into these three populations.

This type of breakdown of community service needs can be helpful in setting priorities in the change process, can help to target efforts for specific service categories and populations, and can, over time, describe changes and trends in community service needs. A similar classification system could be developed within an organization to examine service populations.

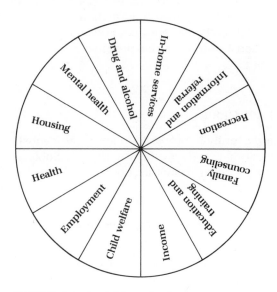

FIGURE 4-1. A social service taxonomy

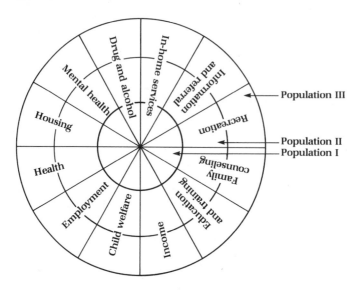

FIGURE 4-2. An expanded social service taxonomy

Needs assessments have become a common activity in all areas of human services thanks, in part, to Title XX of the Social Security Act, which requires that needs assessments be conducted as a condition for funding. Many efforts might be characterized as chaotic or haphazard, with reliability, validity, and sampling questionable. Nevertheless, the trend is encouraging. Statistical data on problems and needs have been seriously lacking. Although many downgrade the value of needs assessment data, they remain one of the few sources available to human service professionals for determining the size and scope of community problems and needs. They can be helpful over time in establishing trends and forecasting. Lacking systematic needs assessment data, the change agent is forced to act on fragmentary information or intuition. Either can dangerously misdirect the change episode. Fragmentary information may distort the true situation. Intuition can fall prey to conscious or unconscious (and unknown) bias.

EXPLORING SUBJECTIVE FACTORS

Clarifying the change opportunity in preparation for analysis must include qualitative as well as quantitative data and information. Subjective data enhance the appraisal by specifying how the problem is perceived and by suggesting strategies for change.

Assessing Characteristics of the Change Opportunity

In exploring the feasibility of a change, the change agent should find out how the problem, need, or issue might be characterized from a variety of perspectives. Much of this necessary information can be collected through interaction with those familiar with the situation. Sometimes these characteristics can be clarified through collection and compilation of additional data from various needs assessment sources identified in the previous section. Factors to be explored include complexity, intensity, urgency, duration, control, barriers, and costs of nonresolution.

Complexity refers to the range of perspectives that need to be considered in identifying and analyzing a change opportunity. The change agent may want to develop a profile, in outline form, of the varying perspectives, highlighting costs, benefits, and concerns from each point of view. A change agent working on the issue of revitalizing a neighborhood might draw up a preliminary outline, a part of which looks like this one:

I. Concerns of community residents
  A. Loss of neighborhood identity and relationships
  B. Impact on organizations such as schools, churches
  C. Fair compensation for homes
  D. Relocation costs and prospects
II. Concerns of local business establishments
  A. Loss of neighborhood marketing base resulting in loss of business
  B. Possible increased traffic resulting in increase in business
  C. Possible increase or decrease in value of property
III. Concerns of the city
  A. Need for expansion of civic center
    1. Current space outgrown
    2. Need to attract more conventions
    3. Need to attract businesses and industry to city
    4. Need to improve image of the city
  B. Need to extend freeway to provide access to area
  C. Need to improve blighted area close to existing downtown area

Such detailing helps dispel simplistic notions about the situation by formulating issues and framing change opportunities from a variety of perspectives.

Questions about *intensity* examine the strength of feelings about the change opportunity. In one situation, clients may be mildly apathetic about a problem or need, while in another the problem may generate extremely strong emotions. A change agent should take careful readings on the intensity of feelings prior to initiation of the change effort. Many union organizers, for example, have discovered that when it comes down to a decision about a strike, the problems do not have the same intensity as they did when they were initially defined. Assessing intensity can be helpful in making decisions about the priority of problems.

Questions about *urgency* examine the severity of the identified problems and needs. Many of the problems that human services deal with can be life threatening or have severe consequences. These situations must be compared with those that are of an enrichment nature. Explorations of urgency can be made using Maslow's (1943) hierarchy of needs (Table 4-1). Problems given highest priority would be those relating to survival, while the lowest priority would go to self-fulfillment activities.

**TABLE 4-1. Maslow's hierarchy of needs as a framework
for determining urgency**

Low-urgency needs	Self-realization
	Esteem (ego)
	Social (belonging)
	Safety, security
High-urgency needs	Physiological (food, clothing, shelter, etc.)

The question of *duration* requires an exploration of the length of time an opportunity has existed. Compared to situations that have a short history, long-standing or chronic situations are often less amenable to change and may require a different approach.

The purpose of exploring *control* is to determine whether the problems or needs identified are within or outside the sphere of influence of those involved in the change effort. The change agent should know where the power lies to make decisions about change. Such a scanning of the environment can indicate where leverage might be found later in the process of intervention. It may also help prevent the investment of resources in no-win situations.

Identifying Barriers to Change

The change agent should also identify important *barriers* to problem resolution. Barriers can be physical (such as the physical condition of housing, a target population, or a neighborhood); social (such as social class, status, gender, or ethnicity); economic (such as income or employment); educational (such as access to good education); or political (such as constituent support on a particular issue). In each instance some individuals or systems may be benefiting from the status quo and therefore support (either actively or passively) the continuation of the existing situation. Even agency staff and other professionals may resist change. From every possible perspective, the change agent should identify factors supporting the continuation of the present situation and barriers to intervention. These should then be laid out for consideration as part of the process of identifying and defining the change opportunity.

The change agent should also consider the *costs* and consequences of nonintervention. If no intervention is attempted, what will happen? Where possible, the costs of early intervention or prevention should be estimated and weighed against the costs of inaction. These data may provide the basis for strong arguments for prevention programs rather than expensive treatment and remedial programs.

Considering Change Approaches

Approach refers to a strategy of intervention. Subjective factors are important in making a preliminary assessment of the strategy that might be pursued. Options include a policy, program, or project approach, or some combination.

A *project approach* focuses on a short-term, time-limited change effort.

Projects disband when they are completed. The change agent should determine why previous efforts to deal with this change opportunity (if there were any) were ineffective. Projects might include such undertakings as a drug-education campaign in the high schools or an effort to improve communication between two units in an agency.

A *program approach* must give greater consideration to existing programs and existing staff and to the creation of a more permanent structure than the project approach. Because of the resources already invested in existing programs, staff are often resistant to program changes. Lewin (1947) points out that a program change process must go through the stages of unfreezing, change, and refreezing (p. 34). A program approach for change would, therefore, require examination of such questions as: Who supports the current design and why? Who would support various alternative program designs and why? How much effort will unfreezing require? An example of a program change might be replacing one-to-one therapeutic intervention in a mental health agency with self-help groups.

Widespread organizational or community support becomes a high priority when a *policy approach* is considered. Depending on whether the change opportunity is identified at the organizational or community level, the focus will be either on agency policy or on service network policy, laws, or regulations. In either instance the change effort moves into a political or policy-making arena where the focus is less on design and more on the extent of support for the proposed change. Questions to be considered include: Who will support the change and why? Who will oppose it and why? Is there a position both sides or third parties or publics will support? How active and strong will the support be? How knowledgeable are both sides about the issues? How much of the support is based on information and how much on emotion? An example of a policy change might be raising the legal drinking age in a state or initiating an aggressive affirmative action policy within an agency.

In many instances, a *combination approach*—usually a combination of policy and project approaches or policy and program approaches—is appropriate. For example, a national policy to address the problem of family violence may be implemented using local projects or programs.

The outcome of this stage—the identification and definition of the change opportunity—should be a written statement of the change opportunity, a working draft to help guide the analysis and planning phases. The written statement should be based on all the data and information collected and compiled, should be brief, and should be used as a basis for securing the agreement of all parties on the definition of the problem.

▬▬▬▬▬ *Case Study*

In a public child welfare agency in a large metropolitan area, problems were beginning to surface in the child protective services (CPS) program. In order to deal openly with the problem of child abuse and neglect in the community, the agency gave wide publicity to the CPS program, explaining the services available to neglected and abused children and their parents. The agency advertised a telephone number to call if more information or help was needed. Within three months, the volume of telephone calls was so great that existing staff could follow up on less than 20%—only those where the caller was able to describe clear evidence of immediate abuse or neglect. Some of the calls came from community professionals such as physicians, nurses, or teachers. Many calls from concerned neighbors or relatives had to go uninvestigated, as did the surprisingly large number of self-referrals. Over 50% of the telephone calls were from parents under a great deal of stress who described feelings toward their children and fears about themselves that clearly put them in a high-risk category, even though there may have been no actual physical abuse or neglect.

The CPS staff members who handled these telephone calls were seriously concerned about these parents, but the entire child welfare program was experiencing budget cuts and loss of positions, and the possibility of an increase in staff adequate to cover this group through traditional investigation, follow-up, and casework methods was out of the question.

Meanwhile an investigative reporter was focusing a great deal of community attention on the problem, and an advocacy group, Children's Rights, Inc., began to mount a campaign in the state legislature to deal with the problem of increasing child abuse. Under pressure from the state legislature, the executive director of the child welfare agency agreed to consider increasing funding but required from the CPS unit a proposal for a new and creatively designed program to deal with the problem.

CPS personnel held a series of planning meetings. During these meetings they reviewed their own program data, statistics from other agencies (including local private agencies), as well as published reports about innovative child abuse programs. They considered various interpretations of the problem facing the agency and the community, reviewing the theoretical understandings proposed by authors in a number of disciplines (law, medicine, social sciences).

Based on these deliberations, one of the caseworkers suggested that, at least for the self-referrals and possibly for others, a specialized program of group work, parent education and mutual support might work. Recognizing that stress needs an outlet, she proposed regular classes and training sessions focused on building parenting skills. The CPS workers formed task forces charged with the following responsibilities: data collection on the size and scope of the problem and need, strategy development (who to involve and how), identification of proposed program content and structure, and budget development.

Case Study Discussion Questions

1. What would you define as the problem? the need? Is there an issue involved? Is there an organizational or community change opportunity involved?

2. Whose problem, need, issue or opportunity is it?
3. How is the need a normative need? a perceived need? an expressed need? a relative need?
4. Identify the individuals or groups which make up the following systems: initiator system, client system, target system, change agent system, and action system (including planning system and implementing system).
5. Assuming that input from all individuals and organizations will be solicited and accepted, which ones should have major input in framing the definition of the change opportunity? Who must agree on a definition of the change opportunity before the change effort proceeds?
6. To what data sources would you turn to learn about incidence and prevalence, complexity, intensity, urgency, duration, control, barriers, and costs of nonresolution?
7. To what extent would you consider project, program, or policy strategies in preliminary strategy development?

SUMMARY OF PHASE I

I. Definition
Identification of the change opportunity is the phase in which conditions, problems, needs, issues and opportunities are explored, participants are identified, input is solicited, and data are collected for the purpose of developing a precise and highly focused definition of the change opportunity.
II. Information needed
   A. Will the situation under consideration be defined as a problem, a need, an issue, or an opportunity?
   B. What are the boundaries of the change opportunity?
   C. Who make up the initiator system, client system, target system, change agent system, and action system (including both planning system and implementing system)?
   D. By what process will the situation be defined? How will decisions about the definition be made?
   E. What do we know about the significant characteristics of the situation?
      1. The need for change
         a. Incidence
         b. Prevalence
      2. Subjective considerations
         a. Complexity
         b. Intensity
         c. Urgency
         d. Duration
         e. Control
         f. Barriers
         g. Costs of nonresolution

III. Tasks to be accomplished
  A. Outline the situation including major areas of concern and subparts
  B. Specify the membership of each change episode system
  C. Develop a data collection plan
  D. Collect data
  E. Begin preliminary consideration of the focus of the change effort
IV. Products to be developed
  A working draft of a problem identification statement that covers the items in II and III
V. Next steps: transition to Phase II
  Prepare data for analysis

SUMMARY OF MAJOR POINTS

1. Opportunities for change require careful and systematic definition.

2. Framing a definition includes examination of the concepts of *condition, problem, need, issue* and *opportunity* as they relate to the situation at hand.

3. Defining a change opportunity requires the delineation of boundaries.

4. Defining the change opportunity requires a careful sorting out of the individuals, groups, organizations, and communities who make up the initiator system, client system, target system, change agent system and action system.

5. Defining the change situation calls for extensive and intensive dialogue among participants in the interest of achieving mutual understanding of all the different values involved.

6. Defining a change opportunity requires an examination of both quantitative and qualitative data and information.

7. Data collection helps to build a base of information for use in defining and analyzing the change opportunity.

8. Even at this early stage of the change process, consideration should be given to the change approach because decisions about approach will help to guide data collection and analysis, and may influence the way the situation is defined.

DISCUSSION OR SELF-STUDY QUESTIONS

1. Concern is often expressed by human service professionals that existing service systems are perpetuated because we assess needs for service and not problems. How would you explain the connection between problem and need?

2. A group of poor, elderly men and women are living in a run-down hotel in the downtown area. The hotel owner takes their full Social Security or welfare checks in exchange for board and room. Health and sanitary conditions are below standard. Nutrition is poor. But the group has not asked for help. You, as an adult protective services worker, discover this situation and

decide to intervene. Identify the probable membership of the initiator, client, target, change agent, and action systems.

3. What change approach would you propose for the situation described in the previous question?

4. In your opinion, can a male change agent act on behalf of a women's group on women's issues (or can a nonminority change agent act on behalf of a minority group on minority issues)? Why or why not? If so, describe the process for defining the situation.

5. Identify several existing service taxonomies currently used in your community (for example, United Way of America Service Identification System). What are their strengths and weaknesses in depicting the needs of clients in your community?

SUGGESTED READINGS

Cohen, N. E. (Ed.). *Social work and social problems*. New York: National Association of Social Workers, 1964.

Etzioni, A. *Social problems*. Englewood Cliffs, N.J.: Prentice-Hall, 1976.

Gates, B. L. *Social program administration: The implementation of social policy*. Englewood Cliffs, N.J.: Prentice-Hall, 1980.

Moroney, R. M. Needs assessment for human services. In W. F. Anderson, B. J. Frieden, & M. Murphy (Eds.), *Managing human services*. Washington, D.C.: International City Managers Association, 1977.

Reid, W. J. Target problems, time limits, task structure. *Journal of Education for Social Work*, 1972, *8*, 58–68.

CHAPTER FIVE

Analyzing the Change Opportunity

$\mathbf{L}$he identification phase describes the nature and characteristics of the change opportunity. Analysis probes to explain why the opportunity exists and to define its aspects and implications. Analysis gives the change agent a sound basis for determining appropriate objectives and interventions. Analysis, then, provides the link between identifying a change opportunity and deciding how to respond to it.

After identification of a change opportunity, pressure often mounts to do something about it. To move directly from identification to setting goals and objectives is to skip a crucial step in the change process however. The danger inherent in bypassing the analysis phase is illustrated by Warren's (1971a, p. 151) critique of the Model Cities program:

> All [nine cities studied] skipped directly from problem identification to program planning without attempt, good or bad, to relate their programs to a diagnosis of the causes of the problems. As a result, the programs were almost completely remedial. They chiefly provided services to people victimized by the problem rather than even claiming to attack the problems themselves.

Analysis is the process of assessing and interpreting the data generated and collected during the identification phase. It entails systematic study of the change opportunity together with exploration of relevant knowledge in the social science field. The purpose of analysis is to examine underlying dynamics of the situation, to postulate causal relationships, and to reveal patterns, connections, and meanings that will inform planning for action.

The role of analysis in the development of a planned change effort is crucial. In the identification phase, the participants have developed an awareness of the problem. Analysis heightens their understanding of the problem, which in turn prepares them for undertaking effective and responsive action. Figure 5-1 diagrams this progression.

CHARACTERISTICS OF ANALYSIS

Analysis uses scientific methodology: a systematic, rational, critical appraisal of the phenomenon under investigation based on empirical facts (Babbie,

(Phase I: Identification) Awareness	(Phase II: Analysis) Understanding	(Phase III: Setting of Goals and Objectives) Readiness for action (identifi- cation of more desirable future state or condition)

FIGURE 5-1. Progression of consciousness regarding the change opportunity

1983; Moroney, 1976). Analysis in the social sciences is different in some respects from analysis in the natural sciences, which take a much narrower view of what can be measured and known. However, the basic motivation—to understand and to establish control over the environment—is the same, as are the essential methods. The distinction between analysis in the natural and social sciences lies in the kinds of questions explored (Wrong, 1970, p. 11):

> In the study of human affairs, man is both the subject and the object of inquiry. Social science is self-knowledge, and man's relation to his own motives, beliefs, and customs is more intimate than his relation to stars, amoebas, or molecules. Thus [Max] Weber argued that one of the major goals of social science—for him it was clearly *the* major goal—was to achieve *clarity.*

The intellectual activities of analysis are directed toward practice issues and practical application. Assessment of the data and the search for relevant research and theoretical constructs are part of a progression toward action. The goal is to enable the change agent to make informed choices.

In addition, analysis is carried out within a social context and involves subjective judgments, preferences, and values. Neutrality and disinterested inquiry are not characteristics of social science analysis. Ideologies, beliefs, and assumptions affect both the perception and the interpretation of empirical data. Rein and Peattie (1981) contend that knowledge is shaped by experience and by expectations. Levy (1983, p. 59) identifies ideology as the premise on which policy is founded and sees its impact in every phase of planned change including the choices of change strategies (prevention, treatment, or rehabilitation) and of targets of change (individuals or institutions).

Rein and Peattie (1981) even suggest that problem or policy analysis typically begins with a solution in mind and is carried out in the search for validation and for meaning and in order to legitimate proposed action. Recognizing this reality, they nonetheless see an important role for analysis: "But we also use research to improve the world of action. By reflecting on the world of action, we identify both the desirable and undesirable, and then generalize them into values grounded in experience. We also refine our understanding of the circumstances in which values can be attained" (p. 527).

The purpose of analysis in the planned change process is to facilitate decision making. Analysis clarifies the nature and dynamics of the change opportunity and the relevance of possible responses. However, it is not realistic to expect analysis to provide "the answer." As Moroney (1976) points out, "Different planners can assess the same situation and produce quite different analyses insofar as each shapes the problem in terms of his background, training, experience, and values" (p. 11). The reality of competing views of human service conditions, problems, needs, issues, and change opportunities in no way lessens the importance of analysis. Enthoven and Smith (1971, pp. 63–64) cite the role of analysis in defining issues and alternatives clearly:

> Analysis in a policy environment calls for more than simply applying the scientific method. Too many of the underlying assumptions of policy decisions are not rigorously verifiable, or cannot be verified at all. Many of them involve value judgments by policy makers as to what an uncertain future is likely to be or should be. The point of analysis is not to give the answer but rather to show how the answer depends on various assumptions and judgments.

Analysis, then, may be expected to clarify options, trace implications, and provide grounding for judgments. Useful analysis will be critical, thorough, and systematic and will be oriented toward practical application.

APPLICATION OF ANALYSIS

An example will illustrate the link between identification and analysis and the tasks involved in each. A substantial increase within one year in the number of elderly persons referred for nursing home placements alarmed the administrator of the county nursing home. Data collected during the identification phase provided information about the clients, about the community, and about service-delivery systems:

I. Client data
   A. Age, sex, ethnicity
   B. Length of time in community
   C. Family ties and location of family members
   D. Organizational affiliations
   E. Economic status and financial resources
   F. Type of housing
   G. Status of physical and mental health
   H. Perceived needs
   I. Reason for referral
II. Community data
   A. Census data
      1. Demographic information
      2. Economic indicators
      3. Housing information
   B. Rate of women entering labor force
   C. Availability and changes in major medical insurance programs
   D. Unemployment trends
III. Service-delivery data

A. Availability and utilization of human services designed for the elderly
   1. Housing (including subsidized)
      a. Institutional
      b. Own home
   2. Home health aides
   3. Meals on wheels
   4. Visiting nurses
   5. Homemaker services
   6. Special-needs transportation
   7. Day care and senior centers
   8. Other
B. Financing of each type of service
C. Effectiveness of service or program
D. Client satisfaction with services

Human service providers, community resource allocators, human service planners, influential people in the community, and representatives of various elderly groups participated in the analysis process. They studied the demographic and resource data in an effort to identify patterns and interrelationships. They looked for interpretive frameworks to explain the phenomenon. Their analysis sought to answer some of the following questions:

1. What significant populations emerge based on
   a. Age
   b. Gender
   c. Ethnicity
   d. Socioeconomic status
   e. Family composition
   f. Other relevant characteristics
2. What trends in service utilization, outcome, and client satisfaction can be identified by population?
   a. Who tends to use each type of service or cluster of services?
   b. Who does not use each type of service or cluster of services?
   c. What measurable results have been achieved by each type of service or cluster of services?
   d. Who is satisfied (or not satisfied) with each type of service or cluster of services?
3. What service gaps are identified? What are the implications of these gaps for admissions to the county nursing home?
4. What is known or can be hypothesized about the interrelationships among 1, 2, and 3 above? What local trends are identified? What are possible explanations for these trends?
5. What theories or concepts might help to explain the observed phenomenon?
6. What are the findings of empirical studies related to this change opportunity?

7. What values, beliefs, and perceptions are involved? How do the values, beliefs, and perceptions of various participants influence their understanding of the current change opportunity?

The analysis helped the participants understand the nature and dynamics of the change opportunity and suggested strategies for intervention. Should the change strategy involve funding more nursing homes, creating day care and co-op housing programs for the elderly, or strengthening home care, nutrition, home health, and other assistance programs—or all three? Should there be increased enforcement of eligibility requirements for nursing homes?

Analysis of the change opportunity helps the change agent discard some options as invalid because they would not be responsive to the problem or need. Other options may be assessed as relevant. Analysis will not always provide clear answers. However, systematic analysis will clarify facts, values, and interrelationships, and will assist the change agent in weighing the implications and likely impact of different choices.

The processes and activities involved in analysis of the change opportunity include technical and interpersonal tasks. Technical tasks include the assessment and interpretation of data as well as connecting the data to analytical frameworks. Interpersonal tasks include the involvement of participants and the mobilization of support for the change effort.

TECHNICAL ASPECTS

What can participants learn from examining the data that will help them clarify or explain the change opportunity? How can they relate the data to analytical frameworks to further enhance understanding and evaluate courses of action? The technical aspects of analysis address these questions. Three aspects will be discussed: identifying etiological and theoretical perspectives, discerning patterns and relationships in available data and information, and incorporating relevant cultural and gender perspectives.

Identifying Etiological, Theoretical, and Research Perspectives

Etiology.   When events or factors tend to be found together or to follow each other with great frequency, they are associated. Postulating and testing associations is one of the major activities in analysis. The change agent seeks causal and contributing factors, or the etiology of the situation, in order to plan the most effective action possible. Zweig and Morris (1966) contend that "the entire perspective of the plan is oriented around how the planner explains the etiology and dynamics of the problem," and they go on to state (p. 16):

> The major point is that in a planning process the causal explanation of the problem implicitly shapes the plan. Tracing out the available explanations utilizing the best available social science orientations provides motive force for different directions for action. Scarcity of resources often makes manda-

tory a selection of a few solutions from a large range of solutions. When the social planning practitioner makes such a choice, it is his professional responsibility to select alternatives that can be based on the most clearly stated conceptual formulations of problem causation.

A variety of broad etiological perspectives might be applied to a change opportunity. Stein and Sarnoff (1964) developed four major etiological categories for use in problem analysis:

1. Inherent in social structure—that is, problems arising from sociopolitical or economic systems. An example is the unemployment that results from technological change.
2. Inherent in individual personality—that is, deficiencies in the coping processes of persons. An example is a person who is unemployed because of personal characteristics that interfere with working relationships.
3. In existing organizations designed to cope with the problem—that is, the inadequacies of human service institutions. An example is the lack of vocational-training programs available to deal with skill deficiencies.
4. In transitory social phenomena—that is, unusual disruptions that can be expected to be remediated or terminated without specific social intervention. An example is a recession leading to temporary unemployment.

For some social problems, several different causal explanations are advanced by different researchers and theorists. Table 5-1 illustrates how the etiology of child abuse and neglect is attributed by various researchers and different models.

Etiological explanations of the same phenomenon have varied at different periods in history. Once mental illness was thought to be caused by demons. Shifts in explanations have been affected by the expansion of research and knowledge and also by social norms, values, and prevailing ideologies. More than one etiological perspective may have adherents at the same time. Today, some see the roots of mental illness in heredity or childhood experiences, others in biochemical imbalances, still others in social learning. In addition, different persons may experience a social problem for different reasons.

TABLE 5-1. Various etiological perspectives on child abuse and neglect

Perspective	Explanation
Social structure	Low value placed on children because they are dependent nonproducers in a capitalistic society
Individual personality	Poor impulse control and inadequate parenting skills of perpetrators because of maternal deprivation, immaturity, or lack of social learning
Organizational	Absence of low-cost child care and extended-day school programs for children of working mothers because of low priority on needs of children
Transitory social phenomenon	Familial stress accompanying high rates of unemployment because of short-term economic crisis

Persons may be unemployed because of structural unemployment caused by technological change or a recession, while others might lack the interpersonal or technical skills needed for employment. And, of course, more than one factor may contribute to a social problem. Racial discrimination or sexism may combine with a recession to contribute to high rates of unemployment for minorities and women.

Two cautions should temper the way one uses causal analyses. First, given available research techniques and available knowledge, it may be possible to determine several contributing factors associated with a complex social problem. Yet it may be almost impossible to verify causal relationships, much less a single cause. Second, change agents must recognize the impact and influence of their initial formulation of the opportunity on the subsequent analysis. Meenaghan and Washington (1980, p. 39) clearly describe this interaction:

> Causation analysis is obviously contaminated by the very concepts selected in the original problem description. For example, if the definition of the problem of income deficiency heavily stresses the skills, behavior, attitudes, and motivations of poor people, then there is a great likelihood that the attributed cause of income deficiency is going to emphasize individual and cultural deficiencies. However, if initial assessment of the problems stresses the nature of the job markets available to people, there is a probability that the society will stress opportunity structures and barriers to economic mobility in "explaining" the social problem. Thus the relationship between problem definition and causal explanations is dynamic in nature and . . . heavily influences subsequent intervention strategies in the areas of social-welfare policy and program responses.

Theory.   Closely related to etiology is theory. A theory is a set of concepts, propositions, and laws that describe and explain a phenomenon. Theories are helpful in problem analysis because they order, codify, and integrate data. They enable the user to understand the underlying dynamics of a situation and to make predictions. Models, which, according to Kettner (1975), provide coherent sets of directives for practitioners, are built on theoretical frameworks.

In the analysis phase, the change agent seeks relevant theories and models to assist in understanding the change opportunity and in formulating effective interventions. However, Etzioni (1976) cautions about expecting a linear relationship from data collection through the application of theoretical frameworks to determination of the appropriate solution. He identifies the limitations of guidance provided by theories in the human service arena (p. 62):

> When it comes to formulating interventions to overcome social problems rather than merely constructing analytic models of the world, social science theories are particularly vulnerable. Theories advance by breaking up the phenomenon under study into analytic slices and then examining one slice—in effect, disregarding the others. Thus econometrics assumes that "all other things" (for example, values, tastes, institutions) will be "held constant;" experimental psychology assumes that economic and social con-

ditions are "controlled," and so on. Such specialization is essential for the abstractions typical theory building requires. Interventions, however, must be introduced into the real world, where all these factors—the economic, psychic, social, and the rest—play a role, and where very few, if any, are ever constant or can be held still. Moreover, factors of various kinds interact and their mutual effects must be taken into account.

Our expectations of the contribution theories and models make to analysis must be realistic. Because theories are based on assumptions and reflect cultural values, the existence of competing and conflicting theories will come as no surprise. Nevertheless, identification of the theoretical underpinnings of proposed policy and program options enables the change agent to see whether there is coherence between the theories used to explain the nature of the problem and those implied in the strategy for its resolution. It also makes the rationales for different choices clearer.

For example, a residential treatment center for adolescents is making policy decisions about resource allocation and treatment. In the course of debate among staff, several different theoretical perspectives emerge. One is a social and personal theory of delinquency that views it as a learned phenomenon transmitted within a deviant subculture. Another theory attributes delinquency to environmental factors such as chronic and excessive youth unemployment, economic depression, and technological changes that require high levels of skill. Finally, there is a theory of delinquency that interprets it as resulting from the way the allocation of resources and opportunity is structured into the society and is maintained by such phenomena as sex and race segregation of jobs, tracking children in the school system, and other institutionalized forms of discrimination. Clearly, the remedies for delinquency differ depending on the theory. Social and personal explanations suggest a need for resocialization, therapeutic, or educational strategies to change the individual. Proponents of environmental explanations might wish to involve youth and staff in legislative advocacy for youth employment programs, extensive vocational training, and changes in the public assistance regulations to allow AFDC households to disregard the earnings of teens in calculating family income. The opportunity theory suggests coalitions to work for restructuring schools and combating racism and sexism.

Initially a broad range of potential etiological and theoretical frameworks should be considered. This broad array must be narrowed as these frameworks become the basis for selecting objectives and strategies. In narrowing the range of frameworks, the change agent considers the following factors:

- Which available frameworks are supported by data on the change opportunity?
- Which explanations are testable? Which have been tested empirically?
- Which available frameworks are most compatible with the participants' most salient values, beliefs, and perceptions of the organization, community and change episode participants?
- Which frameworks apply to a sufficiently broad range of events so as to address a significant aspect of the situation?

- Which available frameworks lead to productive interventions, given the current state of intervention knowledge and skills?
- Which frameworks provide the simplest and most logical explanation?
- Which frameworks are internally consistent?

The process of selecting etiological and theoretical frameworks should involve diverse perspectives and interests. Although this process is time consuming, consensus on frameworks forms the basis for achieving consensus in subsequent phases. Failure to agree at this point may lead to later disagreement on goals, objectives, and strategies for intervention.

Research, evaluations, and reports of practice innovations.   Findings from research studies, evaluations of practice, and reports of practice innovations can contribute to understanding the change opportunity. Existing research and practice findings reflect ways that the problem has been conceptualized, illustrate the results of data analysis, and often suggest implications for action. The task of the change agent is to locate—by search of the literature and contact with agencies—research and documented practice innovations that relate to the situation under analysis. Freeman and Sherwood (1970, p. 43) indicate that one of the skills needed is playing detective to find relevant unpublished research reports. Much useful material in the human services falls into this category, especially program evaluations. The change agent finds such material (called *fugitive literature*) through research librarians, agency research and practice staffs, university faculty studying related problems, government agencies that have sponsored research and evaluation studies, and professional groups interested in the area of study. Some annotated bibliographies give information about fugitive literature in selected fields, such as the one on human service management put out by Project SHARE (n.d.).

Blue-ribbon panels or commissions, whose findings give direction to policy and program development, use combinations of existing reports of basic research studies and evaluations of interventions in their deliberations. For example, the 1955 President's Commission on Mental Illness and Health conducted a comprehensive review of the state of knowledge about the problem and the nature of the service delivery system. Their report, *Action for Mental Health* (Joint Commission on Mental Illness and Health, 1961), was the basis for the development of community mental health centers and other mental health programs. Coleman's *Equality of Educational Opportunity* (1966), which summarized the proposals of a commission, influenced judicial and legislative decisions and subsequent projects and programs relating to school integration. *A Nation at Risk*, by the National Commission on Excellence in Education (1983), resulted in proposals for improving the quality of teaching in U.S. schools.

Several kinds of research contribute to analysis. One type increasingly used in the human services is cost/benefit (or cost/utility) analysis. It is a process designed to compare investments with expected results so that different alternatives may be weighed. A cost/benefit analysis of two alternatives for dealing with families in poverty was conducted by the Department of Health, Education, and Welfare. The analysis compared income maintenance grants to a work incentive program (WIN) that included training, placement, and day-care services. Results revealed that, in the initial years, the income maintenance program was less costly, but after mothers had been in the work incentive program for five to six years the work policy saved money for the government (Rivlin, 1971, p. 62).

Cost/benefit analysis is a quantitative process that depends on the calculation of monetary values. In the human services, however, practitioners also consider qualitative aspects of the situation. For example, in examining the alternatives of home health care services and institutional care for the elderly, one of the qualitative costs of institutionalization is the stress and insecurity suffered by the client when removed from familiar surroundings and a neighborhood support system. This cost must be considered against the benefits to be expected from the institutionalization—for example, constant medical or nursing surveillance.

A second kind of research, evaluations of social interventions, may also contribute to analysis. Care should be exercised in drawing inferences from such research, however, because the context of a particular evaluation may limit its applicability to other situations. Moreover, as Rivlin (1971) points out, the social interventions might not have been designed to facilitate research or the research might not ask the appropriate questions. She cites evaluative research on Project Headstart (early education for poor children) as an example of these limitations (pp. 84–85):

> Headstart was conceived and started with remarkable rapidity. An appealing idea, it caught the imagination of Congress and the public. Everyone wanted to move ahead fast. There were varying ideas about what kind of program was appropriate, what ages were best for it, how long it should last. In effect, local Headstart projects were free, within budgetary limits, to try any approach that seemed reasonable. Tremendous political pressure was exerted to involve more children in short summer programs rather than fewer children in more expensive all-year programs. After the fact, an evaluation attempted to uncover whether the program had had an average effect, discernible in test scores at the first- and second-grade levels. But the program was not designed to answer the really important and interesting question: Were some more successful with particular types of children?

A third type of research, reports of practice innovations, may also offer useful input for analysis of the change opportunity. An agency or a practitioner sometimes develops an innovative approach or design for providing services that turns out to be particularly effective. Limited formal research may have been conducted, but the program may have gained some positive recognition through reports of clients and professionals. The method or design is often then shared in workshops, conferences, or journal articles.

In looking for applicable research, evaluations, and reports, the change agent should recognize the difficulty of conducting systematic research and evaluations. First, research and evaluations can be expensive. The Coleman study on equality of educational opportunity, cited earlier, cost nearly a million dollars (Etzioni, 1976, p. 52). Second, researcher bias is a problem. In the social sciences, research may be undertaken to "prove" the validity of a particular treatment approach. Even when the bias is not conscious or blatant, it may shape the way questions are framed and data are sought and analyzed. Third, sometimes valid research on policy issues does not result in action because it does not fit the dominant political ideology (for example, income maintenance studies; Office of Economic Opportunity, 1970). Fourth, research and evaluation designs often must compromise rigor for feasibility. The most rigorous research design is the controlled experiment, but it is rarely possible to use this design with human subjects experiencing social problems. It is not ethically acceptable intentionally to deny treatment to one group of persons while providing it for another in order to find out how the illness or difficulty progresses in the absence of intervention (Jones, 1981). Fifth, the complexity of problems makes isolation and control of variables difficult if not impossible. Sixth, findings may be misinterpreted.

Change agents should not, therefore, expect research and evaluation to suggest clear-cut solutions to problems. Research and evaluation used in human service planning and analysis cannot be characterized as purely scientific, neutral, and disinterested, nor should they be. They are shaped by the cultural and political context, by value perspectives, and by experiences. In actuality, research and problem analysis often begin after a solution or approach is at least partially in mind. The research then serves the function of supporting and legitimizing the proposed policy, program, or project. Such bias is not malicious or manipulative or even necessarily intentional; it is a result of the way social science knowledge develops.

Awareness of the nature of social science research and knowledge suggests the importance of viewing it with a critical eye. The assumptions on which research is based should be clearly stated, and the validity of key assumptions should be subject to scrutiny. Not only is there a natural tendency for research to be used (and misused) to justify dominant world views, existing programs, or favored interventions; but there is also a tendency for research to support incremental change because research usually derives from existing programs and dominant ideologies. Incremental approaches to change are further supported by the frequently mixed or ambivalent findings from research. Rein and Peattie (1981, p. 541) advocate a critical perspective on research and suggest some of the questions to consider:

> More than content and methodology must be addressed if we are to understand the problem-setting process. Since its inception, social science has sought an adjudication role through which research could rise above particular claiming perspectives and become the means of discovering some general interest within which competing claims would be assimilated. We believe this is illusory. Believing this leads to questions as to the social organization of research. Who frames the problems? To whom are the findings useful? What is the sponsorship of research? What new, alternative bases for research are possible? And what problem formulations would they employ?

Despite the limitations on the validity and reliability of social science research and social intervention evaluations, their potential contributions should not be discounted. Research and evaluations have utility in analysis of the change opportunity. They contribute to our systematic examination of the situation. They may provide data for comparison; they may suggest alternative conceptualizations of the problem; they may help clarify implications of different courses of action.

The task of the change agent is first to locate research and evaluation findings and reports of practice innovations, then to assess their applicability, and finally to use their implications in analysis of the change opportunity.

Discerning Patterns and Relationships in the Data

The data collected in the identification phase have little meaning in their raw form. They must be analyzed through study, compared, and interpreted. Care must be taken to examine the most important and revealing relationships. Deciding how to organize and handle the data is a complex and difficult undertaking. The choice of variables to be isolated and comparisons to be made will influence the direction and usefulness of the analysis.

Several kinds of operations are basic to data processing. Data may be broken down so that the component parts can be studied and so that different variables can be correlated. Breaking data into subcategories is called *disaggregation*. For example, monthly figures on juveniles apprehended by the police may be disaggregated by type of offense, demographic characteristics of offenders, identity of officers, and other factors. These figures may be cross-tabulated to examine the relationship between selected characteristics (see Table 5-2). This breakdown begins to pinpoint sectors of the city where arrests are highest and can help to concentrate efforts toward making detailed analyses of selected sectors.

Data may also be combined to form single measures. Combining data is called *aggregation*. For example, county health officials may have data from many separate treatment centers, each reporting monthly statistics on the number of drug, alcohol, and mental health clients treated. In order to develop a countywide profile of services, data would be aggregated as illustrated in Table 5-3.

TABLE 5-2. Juveniles apprehended in June, by district and type of offense

	N.W.	*N.E.*	*S.W.*	*S.E.*	*Total*
Status offenses	9 (4%)	12 (5%)	16 (7%)	21 (9%)	58 (25%)
Nonstatus offenses	14 (6%)	19 (8%)	98 (41%)	46 (20%)	177 (75%)
Total	23 (10%)	31 (13%)	114 (48%)	67 (29%)	235 (100%)

TABLE 5-3. Individuals receiving drug, alcohol, and mental health services in Jackson County

Clients receiving drug-related services	370	(17.4%)
Clients receiving alcohol-related services	612	(28.7%)
Clients receiving mental health services	1147	(53.9%)
Total	2129	(100%)

In change efforts at both the organizational and community levels, the volume and variety of available data may seem overwhelming. During processing, data must be compiled, organized, analyzed, and presented in a manner that leads to understanding. Computers are valuable for data processing and are increasingly available to the human service professional. Weiner (1982) comments on the potential contribution of computers:

> Too many societal problems receive only simplistic thinking before actions are taken. When manager and planners are bogged down with receiving and processing data stimuli that flow at bombardment rates, there is little time remaining to analyze the data and perceive patterns. Machines can and should receive/process data; in turn, humans should be trained to take advantage of sophisticated computer graphic techniques to discern patterns and formulate response strategies. . . . As societal systems become more complicated and intricately interrelated, there will be a greater need for computer support of strategic planning activities.

Computers substantially enhance data processing capabilities. They enable change agents to calculate in minutes what would require hours or days of manual computation. Cross-tabulation, tests of significance, bar graphs, and many more comparisons and analyses may be secured if the computer has been provided with the necessary data and an appropriate program. Ultimately, however, human judgment is the key, for the change agent must determine what data are to be entered, in what form, and what programs are to be used to retrieve and analyze the data.

In data analysis, the task is to reduce the data to usable points of reference for understanding the change opportunity. Social science research texts include comprehensive presentations of data analysis techniques (Babbie, 1983; Campbell & Stanley, 1963; Miller, 1977; Wallace, 1971). Five basic approaches will be briefly highlighted here: cross-sectional analysis of component parts, time-series comparisons, comparisons with other data units, standards comparisons, and epidemiological analysis. The data to be used in analysis may include data from field surveys, secondary data such as census material, or standards established by experts in the field.

Cross-sectional analysis. Cross-sectional studies describe the change opportunity at a single point in time. One way to analyze and interpret the results of cross-sectional studies is to break down responses within one survey or sample. The total sample may be the focus of the analysis, or subgroups may be identified and their responses examined for similarities or differences from the total. The decennial U.S. Census provides a cross-sectional description of the population. Figures from the most recent census are often used in community planning. For example, the rates of substandard housing in a specific geographical area may be identified, and correlations may be calculated among size of families, age and sex of the heads of the households, and housing standards. Cross-sectional analysis is useful in describing the scope and extent of a problem and in geographically locating high-risk populations. One limitation of surveys is that each is based on information collected at only one point. A single cross-sectional study does not help explain changes over time.

Time-series comparisons. Several observations made over a period of time on the same population reveal trends and developments. Such measures help elucidate the historical and developmental characteristics of the change opportunity. If data were available at the county level on the incidence and prevalence of mental illness and on treatment-utilization patterns for several successive years, a trend toward multiple short hospitalizations for acute episodes of mental illness might emerge. Such information would aid in planning community resources and agency programs for the mentally ill. Time-series comparison is an important technique in program evaluation.

Comparisons with other data units. A third technique for data analysis compares data from one agency or community with data from similar agencies or communities. Such comparisons are often used to identify regional variations that might be significant. They may also be used to address issues of equity in resource allocation. For example, the United Way might be concerned about high rates of staff turnover in member agencies. Comparative data from other communities or agencies would help reveal whether this was a general phenomenon or whether it appeared to be more severe in specific agencies. If there were substantial variations, an effort could be made to identify variables associated with higher or lower staff-turnover rates.

The growing availability of community information systems, which collect and store information on a number of variables—for example, employment, health, rates of arrest and conviction for various crimes—facilitates comparisons between geographical units. Human service organizations are also increasingly developing data systems with information on service utilization, client characteristics, and service outcomes. Ensuring that the same or similar definitions and formulas were used to derive the data is crucial for the validity of comparison between units. Some national data sources, such as the census, are available to establish a comparative base from state to state, county to county, city to city, and district to district.

Standards comparisons. Another analysis approach compares data on a change opportunity to established standards. Standards comparisons often occur during an agency evaluation or accreditation process. The expertise of the evaluator or reviewer can be enlisted to enhance understanding of the change opportunity and to suggest potential intervention strategies. A number of national organizations in the human service arena promulgate standards related to their areas of expertise. For example, the Child Welfare League of America publishes comprehensive sets of standards related to community and agency programs for child abuse and neglect, adoption, and other child welfare services. The National Association of Social Workers and other professional organizations have goals for public social policy that provide a basis for comparison of existing situations to an ideal standard (National Association of Social Workers, 1983).

Comparison of the situation at hand with a set of standards helps the change agent determine change objectives. Standards also provide sanction for change efforts because they are set forth by respected professional bodies concerned with quality control and accountability. However, the change agent needs to understand that the orientation and possible subjectivity or bias of the standard-setting body may bring into question any set of standards.

Epidemiological analysis. In the public health field, epidemiology is the study of the distribution and dynamics of disease in human populations. *Distribution* refers to the prevalence of a disease or, in the human service perspective, of a status, condition, need, or behavior in human populations. Distribution factors—demographic variables as well as time and place—are analyzed to discern patterns. This element of epidemiology has been referred to as descriptive. Analysis of *dynamics or determinants* involves the study of the causes or contributing factors that form the etiological basis for the disease, status, condition, need, or behavior. This aspect of epidemiology has been referred to as analytical. *Human population* refers to any grouping of humans by a characteristic or set of characteristics (Burton, Smith, & Nichols, 1981, pp. 470–473; McMahon & Pugh, 1970, pp. 1–5). Minority groups, women, human service professionals, the elderly, the handicapped, and others may be identified as separate populations for analysis. The change agent recognizes that each of these populations may experience a change opportunity differently from the general population.

Epidemiological analysis is useful in understanding who is affected, historical trends in the change situation, and factors causing or contributing to the current situation. These understandings form the basis for the subsequent planning and implementation activities.

Moroney (1976) advocates the application of epidemiological methods to analysis in human services but notes that the model is more applicable to situations where there is a single causal agent than to multicausal problems. He cautions against simple solutions based on analysis of limited data. The apparent need for more hospital beds in the 1970s was deceptive (pp. 14–15):

> Hospital administrators and physicians have been arguing for expansion and cite growing populations, dangerously high occupancy rates, and long waiting lists for elective surgery. While some planning agencies accepted the analysis and recommended additional beds, others examined the situation more closely. Hospital utilization surveys showed that up to 25% of beds were being used by chronically ill patients, usually the elderly, and that many of these beds could be released for the care of acute patients if lower level care could be provided. . . . The solution, then, was not to add more hospital beds

but to develop a community support system. The cause was in placement and utilization.

Incorporating Cultural and Gender Perspectives

Data analysis also incorporates relevant cultural or gender perspectives in order to determine whether the change opportunity affects a minority population differently from nonminority individuals or women differently from men. Similarly, other oppressed populations have distinct experiences and perspectives to contribute to the definition and analysis of the change opportunity. The change agent must be sensitive to the role of discrimination as well as to diverse cultural values in analyzing data on the change opportunity. Knowledge and information can be introduced from a variety of sources. A growing body of literature is available to aid in the understanding of cultural and gender differences. Expert input is often also available from people knowledgeable about the critical cultural and gender issues.

It should be recognized, however, that perspectives on minority and women's issues vary significantly. Further, any subgroup of the population, by definition, shares specific characteristics and perhaps even experiences and perspectives. Yet each population cannot be treated as homogenous. Few, if any, populations agree on one perspective and recognize one spokesperson. It may be prudent and politically sound, therefore, to consider a range of perspectives.

It is also important that efforts to incorporate cultural and gender perspectives focus on strengths of a population rather than deficits. Much of the literature on women, for example, tends to emphasize victimization without an equally strong identification of positive factors. Interventions should not be designed to deal only with deficits, without building on strengths. And, finally, the analyst must determine whether a particular analysis leads only to hopelessness and dead ends. If so, that analysis cannot be used as the basis for intervention.

INTERPERSONAL ASPECTS

The technical aspects of the analysis phase assure that the process is systematic, rational, and thorough in its approach. Interpersonal aspects assure that the process is participatory, that values and preferences are considered, and that support for action is mobilized and opposition is reduced. This section discusses interpersonal, political, and economic considerations, and analysis of the force field.

Identifying Relevant Interpersonal Relationships

The relationship aspect of analysis refers to an understanding of the ability to develop cooperative working relationships despite differences of opinion. Good working relationships depend heavily on clear and accurate communication. Individuals develop unique perceptions and perspectives as a result of their personal experiences. These perspectives act as filters in sending and receiving communications. Communication is defined by Robbins (1980) as "the transference and understanding of meaning" (p. 356). Robbins identifies seven parts of the communication process: the communication source or sender, the message, encoding, the channel, decoding, the receiver, and feedback. Four conditions, he says, affect the encoding of messages: skill, attitudes, knowledge, and sociocultural system. The way messages are encoded and decoded will, therefore, vary greatly from person to person.

Initiators, clients, the change agent, and other relevant parties may have different attitudes, beliefs, perceptions, and perspectives about the change opportunity. Their personal ideologies will affect their viewpoints and their openness to different understandings of the change opportunity. Part of the purpose of analysis is to bring to the surface these different values and their strength or importance to different participants in the process.

It is important that the change agent deal with interpersonal differences sensitively. Openness and discussion should be encouraged. The change agent attempts to maintain an analytical focus and avoid conflicts. The goal is to reach consensus based on careful consideration of all the technical aspects of analysis, while recognizing that interpersonal conflicts are powerful barriers to consensus.

Incorporating Political and Economic Considerations

Political and economic considerations also weigh heavily in analysis. The availability of resources, the political climate, the level of awareness of the general public and of leaders all influence the acceptance of particular analyses and their implications. Political and economic considerations become particularly important as the process moves from analysis to action and as objectives and strategies are considered.

The change agent's task in the analysis phase includes assessment of political and economic considerations. Four processes are important: assessing the impact of the proposed change on other systems; cultivating sanction for a change-oriented analysis; assessing economic resources; and building support and minimizing opposition. If these considerations are ignored, the chances of developing successful planned change intervention are reduced. Each of these four considerations is discussed in the following sections.

Assessing the impact of the proposed change on other systems. Other systems might gain or lose clients or other resources, have their policies or procedures modified, or experience other changes central to their mission or ways of doing business. The establishment of a free clinic will have an impact on referrals to medical specialists at the county hospital and on referrals to community mental health clinics. The creation of a centralized hospital social service department will change lines of authority and patterns of communication and access if social workers were previously responsible only to separate medical services. These anticipated side effects need to be identified. Representatives from these systems may in many instances participate in the analysis phase. They are particularly important in assessing links with other parts of the community, organization, or human service network. To the extent that these other systems share in refining the problem definition and shaping initial understandings of the change opportunity, they become potential members of a support group for action. However, if their participation in analytical activities results in opposition to a proposal for change, their positions will be known and can be taken into account in developing strategies. Failure to involve them may contribute to counterproductive territorial or ideological disputes. If crucial perspectives are not considered, rational resistance to an inappropriate analysis may develop.

Cultivating sanction.   Developing sanction for a change-oriented analysis is not always easy, especially where no previous human service intervention exists. The general public and existing political structures often support and rationalize the status quo. Nonetheless, particularly if the change effort is focused on a problem, a number of professionals and citizens will perceive the need for change and have a different vision of the future. If they find none of the organizations, communities, groups, or service networks most directly involved receptive to their ideas, they may look for another approach to initiating change. An interesting historical example illustrates how, in a time when children were viewed as the property of their parents, change agents found an acceptable point of entry for intervention. A child named Mary Ellen came to the attention of community leaders in 1875. She was being severely beaten and neglected by her foster parents. Lacking child abuse and neglect legislation as a sanction, community leaders used existing laws against abuse of animals as the basis for intervention (Kadushin, 1974, pp. 225–226).

Assessing economic resources.   Economic resources—especially in times of limited growth or recession—play a crucial role in determining the acceptability and feasibility of a proposed change. Creation of new services will be difficult unless the analysis can demonstrate cost savings or other important benefits. Analysis must address economic issues. Who should pay (the recipient of service, the employer, the taxpayer, other third parties, or some combination) and which level of government or which nongovernmental source should provide resources are important issues to consider. Where there is competition for limited resources, the strengths and weaknesses of potential alternatives should be addressed. During the analysis phase, practitioners should examine several alternatives and their implications. The availability of data on more than one option preserves flexibility.

Building support and minimizing opposition.   Identifying potential support for and opposition to change facilitates successful action. The change agent can cultivate positive forces and anticipate resistance. Clues regarding which groups and individuals will be supportive and which will work against the change have been emerging since the change process began. Who has participated in discussions and meetings to identify and analyze the problem, and who—although invited—hasn't? What different definitions and understandings of the situation have been proposed, by whom, and what are their implications? Which systems and groups have tended to legitimate the status quo and why? Which will need to give sanction to a change effort?

Building support and minimizing opposition may be accomplished through involvement of key persons, groups, and organizations. Identifying common interests and establishing the basis for a mutually beneficial exchange of resources encourage reciprocity as well as the recognition of interdependence. Brager and Holloway (1978, p. 187) underline the importance of human relationships, values, attitudes, and beliefs:

> In social work, assessment has tended to focus either on the service needs of specific individuals and groups or on the technical aspects of services and systems affecting categories of clients. While these are significant areas of professional activity, we believe that a set of concerns that might be called "political"—including the tasks of identifying potential opposition and support, negotiating an exchange of rewards, and the like—is no less important although it has been largely neglected.

In this process, the change agent recognizes the value of wide participation and uses a number of methods and techniques. Participants should have an opportunity to learn about, shape, and validate the understanding of the change opportunity and its implications. Although data processing and making links to theories and research often require special expertise and resources, the initiators, clients, planners, and implementers all have an interest in the analysis phase. It is important to establish mechanisms to involve these change systems in developing and reviewing the analysis. In a transactive planning process, as discussed in Chapter 4 (Friedmann, 1973), the change agent and other participants engage in an intensive dialogue in which they exchange perspectives. Mutual learning and sharing during the analysis phase help prepare participants for acceptance of change.

Delbecq, Vandeven, and Gustafson (1975) describe a number of group techniques for decision making. Two approaches are the Nominal Group Technique (NGT) and the Delphi Technique. NGT and Delphi are useful for involving various participants early in the analysis phase and helping them identify problems, clarify issues, and express values and preferences.

Analyzing the Force Field

Participatory group techniques and transactive processes involve those affected by the change episode in the development of an understanding of the change opportunity. Force-field analysis assesses potential support for and opposition to these shared understandings of the change opportunity.

Force-field analysis is derived from theoretical constructs developed by Lewin (1951) and applied by human service practitioners. Brager and Holloway (1978, p. 108) illustrate its use in analysis, introducing their discussion with a statement of the basic concept:

> At the heart of his [Lewin's] "field theory" is the conception that stability within a social system is a *dynamic* rather than a static condition. Seeming stability among the elements of social systems is, in this view, the result of

opposing and countervailing "forces" that continuously operate to produce what we *experience* as stability. Change occurs when the forces shift, thus causing a disruption in the system's equilibrium.

Lewin called the systematic identification of opposing forces a "force-field analysis." In analyzing a field of forces, a range of variables is identified which have a probability of influencing the preferences of significant organizational participants with respect to the desired change.

The process of force-field analysis requires several activities (Brager & Holloway, 1978, pp. 112–128):

1. The change agent must specify the understanding of the change opportunity. Clarity is essential.
2. The change agent then identifies critical and facilitating actors. *Critical actors* are those whose support is crucial for a change effort to succeed; they hold the power necessary to cause the change to happen. *Facilitating actors* are those who wield important influence with—or control access to—critical actors.
3. The next step is to specify driving forces and restraining forces. *Driving forces* are those variables that, when activated or enhanced, promote or support the analysis. *Restraining forces* are those variables that, when activated or enhanced, hinder or create resistance to the analysis or strengthen commitment to the status quo.
4. Once the forces are identified, the change agent analyzes each to assess three factors: amenability to change, potency, and consistency. *Amenability* refers to a force's potential for modification, *potency* to its anticipated impact on the problem, and *consistency* to its likelihood of remaining stable throughout the change process.

Figure 5-2 is a chart that a change agent might use to record a force-field analysis.

Force-field analysis is useful at this stage of the change process because this is the earliest point when full understanding of the change opportunity is to be expected. During the identification and definition phase, incomplete appreciation exists. Conceptual frameworks have not been rigorously tested by empirical evidence during identification and definition. During analysis, key participants can see the implications of this choice of understandings for subsequent choices of objectives and strategies.

The force-field analysis developed during the analysis phase is intended to be a working document. The change agent expects to reconsider and revise the force-field analysis at key points in the change process: when specific goals and objectives are selected, when strategies are chosen, and during the implementation process.

THE ANALYTICAL PROCESS

Analysis in the social sciences in many cases is more art than science. Although an attempt has been made here to systematize a process for collect-

Support of
change opportunity

Opposition to
change opportunity

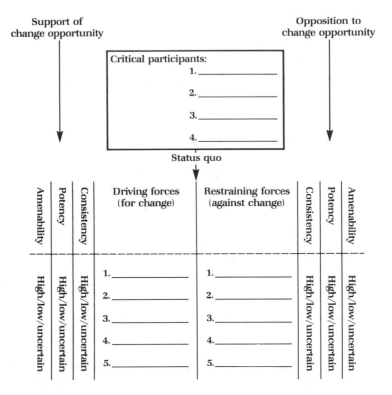

FIGURE 5-2. Force-field analysis chart. *Adapted from Changing Human Service Organizations: Politics and Practice, by G. Brager and S. Holloway, p. 127. Copyright © 1978 by The Free Press, a Division of Macmillan Publishing Company.*

ing and analyzing data and information, the analyst should not expect that a clear and concise understanding of the situation will readily emerge or that the process will proceed in a neat, orderly manner. Development of several working hypotheses is a more reasonable expectation than establishment of a common understanding. Analyzing these hypotheses, the change agent and other participants continually test for a fit among a range of considerations including theoretical frameworks; research and practice findings; data and information; interpersonal, political, and economic considerations; and cultural and gender perspectives. In this analytical process, those involved continually move toward some understandings and away from others, as each of the working hypotheses appears to provide or fails to provide an explanation of the current situation.

Analysis involves a thinking through and ordering of the data and information gathered in the identification phase of the process. Since, in reality, identification and analysis are interactive processes, awareness of a framework for analysis permits efficient collection of data and information. Developing etiological, theoretical, cultural, and gender perspectives involves consideration of all the components of identification for their fit to the situation at hand. Discussing patterns in data involves analysis of the data that document the need for change. Force-field analysis attempts to weigh the human factors, values, preferences, and their relative strengths in supporting or resisting change. These processes may be undertaken simultaneously. The change agent can involve members of the initiator, client, and action systems as appropriate. The goal is clarity, a common understanding by the major participants of the change opportunity. Graphic presentation of the components of identification and analysis may be helpful to the change agent. Table 5-4 illustrates the interrelationships of these components.

Effective analysis is systematic and comprehensive. It produces a statement or picture of the central elements of the change opportunity and their interrelationships and dynamics. It suggests next steps. As the analytical work moves toward completion, the need begins to become clear. Need implies a deficit on the part of the target population. Meeting a need requires some form of intervention. Before the analysis phase is complete, data should be ordered to depict the size and scope of the target population and the normative, perceived, expressed, and relative need. These data, together with the components of analysis, form the basis for consideration of goals and objectives.

Case Study

Jan Simpson was one of 7 women and 18 men on the professional staff of the Sunnyvale Community Mental Health Clinic (SCMHC). She had worked there for a year. In preparing a statistical report, she became aware that the dropout rate from treatment in the crisis unit was higher for women patients than for men. She had been aware of some other indicators of women's dissatisfaction with SCMHC services, such as the patient who alleged that a male therapist made sexual overtures and the complaint from a women's group in the community that women patients receive medication more frequently than men.

Jan talked with a few other women staff members, learned of their confirmation of some of her impressions, and decided to pursue the question. She requested and received permission from the director to explore this situation further using clinic service data.

Jan began to analyze data about women clinic patients. Her initial impressions were confirmed by the data, which showed higher rates of medication and lower rates of other treatment for women patients. More dropouts from the crisis clinic were women, but their length of time on the in-patient unit was longer. No patient satisfaction survey had been conducted in the past five years, so she could not find systematic evidence to confirm her impression of dissatisfaction among a subtantial number of women patients.

Before deciding on next steps, Jan returned to the director and explained her initial finding to him. He was receptive and decided to set up a task force, composed of three therapists and two administrators, to analyze the issue and make recommendations based on their analysis. He wanted to have a

TABLE 5-4. Components of identification and analysis of a change opportunity

Identification of a condition →	Leads to identification of a problem or opportunity →	Which leads to analysis of a problem or opportunity →	Which leads to a shared understanding of the need for intervention →	Which leads to subsequent phases in the change process
A statement describing the current situation, based on existing data and information	• *Problem statement:* A statement about why the condition is seen as a problem and by whom • *Boundaries:* The geographical or population limits for study of the problem • *Specification of participants:* Identification of initiators, clients, targets, change agent, planners and implementers • *Documenting the need for change:* Identification of relevant data that support the problem statement • *Interpersonal, political and economic considerations:* • *Complexity:* identification of all relevant perspectives and considerations • *Intensity:* level of feeling and commitment from each relevant perspective • *Urgency:* degree to which problem is life threatening • *Duration:* length of time the problem has been in existence • *Control:* identification of sources of control over change • *Barriers:* identification of barriers to resolution • *Cost of nonresolution:* calculation of what the costs will be if nothing is done	• *Etiological and theoretical perspectives:* • *Etiology:* identification of cause/effect relationships and development of consensus about causes • *Theory:* identification of relevant theoretical frameworks and development of consensus • *Research, evaluation, and practice findings:* identification of relevant research, evaluation, and practice findings • *Patterns in available data:* Utilization of data collected for cross-sectional analysis, time-series comparisons, comparisons with other data units, standards comparisons, and epidemiological analysis • *Cultural and gender perspectives:* Incorporation of special considerations based on culture and/or gender into the analysis • *Interpersonal, political, and economic considerations:* Analysis of interpersonal differences, political implications, and economic considerations; examination of forces moving toward change and forces resisting change	• *Normative need:* Deficits in relation to standards established by experts • *Perceived need:* Deficits in relation to standards established by the respondent • *Expressed need:* Deficits established by demand for services • *Relative need:* Deficits established when needs and resources in one area are compared with needs and resources in another area	Goals and objectives are established, a plan is developed, intervention takes place, and evaluation (if intervention is effective) reveals a changed condition

thorough review of existing data before recommending any commitment of clinic funds to other actions, however.

The task force divided the responsibility, with two members conducting further analysis of the clinic data and the other three locating published reports on women and mental health. They learned that the patterns identified at SCMHC were similar to, but slightly more pronounced than, patterns found in many community mental health centers. Women were disproportionately represented in the patient load, with heavier prescription rates for medication, more serious diagnoses, and less effective treatment outcomes.

The task force became quite concerned about its findings and requested time during a staff meeting to make a report. At the meeting, a number of the staff members were not convinced that a problem existed. They felt the statistics reflected a naturally occurring reality: more susceptibility to some types of mental illness among the female population. They saw no reason to spend clinic funds on an evaluative survey on women's perception of treatment since the staff was made up of professionals who were performing their jobs competently and responsibly.

Case Study Discussion Questions

1. Which aspects of data analysis did the task force cover well, and which did they neglect? What would you have done differently and why?
2. What are Jan's options if the administrator opposes any further pursuit of this issue? Which option would you attempt? Why?
3. If the change episode is to move ahead, what next steps might the administrator, the change agent, the task force, and staff take, and why?
4. Identify a perspective and interpretation that might be developed within each of the four etiological categories.
5. Identify those who should be involved in the analysis phase.
6. Examine the interpersonal, political, and economic considerations and construct a force-field analysis. Was it helpful? Where did it lead you?

SUMMARY OF PHASE II

I. Definition

Analysis of the change opportunity is the phase in which the definition of the change opportunity and the data gathered during Phase I are further studied for the purpose of developing clarity, understanding, and an explanation of the dynamics and causes of the change opportunity. This phase provides an analytic statement, which is the basis for developing appropriate and meaningful objectives and strategies.

II. Information needed

A. Are there etiological perspectives and theories that help explain the phenomenon or suggest change objectives and strategies?

B. What is known about the causes or treatment of this phenomenon? What do research studies, evaluations, and reports of practice innovations say about this change opportunity?

C. As the data are processed, what patterns may be discerned? What is

the distribution and what are the determinants of the phenomenon?
   D. Which variables appear to be associated? Can causal patterns be discerned?
   E. Are there particular cultural or gender perspectives relevant to this situation?
   F. Which interests, actors and change systems should have input into framing or responding to the analysis?
   G. Who might support or oppose a particular understanding of the change opportunity and which forces can be utilized in the direction of desired change?
   H. What values and perspectives are involved and how can they be used to mobilize for action?
III. Tasks to be accomplished
   A. Analyze and synthesize data to discern patterns, including distribution, association, and etiology
   B. Locate relevant reports of research, evaluations, and practice innovations, and theoretical frameworks for analysis
   C. Process data already collected and collect additional comparative data if available
   D. Identify gender and cultural perspectives and their implications
   E. Identify relevant change systems to be involved in the analysis of the change opportunity, noting roles appropriate to each
   F. Consider interpersonal, political, and economic implications of the analysis
   G. Conduct force-field analysis of the most promising understandings of the change opportunity
   H. Based on analysis, identify and define need in this episode of change
IV. Products to be developed
   An analysis of the problem, including identification of the contribution of research and theory to understanding and explaining the change opportunity; discernment of significant patterns, relationships, and causal factors; consideration of interpersonal, political, economic, cultural, and gender perspectives on the situation; assessment of alternative understandings and their feasibility and selection of a particular alternative; and assessment of need in relation to the tentatively planned intervention.
V. Next steps: transition to Phase III
   The common understanding of the change opportunity provides the basis for the subsequent selection of objectives and strategies.

SUMMARY OF MAJOR POINTS

1. The change opportunity, once defined, requires thorough analysis.
2. Developing etiological perspectives helps identify important variables and conceptualizations related to the situation.
3. Theoretical frameworks give direction to the analysis.
4. Findings from research studies, evaluations, and reports of innovative

human service interventions provide additional data for the analysis, suggest conceptualizations, and add to understandings of relationships.

5. Processing data allows patterns, trends, and relationships to be examined and comparisons to be made. Techniques for data processing include cross-sectional analysis, time-series comparisons, comparisons with other data units, and standards comparisons.

6. The analysis takes into account gender and cultural considerations so that intervention may be responsive to diversity in society and to social justice.

7. Analytical activities are conducted by change agents in interaction with initiators, clients, planners, and implementers. Interpersonal and political factors such as the attitudes, beliefs, and value perspectives of major participants and the availability of resources affect the analysis and how it is used.

8. Analysis provides the understandings of the change opportunity that are the basis for subsequent change episode decisions and activities. A significant aspect of these understandings is feasibility: understandings must lead to action with a reasonable prospect for success.

DISCUSSION OR SELF-STUDY QUESTIONS

1. What pressures contribute to the tendency of human service professionals to bypass analysis and respond to symptoms with immediate action? What arguments might you give for investing time in analysis?

2. An administrator of a major, public human service agency is aware of persistent high turnover among entry-level professional staff. It is time for budget submission and the deputy director suggests submitting a request for a 15% pay increase to counteract turnover. The deputy suggests justifying the increase as economical since a reduction in turnover will save their having to constantly orient and train new staff. The administrator believes further analysis should be made before a solution is proposed. What kinds of data might be sought, from what sources? How might these data be analyzed?

3. Suggest three different etiological perspectives on substance abuse. How would you decide whether each was relevant to planning services?

4. A newspaper expose on hunger has alleged that there are severely malnourished children in the community, that some families are eating out of garbage cans, and that some elderly are subsisting on dog food. The public welfare department and the court health department each looked into this situation and reported that the media had exaggerated a few cases of "mentally disturbed individuals, who refused to seek help from agencies." You are a children's advocate working for a nonprofit agency, and you are concerned about the needs of the children involved. How might you proceed?

SUGGESTED READINGS

Campbell, D. T., & Stanley, J. T. *Experimental and quasi-experimental designs for the social sciences.* Washington, D.C.: American Educational Research Association, 1963.

Meenaghan, T., Washington, R., & Ryan, R. *Macro practice in the human services: An introduction to planning, administration, evaluation, and community organizing components of practice.* New York: Free Press, 1982.

Nagel, S. *Improving policy analysis.* Beverly Hills, Calif.: Sage, 1980.

Weiner, M. E. *Human services management: Analysis and application.* Homewood, Ill.: Dorsey Press, 1982.

CHAPTER SIX

Setting Goals and Objectives

OBJECTIVES

Studying the contents of this chapter should enable the reader to:

DEFINE AND DISCUSS THESE KEY CONCEPTS

Goal

Objective

GIVEN A WELL-DEFINED ORGANIZATIONAL OR COMMUNITY CHANGE
OPPORTUNITY, DRAFT ONE OR MORE GOALS FOR AN EPISODE OF PLANNED
CHANGE

GIVEN A GOAL, DEVELOP A SERIES OF PROCESS AND OUTCOME OBJECTIVES
FOR THE CHANGE EPISODE

IDENTIFY AND DISCUSS THE TECHNICAL, THE INTERPERSONAL, AND THE
POLITICAL ASPECTS OF GOAL AND OBJECTIVE SETTING

DEVELOP A COMPLETE ACTION PLAN

"**W**ould you tell me, please, which way I ought to go from here?"

"That depends a good deal on where you want to go," said the Cat.

"I don't much care where," said Alice.

"Then it doesn't matter which way you go," said the Cat.

Lewis Carroll, *Alice in Wonderland*

A clear definition of the direction in which a change effort is to move is critical to the success of that effort. Although past attempts at change have typically had at least a vaguely defined sense of direction, many have failed for lack of specificity and consensus. The "crisis of accountability" given so much coverage in human service literature during the late 1970s stimulated interest in goal and objective setting. As it became apparent that continued funding for human service programs often was contingent on prior specification of outcomes and rigorous evaluation, objectifying outcomes gained increased importance (Daley, 1976, pp. 241–251). Human service professionals are accountable for the efficient use of resources in the planning, administration, and provision of those services that meet consumer needs. Goals and objectives can be valuable tools to use in fulfilling this requirement. They can tell us where we want to go.

ROLE OF GOALS AND OBJECTIVES IN THE CHANGE PROCESS

Deliberate, planned approaches to organizational and community change are essentially future oriented. In this sense, planned change is proactive—it attempts to gain control over subsequent events and conditions. Setting goals and objectives moves the change process from concern for past and present events and conditions to concern for desirable potential future states. The goals and objectives selected have far-reaching implications for the subsequent phases of the change process. They set the direction and describe the proposed destination. Later in the change process, objectives will be used to focus monitoring and evaluation activities. Objectives direct the evaluator to the key results the change episode intends to produce. Daley (1980, pp. 58–59) provides a model reflecting the integrative and linkage functions of goals and objectives during an episode of intervention.

A community situation will illustrate the function of setting goals and objectives. In Springdale, a series of teenage traffic deaths involved intoxicated drivers. Local police reported a 340% increase in driving-while-intoxicated arrests during the past three years. A newly organized chapter of Mothers Against Drunk Drivers (MADD) pointed out that nationally over 500 persons per week are killed by drunk drivers.

The mayor appointed a blue-ribbon community panel to look into the situation and make recommendations. The panel consisted of the high school principal, the county sheriff, the director of the mental health center, the president of MADD, and a business, a civic, and a political leader. During the definition and analysis activities, two distinct views of the situation emerged. One group (the MADD president, the school principal, the sheriff, and the political leader) saw the situation as essentially a law-enforcement problem— Springdale needed to get tough with drunk drivers. The second group (the mental health professional and the business and civic leaders) saw the situation in essentially behavioral-health terms—the intoxicated drivers needed to be off the roads and in treatment. The problem statement incorporated both views of the situation.

When the panel began to set goals and objectives, the differences between the two views became crucial. All members could agree on the general goals of getting drunk drivers off the road and decreasing traffic deaths caused by intoxicated drivers. However, those who favored strict law enforcement proposed quicker prosecution, no plea bargaining, and longer mandatory jail sentences. Those who favored a behavioral-health explanation proposed prevention and treatment programs for alcoholics. With limited resources, choices would have to be made.

This illustration of the relationship between the definition and analysis of the planned change opportunity and the setting of goals and objectives highlights several key points. First, although we have suggested that a single, consistent definition and analysis statement be developed before facing the task of goal and objective setting, at times this statement is not produced, lacks necessary specificity, or addresses multiple problems. Second, when resources are limited, choices must be made between or among possible future states. Finally, for the planned change process to move forward effectively and efficiently, these choices must be reflected in goals and objectives.

The change agent develops frames of reference during the definition and analysis steps to facilitate understanding of the change opportunity. To ensure continuity, these same frames of reference are used in setting goals. In the Springdale illustration two frames of reference—law enforcement and behavioral health—were developed. These ways of looking at the change opportunity shape the nature of the goals and objectives selected. A variety of frameworks—or multidisciplinary frameworks—provides the rich background needed to deal effectively with many organizational and community situations needing change. Alcoholism and drunk driving are complex phenomena involving biological, psychological, social, and economic factors in their development and in their resolution. Piecemeal law-enforcement approaches to the Springdale situation may contribute to the development of even more serious problems—for example, long-term economic dependency and family instability if the drivers are given lengthy jail sentences. Therefore, our change model anticipates the need for multiple or multidimensional sets of goals and objectives when dealing with complex phenomena. In the case of drunk driving, goals and objectives might address desired future legal biological, economic, social, and psychological states for the driver, his or her family, natural community helping systems, and other significant persons and systems.

In summary, the purpose of setting goals and objectives is to move the focus of the change process from what presently exists to a desired future state. The logic of the planned change process requires that both the present situation (condition, need, problem, issue or opportunity) and the desired future state (goals and objectives) fit within the same framework because those factors that have contributed to the existence of the present state need to be addressed as the change process moves toward the desired future state. By the end of this phase of the change process, the key results of the change episode will have been specified and accepted by all participants.

SETTING GOALS

The terms *goal* and *objective* have specific meanings as used in this book. Different authors define these terms in different ways. Some transpose the meanings used here. Others treat the terms as synonymous. When exploring the literature on this topic, readers therefore must examine how a particular author uses each of these terms if they are to understand that author's ideas.

Statements of Purpose

Goals and objectives are part of a hierarchy that begins with a statement of purpose (a mission statement). Statements of purpose provide a continuing philosophical perspective and make explicit the reason for the existence of an organization or a community service system. Statements of purpose establish broad and relatively permanent parameters within which goals are developed (Morrisey, 1970, pp. 19–27). A state department of social services might have the following statement of purpose: "to increase the economic self-sufficiency of disadvantaged populations in the state." A statement of purpose will never change unless the reason for the existence of an organization or a community service system changes.

Definition

Describing goals in a human service agency, Daley (1980, p. 58) notes:

> Goals describe desired future states. They are broad statements intended to provide a general direction, and they are brief general statements to the

community that reflect that agency's interests and identity. Goals are not sufficiently specific to provide guidance for agencies' day-to-day operational decisions; they are long range and frequently do not include an explicit time frame. Goal statements may be formulated in quantitative or qualitative terms and may or may not be attainable. It may or may not be possible to measure their achievement or even to know if a goal is achieved.*

Goals may be developed at the community, organizational, program, and service-delivery levels. All three approaches to planned change—policy, program, and project—include goal setting. Goals developed at higher levels and for more broadly defined units tend to be more encompassing, while goals at the organization, program, or client service level are more narrowly defined. An illustration may help to clarify the scope of goals at different levels:

Statewide or community goal: To reduce the incidence of alcohol abuse in the state (or county).
Organizational goal: To reduce alcohol dependence and increase economic self-sufficiency for those clients who are served by this organization.
Program goal: To increase the self-esteem of those clients who participate in this program.
Service-delivery goal: To improve Mr. Franklin's interpersonal-relationship skills.

Stepping back from day-to-day concerns to set new goals might be done every three to five years on a formal basis at the community and organizational levels. A longer time frame might be appropriate if facility planning is involved—for example, when a boys' and girls' club contemplates building a new sports complex with an expected life of 20 years. Setting goals is not costly and is a wise investment to ensure responsiveness to changing client and consumer needs and preferences. Although the formal process of goal setting may occur every three to five years, goals may be reviewed in intervening years as annual objective setting takes place to ensure that the goals remain responsive to current client needs. At the program and service-delivery levels, goals are usually set for the duration of the program, service, or change episode.

Functions of Goals

Goals have multiple functions: They are general guides or beacons for the change episode. They provide brief statements of the intended area of intervention. And, in a political sense, abstract goal statements provide the umbrella under which individuals, groups, organizations, and interests holding diverse views can be mobilized to support activities in a general interven-

*From "Setting Objectives in the Human Service Agency," by J. M. Daley. In K. Dea (Ed.), *Perspectives for the Future: Social Work Practice in the 80's.* Copyright © 1980 by the National Association of Social Workers, Inc. This and all other quotations from the same source are reprinted by permission.

tion area. Goals do not address the why (rationale) or how (methods) questions of change efforts.

Goals should therefore describe the major directions of the change effort, be concise and clear to ensure comprehension by the intended audience, and be likely to elicit a positive response. Thus content, clarity, and political attractiveness guide goal selection and formulation. The change agent needs to identify the parties and interests that must be involved, understand how each will react to various formulations, and tailor the statements to obtain approval of the necessary parties. The change agent often uses negotiating skills in helping the initiators, targets, clients, planners, and implementers to reach agreement on the goals of the change episode. Successive drafts may be circulated among the various participants until a version captures a direction acceptable to all parties.

Goal statements are vital in the public debate about human service interventions. Goal statements are the public banners under which competing interests attempt to mobilize support for change efforts. Interest groups invoke strongly held values in their goal statements. Consider the debate on abortion services. The public is asked to support movements advocating "the right to life" or "freedom of choice." Each slogan expresses a broad and highly valued conviction in order to attract widespread support. In attempting to influence an organization's or a community's agenda, the change agent must be keenly aware of the values implicit in goal statements.

The politics of goal setting involves interest-group competition for scarce resources in addition to value conflicts. Rivlin (1971, pp. 46–47) discusses the nature of the conflict over policy goals (which she calls objectives):

> The bitter argument that rages among the radical right, the middle, and the new and old left over social action programs is not primarily about the objectives themselves. The real issues are the relative importance of these and other objectives (curing poverty versus preserving self-reliance, for example) and the means of reaching them. Almost all the participants in the argument genuinely want healthier, better educated citizens, and less poverty. These are not empty slogans. They suggest indicators—a set of measurements—that most people would accept at least with respect to the desirable direction of change. Most people believe infant-mortality rates should go down, reading levels should go up, and the number of people with low incomes should decline. They are not agreed on what they would give up to achieve these changes, how to achieve them, or which ones are most important.

Participation in Setting Goals

Individuals formally charged with setting the directions for communities, organizations, and programs select goals. These individuals typically are members of governing boards (boards of directors, trustees, oversight committees, or legislative bodies). Daley (1980, pp. 61–65) proposes an expanded goal-setting task force for a human service agency; such a task force could be used in community and program goal setting as well:

Intense participation by a broad spectrum of actors ensures that the institutional goal-setting process avoids an inadvertent continuation of the existing goals and programs of the agency. A mechanism frequently used by agencies to accomplish this is some form of organizational retreat . . . [involving] as key contributors persons who are not traditionally included in retreats. Middle managers; service delivery staff; nonprofessional employees, including clerical staff; consumers; and other community persons have substantial contributions to make to the deliberations concerning "images of the future"—the future shape of society and the community's and agency's role. . . . Facilitative techniques and trained group leaders further assure the accomplishment of the necessary tasks. Outside stimulators can provoke the thinking of participants. For example, futurists might discuss what they think the community will be like in five or ten years; faculty members can present their views of knowledge or skill breakthroughs likely to be available to the helping professions; government representatives might discuss changes likely in government involvement in meeting human service needs; or social demographers might describe the community's population of the future.

SETTING OBJECTIVES

Purpose of Objectives

Although goal statements provide useful general guides or beacons, specific objective statements are needed to guide subsequent implementation and evaluation decisions in the change process. Goals provide the context for gaining public recognition and political support. Objectives direct intervention and evaluation activities in a highly specific manner.

Consider this situation: A board of education has directed the superintendent of schools to look into the problem of the high dropout rate from the high schools and the many academic and social problems experienced by marginal students. A task force made up of teachers, parents, students, administrators, and board members explores the problem and identifies a variety of perspectives on it. Teachers express concern about the low level of effort expended by academically marginal students and feel parents need to take responsibility. Parents question the placement of students experiencing academic difficulty in the same classes with average or exceptional students. Administrators raise questions about the ability of the school district to add another special program when funding is being reduced. Students feel that an effort should be made to involve marginal students in extracurricular activities. In spite of different perspectives, however, all members are able to agree on a goal statement. The goal is "to improve the academic performance of students experiencing academic difficulty." It describes a future state. It is a broad statement intended to provide general direction. It can act as an umbrella under which many different perspectives can be incorporated, and it is politically attractive in that it reinforces a strongly held set of values.

Following agreement on a goal statement, however, divergent perspectives must be identified, reconciled, and ordered according to importance. This task is accomplished by setting objectives. For example, what is meant by "academic performance"? What is meant by "improve"? How will "academic difficulty" be defined? What kinds of efforts should now be undertaken to move toward the goal? Options include counseling, tutoring, providing Parent Effectiveness Training, reorganizing class structures and teaching assignments, and expanding extracurricular activities. Obviously the goal statement does not provide sufficient direction to guide preparation for action or to indicate how success will be evaluated. This direction is provided by objectives.

Any number of objectives can be incorporated under a goal. The guiding factor is what is realistic and manageable, given the severity of the problem and the time and resources available. One objective under the stated goal might read: "By June 30, the reading level of at least 100 high school seniors defined as experiencing academic difficulty will be improved to a minimum of 9.6 years as measured by a standard reading achievement test." This objective establishes one clear direction in the move toward the stated goal.

With this objective as a guide, planning can go forward. This is the primary purpose of objective setting—the desired future state is identified in specific detail in order to guide subsequent planning, implementation, and evaluation activities. Objectives facilitate a meeting of the minds about important decisions. When written, objectives also help the various participants to understand their responsibilities in the activities. Therefore, objectives should be written in language that is clear, concise, and commonly understood by those expected to use them as guides.

Later in the change episode, objectives will serve as criteria and standards against which effectiveness is measured. Well-formulated objectives are vital to the productive evaluation of planned change efforts and results. Objectives identify in specific language the intended outcomes of the planned intervention; they describe the results the evaluation will seek to measure and judge. Carefully selected and formulated objectives structure evaluation efforts. Therefore, the use of resources during this phase of the change process can be viewed as an initial investment in evaluating the process and results of the planned intervention. The objectives indicate to the evaluator what to look for (results and criteria) in which population and when.

Definition

Contrasting objectives and goals in human service agencies, Daley (1980, pp. 58–59) states:

> [In contrast to goals] objectives describe desired future states that are the intended result of interventions. Objectives reflect shorter time frames, seldom exceeding one year in the human service field. They typically have an explicit time frame. It is important that the objectives be articulated in quantitative terms because it is necessary to know when objectives are achieved and to measure their achievement. . . . Objectives focus on key results—the important products of the professional intervention. As such,

the identification of an agency's predicted key results is a vital step in the process of setting objectives and, for an agency, serve a crucial function in its program decisions.

Objectives may be set at the community, organizational, program, and service-delivery levels for change episodes using policy, program, or project approaches. However, change objectives are less frequently encountered at the community level and with policy approaches in the human service field. Because of the complexity and breadth of most community-level and policy changes, only goals are specified, with objectives left to the specific implementation programs or projects.

Content.   Authors vary in their opinions about what should be included in statements of objectives. Consensus exists that the how (methods and activities) and why (rationale) questions of change are not addressed in statements of objectives. The rationale is examined during the definition and analysis phases of the process; the methods and activities are explicated in the design and implementation activities, which follow objective setting.

Mager (1962, p. 12) appears to propose the fewest elements in a statement of objectives. Speaking of learning objectives, he proposes that an objective identify the terminal behavior expected of the student, describe the significant conditions under which the behavior is expected, and identify the criteria for acceptable performance. Mali (1972), Morrisey (1970), Raia (1974), and Reddin (1971), suggest other components of objectives including an explicit time frame, a statement of the resources needed, and identification of the agent responsible for accomplishing the objective.

As used here, an objective includes the following components:

1. Time frame—date by which the objective will be completed
2. Target population—the population that will evidence the desired change
3. Result—the intended key consequence, which includes the variables to be changed and (possibly) the direction and magnitude of the change
4. Criteria—standards for use in measuring successful achievement of the result

Types.   It is necessary to utilize two types of objectives—outcome objectives and process objectives. *Outcome objectives* refer to a quality-of-life change for the target population. Millar and Millar (1981) define outcome as "the condition of the client after services have been provided (preferably after they have been completed) and the extent of change in the client after they are provided" (p. 2). A quality-of-life change can be a behavioral change (reduction in unexcused absences), a change in status (unemployed to employed), an improvement in skills (ability to read at a higher level), a change in self-perception (heightened self-esteem), or many other types of change. Outcome objectives must describe an improved and more valued state for the target population in the future. In the case of organizational change, this population might be selected staff members; outcomes would then be stated as quality-of-life changes for those staff members. Outcome objectives ensure that the change effort will focus on some measurable improvement for the designated population and not be limited to the completion of an activity or the simple delivery of a service. To ensure this focus, every goal should always have an outcome objective.

The second type of objective—*process objective*—has a different purpose. Process objectives have a management function—monitoring and controlling the process and progress toward achievement of outcome objectives. They establish major areas of effort and identify interim points in the change process. Process objectives are effective tools for making implementation manageable, and they provide a basis for later evaluation of the method of implementation.

Consider the outcome objective "By June 30, the reading level of at least 100 high school seniors defined as experiencing academic difficulty will be improved to a minimum of 9.6 years as measured by a standard reading achievement test." Conceivably this outcome objective could require a range of interventions. Each intervention should be spelled out in detail in one or more process objectives. During the analysis phase, it may have been determined that a four-part effort would be necessary to improve reading: outreach, family orientation and counseling, tutoring, and testing. Corresponding process objectives might be:

1. By September 30, to contact each high school senior with a grade point average of 1.75 or below to encourage participation in the program, willingness or refusal to participate being indicated by a signed form.

2. By November 15, to complete orientation and counseling with all participating families, as indicated by a signed attendance sheet.

3. By May 30, to provide a minimum of 50 tutoring sessions to participating students, as indicated by signed attendance sheets.

4. By June 15, to test each participant's reading level, as indicated by submission of reading achievement test scores.

Cumulatively, achievement of these process objectives will provide a basis for evaluating achievement of the outcome objective as well as a data base for the evaluation of each component of the intervention process. Ultimately, a set of activities or action steps will be developed for each process objective. We discuss these action steps later in this chapter. Taken together, goals, outcome objectives, process objectives, and activities constitute an action plan. The action plan, then, becomes the blueprint for intervention. This is the hierarchy:

Goal
    Outcome Objective
        Process Objective 1
            Activities
                1.1
                1.2
                1.3
                Etc.

Process Objective 2
  Activities
  2.1
  2.2
  2.3
  Etc.

Retaining these components of the action plan together as a package will help in the subsequent phases of design, budgeting, monitoring, and evaluation.

Characteristics of Objectives

A well-chosen and well-formulated objective should be understandable, be specific, be time limited, relate to key results or processes of the intervention, be consistent with frameworks developed in earlier steps of the change process, be measurable (as quantitative as possible), and be realistic and attainable, yet a challenge. Selection of objectives is based in part on their feasibility given the resources available and the nature and scale of the change opportunity. The change agent must be vigilant in assuring that the concern and good intentions of participants do not cloud their judgment about what it is possible to accomplish with the resources (time, knowledge, personnel, techniques, money) available (Mali, 1972; Morrisey, 1970, pp. 51–61; Raia, 1974, pp. 66–67).

Examples of Objectives

Using the components listed above for a well-stated objective, one might write this outcome objective: "By July 1 [time frame], 80% of the 50 previously unemployed but employable developmentally disabled adults who have successfully completed the program [target population] will be economically independent [result] as measured by current monthly pay receipts of at least $100 per week [criterion]." A client process objective might be: "By July 1 [time frame], Mr. Jones [target population] will complete three job applications and interviews in private industry [result] as self-reported to his counselor [criterion]." In both objectives the agent responsible (the program director and the job counselor) is implicit. Tables 6-1 and 6-2 illustrate one system for documenting objectives. Note that the "Responsible Agent" and "Status/Date Completed" columns provide monitoring and evaluation capabilities in this relatively simple system.

Care must be taken to ensure that expected results of the change episode are specified. If results are not specified, the entire change process may be misdirected. To return to the example of students with academic problems, if the formal objective did not define the intended result of improving the reading level, serious conflicts could develop as the planning and implementation activities proceeded. Should the change effort focus on reading, discipline, parent/child relationships, or extracurricular activities? The goal statement does not answer this question. Through a process of consensus

TABLE 6-1. A proposed format for documenting a program objective
Goal Area: Economic Self-Sufficiency

Result	Target Population	Time Frame	Criterion for Success	Responsible Agent	Status/Date Completed
Economic independence	50 employable but previously unemployed developmentally disabled persons who complete job training	July 1	Pay receipts of $100 per week for current month for 80% of persons completing program	Program director	

TABLE 6-2. A proposed format for documenting a service objective
Goal Area: Improvement of Job Hunting Skills

Result	Target Population	Time Frame	Criterion for Success	Responsible Agent	Status/Date Completed
Completion of three job applications and interviews in private industry	Mr. Jones	July 1	Self-report of Mr. Jones to job counselor after applications and interviews have been completed	Job counselor	

building, agreement must be reached on objectives, and they must be formulated and affirmed by relevant parties and interests.

Participation in Setting Objectives

The people and interests most directly involved at a given phase in the change episode should participate in the identification, selection, and formulation of the objectives for that phase and have a role in selecting objectives for the overall episode. Because most episodes of organizational and community planned change involve numerous people and interests, setting objectives is a responsibility shared by many. The change agent is responsible for devising an objective-setting process that involves all participants and for ensuring that drafts of the objectives are prepared and widely circulated among interested parties for review and response. These reviews may be done by exchanging written communications, in individual interviews, in group meetings, or through some combination of these techniques. In this manner the change agent guards against diversion of the change process from the agreed-upon change opportunity by persons who perhaps have not accepted the early consensus on its definition and analysis.

It is obvious that planners and implementers must agree to the overall objectives if the change episode is to be successful. Often overlooked are the targets and clients. Counselors, therapists, administrators, and community workers have experienced the frustration of having the best-laid plans (and objectives) of professionals disrupted by the targets of change or the clients themselves. These frustrations often occur because these other participants and interests were not involved in early decision making (including objective setting), did not agree with the objectives chosen, or did not know of or understand the objectives selected for the change episode. Wide involvement requires more resources, especially skill, time, and patience, than might be required if a more limited group were used to set objectives. However, these additional resources are a wise investment that is expected to pay rich dividends later in the process.

Participants select and formulate objectives based on their unique perspectives and roles in the problem-solving process. Often joint objective setting occurs, as when planners and implementers agree on the outcomes expected of the intervention phase. In the Springdale illustration, law enforcers, mental health professionals, and community resource allocaters might need to agree on a set of workable objectives. These jointly set objectives constitute, in a sense, a professional contract among the parties; negotiations to set objectives cannot exclude any party to the contract. Setting joint objectives thus requires patience, time, and negotiating skills (Daley & Kettner, 1981; Fisher & Ury, 1981).

This participation of diverse actors and interests in setting objectives occurs at various points of time during the change process and at various levels of the community or organization. For example, in a large state social service organization the top administrators may set objectives for the overall organization. Middle-level managers may establish another set of objectives for specific programs. At still another level, within specific programs, supervisors and child welfare workers may set another set of objectives related to client outcomes. Table 6-3 illustrates these levels of objective setting.

Effective and efficient organizational functioning is enhanced when these multilevel objectives form a consistent and congruent network. The relationships of these objective networks through time and among organizational levels are complex. Reddin (1971, pp. 178–179) describes a process by which proposed sets of objectives move up and down among organizational levels,

TABLE 6-3. Levels of objective setting in a state department of social services

Organizational Level	Person Who Sets Objectives
State department of social services	Administrator
Specific programs	Program manager
Specific client outcomes	Supervisors, staff, and clients

with persons from each level interacting with persons from the level above and the level below to select and formulate objectives. Raia (1974, pp. 29–31) describes a "cascade" approach with formal, specific mission statements, long-range goals, and even objectives originating at the top of an organization. These statements form the context for goal and objective setting at the next lower level and so on, with each lower level deriving its own goals and objectives from the statements of the higher levels. Ideally this process should be two way—top down and bottom up—so that lower-level objectives move for consideration to the next higher level. This process can then be used to refine goals and objectives at all levels. It is compatible with the objective-setting process proposed here for the organizational and community planned change process. The change agent deliberately involves people and interests from various organizational and community levels in setting objectives. Participation of these diverse elements helps refine the content of objectives and builds commitment to those selected.

This network of interrelated processes and outcomes ties the present state to a desired state, structures short-term results into a long-range strategy, and blends the results of actors at various hierarchical levels (Mali, 1972, pp. 12–28). Thus, objective setting involves technical and interpersonal or political tasks. In technical terms, the objectives must be clear, concise, and contain specific information. Interpersonally and politically, the objectives must be agreed to by diverse participants if concerted efforts are to be directed to their accomplishment.

Table 6-4 highlights a number of similarities and differences between and among statements of purpose, goals, and objectives. *Program* as used here in "program goals" and "program objectives" refers to a frequently encountered level of large social service agencies and should not be confused with the program approach available to change agents and discussed in Chapter 2.

TABLE 6-4. Goals and objectives

Concept	Definition	Important Characteristics	Time Frame	Who Selects and Formulates
Community or organizational purpose or mission	Provides on-going reason for existence and philosophical base	Believable Desirable	Indefinite, with periodic reevaluation	Policy board, executives, staff, community members, clients, consumers, influential people, and other professionals
Community or organizational goal	In general terms, identifies and describes areas in which outcomes are expected	Believable Desirable	Range: three to five years	Same as purpose or mission
Community or organizational objective	In specific terms, identifies and describes	Believable Desirable Achievable Measurable	Usually one to five years (mixtures possible)	Same as purpose or mission

TABLE 6-4 (continued)

Concept	Definition	Important Characteristics	Time Frame	Who Selects and Formulates
	desired future outcomes and processes to be implemented			
Program goal	In general terms, identifies and describes areas in which program outcomes are expected	Believable Desirable	Usually one to three years or duration of program with yearly reassessment	Executives, program administrators and staff (with input from community members, clients, consumers, influential people, and other professionals)
Program objective	In specific terms, identifies and describes desired future program outcomes and processes to be implemented	Believable Desirable Achievable Measurable	Usually one year or less	Executives, program administrators, and staff (with input from community members, clients, consumers, influential people, and other professionals)
Service or client goal	In general terms, identifies and describes areas in which outcomes are expected with a specific client	Believable Desirable	Duration of service or until change, usually less than a year	Staff and clients
Service or client objective	In specific terms, identifies and describes future outcomes for a specific client and processes to be implemented	Believable Desirable Achievable Measurable	Until achieved or until change, usually less than a year	Staff and clients

Adapted from William R. Conrad & William R. Glenn, *The Effective Board of Directors.* Chicago: Swallow Press, 1976. (Reprinted with the permission of The Ohio University Press, Athens.)

ACTION PLANNING

The final step of this phase is the construction of an action plan. An action plan is a distillation (in writing) of all work completed in the earlier phases; it incorporates goals and objectives, the approach (policy, program, or project) selected, and strategy considerations. The action plan, in essence, is the document that specifies how the future state will be achieved.

Following the selection of goals, outcome objectives, and process objectives, activities (or action steps) are spelled out in detail for each process objective. Activities are generally listed in chronological order together with a time frame for completion and with the name of the person responsible; in this form they constitute a checklist to ensure completion. A simple technique for organizing an action plan is the Gantt chart. Developed in approximately 1910 and named for its originator, Henry L. Gantt, it is one of the simplest of all planning techniques (George, 1968, p. 101).

A typical Gantt chart deals with two variables—activities and time frames. Activities are listed down the left column, time frames across the top of the page as column headings. Figure 6-1 is a Gantt chart that might be used to outline an action plan. This simple planning tool is most helpful in ensuring that implementation of plans keeps on schedule. If any of the activities is not completed as scheduled, it may affect all the remaining activities as well.

FIGURE 6-1. Sample Gantt chart
Process objective: by August 30, the counseling program supervisor will make recommendations about the continuation of an experimental group-counseling program for single parents

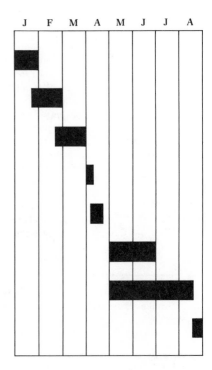

Gantt charting can also be helpful for keeping track of the completion of objectives. Two simple charts—a goal-planning chart and an objective-planning chart—can be used to depict the overall plan at a glance. Let us assume, for example, that a newly created women's center has established the following goal: "to improve self-confidence among the women who partici-pate in this program." Figure 6-2 is a planning chart for this goal. This chart provides a quick overview of all the objectives that relate to the goal. Each objective is then placed on a separate objective-planning chart, and activities are scheduled as appropriate. Figure 6-3 is one of the objective-planning charts that could be devised.

If space permits additional data can be recorded on the chart to increase its usefulness as a management tool, including the status of each activity, the amount of time spent on a given activity, funds expended, and barriers encountered. If space is not available, these items can simply be added at the bottom of the page, as illustrated in Box 6-1.

FIGURE 6-2. Goal planning chart

Goal: to improve self-confidence among the women who participate in this program

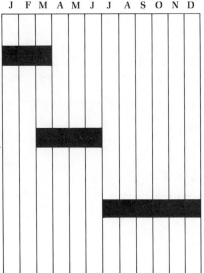

J F M A M J J A S O N D

Objectives

1. By April 1, to complete outreach and screening and assessment of at least 50 women who have been identified as victims of domestic violence, as documented in a report to the program director (process objective)

2. By June 30, to complete at least three groups with a minimum of ten members each meeting on a weekly basis for four months, as monitored by weekly atten-dance sheets (process objective)

3. By December 31, to have at least 75% of the group participants demonstrating an improvement of ten points or more on the Kruger Self-Confidence Scale, as measured by a pretest and a posttest (outcome objective)

FIGURE 6-3. Objective planning chart

Process objective: by April 1, to complete outreach and screening and assessment of at least 50 women who have been identified as victims of domestic violence, as documented in a report to the program director

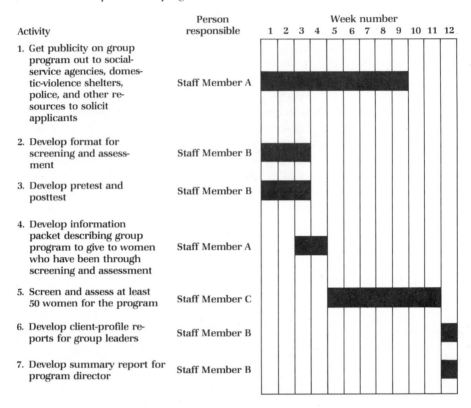

Activity	Person responsible	Week number 1 2 3 4 5 6 7 8 9 10 11 12
1. Get publicity on group program out to social-service agencies, domestic-violence shelters, police, and other resources to solicit applicants	Staff Member A	
2. Develop format for screening and assessment	Staff Member B	
3. Develop pretest and posttest	Staff Member B	
4. Develop information packet describing group program to give to women who have been through screening and assessment	Staff Member A	
5. Screen and assess at least 50 women for the program	Staff Member C	
6. Develop client-profile reports for group leaders	Staff Member B	
7. Develop summary report for program director	Staff Member B	

BOX 6-1 Format for identification of problems and barriers

Please indicate problems and barriers encountered that prevented completion of an activity:

Activity	*Problem or Barrier*	*Recommendations*

The use of these tools can enable human service professionals to anticipate each step in the change process, to ensure that each activity is completed on schedule, and, in general, to exercise control over the achievement of goals and objectives and the elimination of barriers. The development of a comprehensive action plan, although time consuming, is an important function. Written goals, outcome objectives, process objectives, and action steps all contribute to clarity of intent and expectations, to coordination of efforts, and to the establishment of criteria for success. Efforts invested at this stage can pay rich dividends at later stages of the change process.

Case Study

In Sandy Beach, foster care workers and administrators note a persistent shortage of foster homes suitable for special-needs children. The Foster Care Committee of the local Community Council develops a study plan to address this community problem. Study is organized around five major questions: What kinds of special needs do the children have? Why are currently licensed foster parents dropping out? What kinds of homes are needed for special-needs children? Why are new families not signing up? What recruitment and retention methods are most effective? Assuming that these study questions hold up through the identification and analysis phases as the probable significant areas for needed change, they serve as a basis for establishing goals, objectives, and activities.

With no apparent major areas of disagreement, members of the Foster Care Committee establish an overall purpose for the change episode: "to improve adjustment and development of children with special needs who are in need of foster care in Sandy Beach." Goals include the following: "To ensure good adjustment and physical, emotional, social, and intellectual development for special-needs children. To improve the quality of the foster care experience for families who provide such care for special-needs children."

When the committee attempts to set objectives, differences emerge. Members representing minority agencies propose objectives related to minority foster homes; representatives of programs serving adolescents want objectives related to foster homes for teenagers; representatives of the developmentally disabled focus on the needs of their target population.

The Community Council planner who chairs the committee recognizes these areas of disagreement. To reconcile them, the planner conducts a brief study to identify the characteristics of the foster children being poorly served by the present arrangements. This study indicates that about 40% of special-needs children are from the ethnic groups in Sandy Beach, 30% are adolescents, 15% are developmentally disabled, and 15% are physically disabled. With this additional information, the committee decides that ethnic-minority children of all ages should be given priority, and, because of limited resources, only this first-priority population will be considered for now.

Objectives under the first goal are then stated: "(1) By July 1, the Foster Care Committee will identify the components of foster care that are critical for successful placement of minority children, as documented by a committee consensus report. (2) By December 31, the number of foster homes having characteristics defined as being desirable for ethnic-minority children will be increased by 50% as documented in agency records. (3) By September 1, at least 75% of ethnic-minority children placed in specially selected foster homes will demonstrate a positive adjustment, as measured by the Foster Home Adjustment Scale."

Subcommittees of volunteers continue to develop objectives for adolescents, the physically disabled, and the developmentally disabled so that when resources become available, recruitment of homes can begin without delay.

Case Study Discussion Questions

1. What assumptions are implicit in the goal statements? From what kinds of conceptual or theoretical frameworks (utilized in the identification and analysis phases) might these goals have been derived?
2. Does the statement of purpose establish broad and relatively permanent parameters within which goals can be developed? Why or why not?
3. Write three or four alternative goals that might have been selected. Identify their strengths and weaknesses in inclusiveness and political attractiveness.
4. Write a process objective and an outcome objective dealing with social development for adolescents.
5. Write out the action steps for one process objective.
6. Identify significant participants at all levels (client or consumer, staff member, manager, administrator) within this change effort. Describe a top-down/bottom-up process for developing and achieving consensus on objectives. What do you think would be some of the major differences in perspective? How might these differences be resolved in a manner that ensures that all opinions are respected and high-level perspectives are not enforced through the exercise of power?

SUMMARY OF PHASE III

I. Definition

Setting goals and objectives gives direction to the change episode and facilitates its transition from study to action. Goals state the broad aims of the intervention. Outcome objectives are derived from the goals and state the specific, measurable outcomes expected. Process objectives specify the methods of intervention designed to achieve the outcome objectives. Action steps spell out the details of implementation for each process objective. With the successful formulation of goals, objectives, and activities, the participants agree on the expected results of the change episode.

II. Information needed

   A. Have significant parties and interests been exposed to a comprehensive listing of all possible directions (goals) that this process might take?
   B. What areas of agreement about the major goals exist among all parties who have an interest in this situation or condition? What are the areas of potential agreement? What are the areas of disagreement?
   C. Are the conceptual and theoretical frames of reference developed earlier being used in setting goals and objectives?
   D. Are data that were collected and analyzed during the definition and analysis phases (including data on values, preferences, beliefs, and assumptions) being used? Are individuals, groups, organizations, and interests attempting to influence the process in a predetermined direction? Who, and toward what ends?

III. Tasks to be accomplished
   A. Consensus building around goals
      1. Ensure wide circulation of all possible directions (goals) the process might take
      2. Test different formulations of possible goals among significant parties and interests
      3. Provide a democratic process for selection of final priorities
      4. Ensure wide circulation of final priorities selected
   B. Developing objectives
      1. Develop a comprehensive list of possible outcome and process objectives for each goal selected
      2. Ensure a democratic process and wide circulation of the list of possible objectives
   C. Selecting objectives
      1. Make a working list of objectives (subject to modification based on desirability or feasibility or both)
      2. Circulate a working list of objectives
   D. Developing action steps for each process objective
IV. Products to be developed
   A. Statement of goals
   B. Statement of objectives (process and outcome) for each goal
   C. Action steps for each process objective
V. Next steps: transition to Phase IV
   The objectives guide subsequent decisions about how to design and structure the change episode to accomplish the desired results.

SUMMARY OF MAJOR POINTS

1. Setting goals and objectives moves the change process from concern for past and present events and conditions to concern for desirable future states.

2. Selection of goals and objectives is influenced by and should reflect the frames of reference developed during the definition and analysis phases.

3. Statements of purpose (mission), goals, objectives, and activities fit together in a hierarchical relationship with each level providing the outer limits for the next level below.

4. Goals are broad statements of desired future states. Goals give direction and serve as beacons during the change process.

5. Outcome objectives are statements of specific desired future states relating to a quality-of-life change for the target population. These objectives are expected to be achieved as the result of the planned change process.

6. Process objectives are statements of expected results: they specify methods of implementation as the change process moves toward completion and achievement of outcomes.

7. Action steps spell out the details of process objectives.

8. Goal and objective setting requires the accomplishment of technical, interpersonal, and political tasks.

9. To enhance the effectiveness of planned change efforts, diverse people and interests need to be involved. This broad participation requires skill, time, and patience.

DISCUSSION OR SELF-STUDY QUESTIONS

1. How do goals differ from objectives?
2. What is the purpose or function of each?
3. How are goals and objectives selected?
4. Who usually selects goals and objectives?
5. Who should?
6. What can the change agent do to ensure that the participants who should set goals and objectives do in fact set them?
7. An exercise: Given a well-defined and well-analyzed organizational or community change opportunity, develop a set of goals and objectives for an episode of planned change. Be sure there is one outcome objective for every goal. List people and interests you think should be involved in setting these goals and objectives. Note for each participant the particular value perspectives he or she might hold that would influence how the goals and objectives would need to be formulated or worded to get that participant to support the change effort. Use the format shown in Table 6-5.

TABLE 6-5. Format for setting goals and objectives
Purpose of Change Episode: _____

Goals	Outcome Objectives	Process Objectives	Participants	Value Perspectives
1.	1.	1.1		
		1.2		
		Etc.		
2.	2.	2.1		
		2.2		
		Etc.		

SUGGESTED READINGS

Daley, J. M. Setting objectives in the human service agency. In K. Dea (Ed.), *Perspectives for the future: Social work practice in the '80's.* New York: National Association of Social Workers, 1980.

Mager, R. F. *Preparing instructional objectives.* Belmont, Calif.: Fearon, 1962.

Millar, R., & Millar, A. *Developing client outcome monitoring systems.* Washington, D.C.: The Urban Institute, 1981.

Raia, A. P. *Managing by objectives.* Glenview, Ill.: Scott, Foresman, 1974.

CHAPTER SEVEN

Designing and Structuring the Change Effort

OBJECTIVES

Studying the contents of this chapter should enable the reader to:

DEFINE AND DISCUSS THESE KEY CONCEPTS

Policy design

Program design

Project design

Job design

Program structure

Project-design techniques

DEVELOP A POLICY STATEMENT USING THE FOUR COMPONENTS OF POLICY
  DESIGN

DEVELOP A PROGRAM USING THE INPUT, THROUGHPUT, OUTPUT, AND
  OUTCOME ELEMENTS OF PROGRAM DESIGN

DEVELOP A PROJECT DESIGN

As the change process moves toward the point of implementation, progressively greater commitments are made to the change approach (policy, program, or project) and to the details of design and structure. Goals, objectives, and activities set the parameters for design and structure; the action plan spells out the details. Because the action plan represents a commitment to a particular approach or strategy and is tied closely to the budget or resource plan, it cannot be changed easily once adopted. For this reason, careful attention to the intent of the change as well as to the details of the action plan is critical in the designing and structuring phase.

Designing and structuring involves the creation of a system capable of achieving objectives. Although objectives are written in precise terms, they still leave room for decision making about the change approach and the action plan. Take, for example, one of the objectives used in the previous chapter: "By July 1, 80% of the 50 previously unemployed but employable developmentally disabled adults who have successfully completed the program will be economically independent as measured by current monthly pay receipts of at least $100 per week." This objective requires a plan for implementation. The plan may include activities that produce changes through a policy approach, a program approach, a project approach, or any combination of the three. A *policy* approach might entail the specification or enforcement of affirmative action requirements for business and governmental organizations to remedy past discrimination in employment of the handicapped. A *program* approach might focus on the expansion of training resources or the increase of training slots. A *project* approach might focus on a one-time recruitment and public relations effort to increase employment opportunities for graduates of the training program. The goal of the designing and structuring phase is to translate the objective into specific tasks and activities and to ensure the appropriate sequencing and timing of each task or activity. Goals and objectives do not define either the approach or the specific tasks. Final decisions about these components are made after goals and objectives are drafted and are incorporated into the action plan. The tasks of designing and structuring interact in many important ways with the tasks of action planning.

DIFFERENCES BETWEEN DESIGN AND STRUCTURE

Designing a change effort includes defining the purpose and nature of the change intended, creating a delivery system, and specifying overall responsibilities. *Structuring* a change effort includes defining specific jobs, positions, or responsibilities and specifying their relationships to each other. Although design and structure are closely related, the elements of design do not necessarily determine the details of structure. For example, a child and family service agency operating within a traditional organizational structure (as depicted in Figure 7-1) may decide to reevaluate the elements of design in each of its programs. As new definitions are developed—definitions of purpose, staff responsibilities, client flow, and expected outcomes—different structural arrangements might emerge for each program.

In family counseling, workers may take cases on a rotating basis, with each worker carrying cases from intake through termination, and all workers performing essentially the same functions. In this program the existing traditional structure may continue. In adoptions, workers may specialize, with some only screening prospective adoptive parents, others working only with pregnant women who wish to relinquish their children, and a third group of specialists working with older children. In this program, a team structure may prove to be workable. In foster care, there may be still a third design, built around process, where one group of workers specializes in recruitment and training, another in licensing, and a third in placement supervision. In this program a linking-pin structure may be the best alternative. We discuss these structural arrangements later in this chapter.

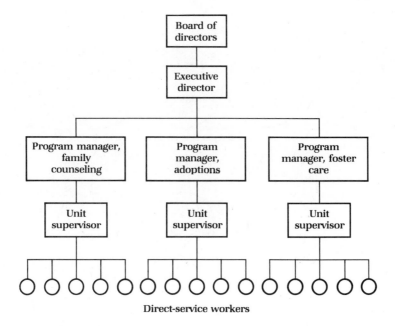

Direct-service workers

FIGURE 7-1. Traditional organizational structure

A different type of structure might be created for a time-limited project developed to determine needs and redesign services for a particular client population. If, for example, services to the transient population of a major metropolitan area were considered to be fragmented, overlapping, and unproductive, a special project might be created to deal with this problem. Key participants in addition to consumers might be staff from the Salvation Army, St. Vincent de Paul, the local alcohol rehabilitation center, the city, and the school of social work, which has agreed to provide students to staff the project. Rather than a traditional bureaucratic structure (which may be counter-productive for such a project) this group may opt for a project-team structure, which allows more flexibility and less dependence on authority than does a bureaucratic structure. A managing board, drawn from the five major organizations, would direct project teams. Each team would focus on a separate area of interest that it pursues independently, while the board ensures coordination of effort. Board members typically lead project teams. In this case teams may focus on needs assessment, resource assessment, study of successful alternative designs, identification of potential funding sources, and other such tasks. Figure 7-2 depicts this project-team structure.

Each of these examples illustrates that structure and design concerns are interrelated yet distinct. Design and structure influence each other and must be compatible with one another. In carrying out the design and structure phase of a planned change episode, participants must make decisions and do developmental work in three areas: selecting the change approach, developing the elements of design, and selecting an appropriate structural arrangement.

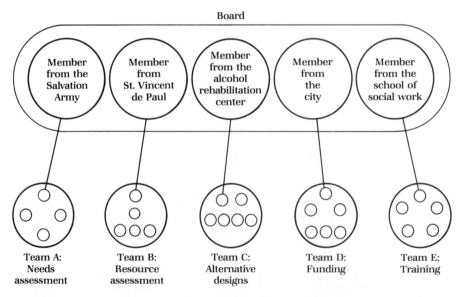

FIGURE 7-2. Project-Team structure (From *Theories of Management* by R. E. Miles. Copyright © 1975 by McGraw-Hill Book Company. Reprinted by permission.)

SELECTING THE CHANGE APPROACH

Approach options in initiating change include the policy approach, the program approach, the project approach, or some combination of the three. As indicated in earlier chapters, preliminary thinking and planning around an approach are important because they help to guide the preparation, data collection, and data analysis phases. In addition, the data collected and the analytical work done in the identification and analysis phases contribute to the decision about an appropriate approach. A formal decision must be made during the structure and design phase.

Because the proposed model of organizational and community change envisions diverse participants, including professionals and consumers, in each step of the change process, selection of an approach will most likely take the form of a planning session or series of sessions. Participants in these sessions examine the data collected in light of the current situation and the barriers that exist to attaining a future, desired condition. Dialogue among the change agent, initiators, planners, implementers, and clients will help clarify issues. Committees and task forces made up of participants can provide a forum for dialogue and formulation of recommendations to the decision-making body. Mutual respect for the expertise of each participant and a genuine exchange of viewpoints will contribute significantly to a sound decision about an appropriate approach.

The change agent facilitates participation by all members of this diverse group. Inexperienced members may need extra assistance if they are to contribute fully to the process. The change agent works closely with these individuals, providing appropriate information and encouragement.

POLICY APPROACH

The expected result of a change effort focused on policy is the formal acceptance of a set of principles and guidelines for action. In many situations these principles and guidelines lead to a redistribution of resources. Policy change can be initiated either in organizations or in communities. In private organizations, formal policy changes are approved by the board of directors, while in public organizations, policies are approved by the appropriate body of elected officials—city council, county board of supervisors, or perhaps the state legislature.

The proposed model of organizational and community change anticipates that efforts to change policy will focus either on organizational policy or on public policy at a local level rather than on social policy at the national level. This focus appears reasonable for the type of change agents we view as the primary users of the proposed model—community workers, managers, administrators, or direct service professionals who may devote only a small amount of total work time to the change effort.

Designing policy is different from designing and structuring programs and projects in several significant ways. Policy establishes principles and guidelines for change, while programs and projects define the details of implementation. Gilbert and Specht (1974, p. 29) identify four dimensions to be considered in policy design: the bases of social allocation (Who is affected by the policy?), the types of social provisions (What is provided by the policy?), the strategies of delivery (How is the policy to be carried out?), and the modes of finance (How is implementation of the policy to be financed?). We address these questions in the following sections.

Who Is Affected by the Policy?

A well-designed policy calls for identification of beneficiaries or recipients. Clear boundaries must be delineated between those eligible to participate and those not eligible, and these boundaries should be able to withstand legal challenges if necessary. If, for example, a new day care program is being proposed for a community, who should be served? Possibilities include all preschool children, all children through age 16 (with services being provided before and after school), children from income-eligible families only, and children of residents only. A well-written statement of policy, such as the following, would define the intended beneficiaries: "Eligibility. Children under age 12 of a parent who is receiving Aid to Families with Dependent Children and is currently enrolled in the Work Incentive Program shall be eligible for day care services under this program."

Gilbert and Specht (1974) propose a series of principles (described below) for making choices about eligibility for benefits: universalism, selectivity, social effectiveness, and cost effectiveness. All these principles are highly value laden, and final decisions about eligibility are often determined or at least greatly influenced by the value perspectives of those who make policy decisions.

Universalism (where benefits are made available as a social right) has the value of inclusiveness—everyone is eligible, so those who participate are no different from those who do not. Universal policies tend to obtain wide societal support and are relatively immune to threats of resource reduction. Public education would be an example of a benefit made available to all as a social right. *Selectivity* (where benefits are made available on the basis of individual need), however, often carries a stigma. Those who participate must first declare themselves in need. Free school lunches, for example, are provided for children on a selective basis following a formal process of determination of need. Selective services, especially if targeted for stigmatized and oppressed populations, tend to be vulnerable to political and economic uncertainties that can influence the quality of these services. As one observer put it, health services for the poor tend to be poor health services. Given the political and economic vulnerabilities associated with policies targeted for stigmatized or oppressed populations, might not universalism be preferred? When all members of a society or community evidence a need—as, for example, the need for general education—universalism is indicated. However, at times a need exists solely or intensely within a specific subpopulation.

In these situations—for example, special education for the handicapped—selectivity is indicated to ensure that the scarce resources reach the intended target group rather than being distributed to a larger but less needy population. Thus, selectivity is a vital mechanism for targeting resources for social purposes.

Social effectiveness and cost effectiveness are important factors in decisions about policy. Policy makers invariably are called on to defend decisions or votes, and their rationale is often built around these two considerations. In human service programs, concern for *social effectiveness* (the extent to which social values are supported) tends to revolve around such issues as work, education, nutrition, safety, and security. Another major consideration in dealing with policy decisions in human services is *cost effectiveness* (the extent to which the benefit is worth the cost). Programs that are self-supporting are politically attractive. Most human service proposals, however, do require additional resources. Careful calculations of costs and expected results can help lead to an informed decision-making process.

What Is Provided by the Policy?

The provisions of a policy define what goods or services will be exchanged during implementation of the policy. These may include specific, tangible goods and services such as money, food, clothing, housing, medical care, day care, or social services. They can also include a wide range of intangible benefits such as licensing or certification, the right to privacy, or access to public documents. As with eligibility, the important issue is definition. Gilbert and Specht (1974, p. 91) illustrate this point in their discussion of the provision of counseling services:

> Among other things, a counseling service may emphasize distribution of information, psychoanalysis, behavior modification, or alteration of environmental contingencies. It may center upon individuals, family units, or groups. It may be short term or long range. And it may be conducted by personnel with a variety of backgrounds and training who base their practice on alternative theories of change.

Clear definitions of provision can increase the likelihood that the intent of the policy will be achieved.

Another consideration is that of the form in which the goods or services are to be transferred to the beneficiary. Gilbert and Specht identify six forms: opportunities, services, goods, credits, cash, and power. *Opportunities* generally take the form of a special consideration not available to all, such as affirmative action programs. *Services* involve the performance of certain functions with, for, or on behalf of the client, such as educational, training, or counseling services. *Goods* are concrete commodities such as food, clothing, and housing. *Credits* can be given in the form of vouchers for goods and services or as tax credits for specialized categories of expenses. Food stamps are examples of vouchers that can be used in exchange for goods. *Cash* is provided through public assistance and social insurance programs. Transfer payments through the use of cash support an important social benefit as well—that of maintaining the right of choice and the dignity of self-determination in decisions about basic care and subsistence. In some situations, however, such as the provision of medical care, cash payments are generally not effective in achieving policy objectives because recipients will spend money on health care only as a last resort. *Power* benefits are intended to redistribute influence over the control of resources. Such benefits as membership on boards of agencies and input into planning and budgeting decisions have been used to involve underrepresented populations in decision making. The extent to which power benefits have achieved the intended redistribution of resources varies considerably.

How Is the Policy To Be Carried Out?

A well-written policy statement typically incorporates a plan for implementation, including the designation of responsible parties. Provisions can be carried out through existing programs or projects, or new mechanisms may be created. Typically an existing department at the federal, state, local, or agency level is made responsible. At the federal level, for example, a section on implementation may begin "The Secretary shall establish. . . . " At the state, county, city, or agency level, "Director" may be substituted for "Secretary." This provision clearly defines responsibility for implementation of the policy. Subsequent sections of the policy may specify the method of delivery and the details of the delivery system. We discuss the components of the delivery system later in this chapter.

In creating or modifying policy, another task is that of selecting an appropriate strategy for initiating change. Gilbert and Specht (1974, p. 111) identify three strategies for designing service delivery. The first is a strategy to restructure authority for and control of policy making. Through the mechanisms of coordination and citizen participation, service delivery systems can become responsive to the needs of consumers without the need for modifications or alternative designs. The second strategy proposed is to reorganize the allocation of tasks. Paraprofessional aides may be responsible for bridging the gap between professionally oriented social service agencies and disadvantaged clients. Or reallocation of tasks may be accomplished by the use of a voucher system, in which clients shop for services in the private sector and pay for them with a government-issued voucher.

The third strategy proposed is to alter the composition of the delivery system. One way is through special attention to client access. Many programs tend to focus heavily on service delivery considerations and to overlook the important consideration of client access. Access can in itself be conceptualized as a social service, with the function of assisting clients to negotiate the whole network of social services available in a community (Kettner, 1973, p. 32). Other mechanisms to alter the composition of the delivery system include competition and separation. *Competition* is the planned introduction of more than one source of a given service to increase client choice. *Separation* is the creation of an alternative network of services designed specifically for populations that have been underserved by existing systems.

The strategy selection process may be lengthy or brief, formal or informal. It must be done with great care. An inappropriate change strategy can doom an otherwise viable change effort. The change agent may use a variety of criteria in selecting the strategy. The following brief list outlines some considerations:

Values. How does each potential strategy relate to significant values held by the various participants?

Political feasibility. Do the participants have adequate power or influence to ensure the implementation of the proposed change? Who controls the resources, including sanction, needed to implement each possible strategy?

Organizational experiences with the change opportunity. How did the current situation develop? How do key participants understand the nature of the situation? What earlier change attempts have been launched?

Readiness. Is the organization more ready to pursue one strategy than another? Why?

Rationality. What is known about the change opportunity? Believed? Assumed? Do these facts, beliefs, and assumptions predispose participants to use one strategy rather than another?

These and other criteria may be used singly or in combinations to select the change strategy.

The strategy selection process can be time consuming. The change agent must explain the importance of strategy choices to participants and encourage careful consideration of the implications of the available strategy options. The change agent may propose a strategy and elicit reactions to it from key participants. Alternatively, the change agent may initially seek strategy suggestions from others. Key participants may then review these proposals either by circulating written drafts or in discussions in strategy meetings. In either case, the change agent retains responsibility for developing detailed strategy proposals for consideration by others.

How Is Implementation of the Policy To Be Financed?

The final consideration in policy design is that of financing its implementation. In some instances no costs are associated with a policy change. The board of a denominational agency may, for example, approve a policy that priority for service in the family-counseling program will be given to those referred by clergy or that food and clothing will be dispensed only to clients screened and referred by local congregations. Costs for implementation of these policies presumably could be absorbed within the existing operating budget.

Often, however, significant costs are associated with policy changes, especially if the changes involve program innovations or modifications. Gilbert and Specht (1974) identify two considerations related to financing. The first is the source of funds. Funds can be generated from recipients (in the form of user charges), from taxes, from voluntary contributions, or through some combination. Each of these finance options is discussed in Chapter 8. The second consideration is the transfer of funds. Implementation requires that funds move from the source where they are generated to the points of implementation. Within our system of government this transfer generally involves a downward flow of funds from federal government to state government to locality. There are a variety of transfer mechanisms including grants and contracts. These are also discussed in Chapter 8.

Box 7-1 is an illustration of a piece of legislation proposed at the state level. It provides for the registration and licensing of day care homes for fewer than five children. If the policy is well designed, the following questions can be answered: Who is affected by the policy? What is provided by the policy? How is the policy to be carried out? How is implementation of the policy to be financed?

PROGRAM APPROACH

In planning programs, decisions about structure should be made only after the design has been completed in order to ensure a good fit between design and structure. For example, in designing and structuring 24-hour crisis-intervention services such as emergency food, clothing, or shelter, it would be counterproductive to structure a traditional hierarchical system, where decision making tends to be concentrated at the upper levels, if supervisors and program managers are not available on nights and weekends. Teams with decision-making authority may be more effective than a traditional hierarchy in such situations. However, a public welfare program with standardized eligibility criteria may need a traditional structure with its built-in check points to keep error to a minimum. In short, in developing programs, design and structure should fit unique needs. For programs, this phase includes decisions about the elements of program design, the job design, and the program structure.

Elements of Program Design

Program components in human services are inputs, throughputs, outputs, and outcomes (Abels & Murphy, 1981; Rosenberg & Brody, 1974b). Decisions about inputs involve consideration of needs, demands, constraints, and resources. Making decisions about throughputs (or conversion processes) includes consideration of the elements of program implementation—specification of services to be provided, methods of intervention, service tasks, standards, and units of service. Deciding about outputs requires consideration of what constitutes completion of a service process. Making decisions about outcomes requires consideration of changes in the quality of life for those who complete the process. We discuss each of these program components below.

BOX 7-1   Sample policy

An Act

Relating to public health and safety; providing for a home day care health registration program; prescribing definitions; providing for health certificates on completion of application and payment of fee and on maintenance of health standards; providing for necessary rules and regulations; prescribing duties of the state treasurer and the director; providing for a certain fund.

Be it enacted by the Legislature of the State, Section 1. Title 36, chapter 7.1, is amended by adding article 3, to read:

Article 3. Home Day Care Health Registration Program

36-896. *Definitions.* In this article, unless the context otherwise requires:

1. "Child" means any person under the age of 15 years.
2. "Day care" means the care, supervision, and guidance of a child or children for compensation, who are unaccompanied by a parent, guardian, or custodian, on a regular basis for periods of less than 24 hours per day in a place other than the child's or the children's own home or homes.
3. "Department" means the Department of Health Services.
4. "Director" means the director of the Department of Health Services.
5. "Home day care" means day care of fewer than five children in the personal residence of the day care provider.
6. "Home day care provider" means any person who provides home day care.

Health registration programs for home day care providers; rules and regulations; fund.

A. The director shall establish in the department a home day care health registration program through which any home day care provider may, on completion of an application prescribed by the director and payment of the required fee, obtain a health certificate. A health certificate may be awarded to each home day care provider who demonstrates the maintenance of adequate health standards, as prescribed by the director, for the provision of home day care services.
B. The director shall promulgate rules and regulations to carry out the purposes of this article, including at least:
   1. Health standard requirements for issuance of a health certificate to a home day care provider.
   2. The fees required for issuance and renewal of a health certificate based on periodic adjustment to maintain the home day care health registration program on a self-supporting basis.
   3. Procedures for renewing a health certificate issued pursuant to this article.
C. The director shall pay fees received pursuant to subsection A to the state treasurer for deposit in the home day care health registration program fund.

Input.   Input includes definitions of the population to be served and the problems to be addressed. *Definitions of the population to be served* are based on several factors: eligiblity, resources available, and appropriateness. Eligibility is typically based on age, residence, income, gender, ethnicity, or other such demographic variables. Limited resources for program implementation also restrict the client population. Appropriateness of the program is a third consideration that may limit the population served. A parent/child counseling program may, because of its nature, be limited to parents with children between the ages of 12 and 18. A simple statement suffices to define the population to be served: "This program is designed for single parents of preschool children who live in Graham County."

Definitions of the problems to be addressed are based on work accomplished in the earlier phases of identification and analysis; they limit the range of needs that can be met by a service or intervention. A classification scheme for problems can aid in the screening process and may help channel clients into the type of service that will be most likely to meet their needs. It should be recognized, however, that even though problems may be conceptualized and listed as separate and discrete, many clients who come for service have multiple problems and therefore need a mix of services.

Throughput. Often referred to as program implementation or the conversion process, throughput encompasses all those elements having to do with the provision of services to clients. These elements are the specification of services, the identification of methods, the identification of service tasks, the enumeration of standards, and the specification of units of service.

Specifying the *services to be delivered* has become an increasingly important element of program design. Early in the history of social welfare programs, services were defined in general terms. Child welfare services, for example, generally encompassed foster care, adoption, child protective services, day care, and others. Although certain provisions were assumed and expected, formal, written definitions were not always available. Such broad sets of expectations may have been adequate at one time, but precision is required in current practice. Planning, funding, and regulating of programs often emanates from federal or state governments, although services may be delivered by local governments or private agencies all over the nation or state. In the absence of clear definitions, it may be difficult to know exactly what services are provided. For example, a 1976 survey (Bowers & Bowers, 1976, pp. 17–20) found that in the 50 state Title XX (Social Security Act) plans there was virtually no agreement on the definition of "homemaker services." Over 100 different activities were listed. Clear definitions can help increase understanding of intent. In the absence of clear definitions, many participants in the change effort may act on different sets of assumptions and therefore may move in different directions. They thus act as barriers to a concerted change effort.

Service taxonomies or classification systems, such as the United Way of America Service Identification System (UWASIS), help to provide a basis for developing common definitions of services. UWASIS identifies eight interdependent human and social goals (United Way of America, 1976, p. 8):

- Optimal income security and economic opportunity
- Optimal health
- Optimal provision of basic material needs

- Optimal opportunity for the acquisition of knowledge and skills
- Optimal environmental quality
- Optimal individual and collective safety
- Optimal social functioning
- Optimal assurance of the support and effectiveness of services through organized action

Service systems are then related to each goal, and a specific service is aligned with its appropriate parent system. For example, income security systems, employment systems, and other related systems would be associated with the goal of optimal income security and economic opportunity. The taxonomy goes on to identify the specific programs designed to achieve the service goals. Each program is given a basic definition, which specifies its purpose and where it fits into the larger system. This definition is provided for the prejob guidance program (United Way of America, 1976, pp. 51–52):

> Prejob guidance is a program designed to help individuals who need to learn the basic tools of obtaining employment to suit their particular skills and talents. Program elements include advice pertaining to some or all of the following: vita or resume preparation; dress and personal appearance; filling out applications and writing letters applying for a job or responding to a job ad; interview techniques; taking employment tests; and providing general orientation to occupational choices. The program may operate on a one-to-one or on a group basis.

This type of definition can be helpful in developing a clear understanding among all participants in the program about what services will be provided.

A second throughput element is identification of the *method of delivery.* This element involves a range of options, depending on the type of service. Counseling services can be delivered individually, in families, in groups, or through some combination. Nutrition services can be delivered to the home in such programs as Meals on Wheels or can be delivered in congregate meal settings. Education and training can involve first-hand experiences, simulations, or didactic presentations. Method of delivery is an area of program design that calls for a high level of creativity and a thorough familiarity with the potential client or consumer population. Before selection of a method of delivery, it is helpful to identify assumptions about service delivery in the program being designed. For example, in a study conducted by Rosenberg and Brody (1974a) of four public social service agencies, method of delivery was built on some combination of the following assumptions (pp. 6–8):

1. Client self-demand. Clients are capable of identifying and articulating their own needs or problems and of making choices and decisions regarding services offered to them.
2. Joint planning. Services are mutually agreed on by consumers and staff.
3. Emphasis on tangible services. Although some clients might need therapeutic counseling services, most low-income clients require tangible services related to employment, housing, education, and legal and health problems.
4. Responsiveness. Agency services are to be made visible and responsive to

the community through outreach efforts, publicity, and, where financially feasible, stationing staff in outside agencies.

5. Goal-oriented services. Services are designed to accomplish specific goals and objectives.
6. Time-limited services. Most objectives can be accomplished in 90 days or less, although exceptions can be made.
7. Assurance of service delivery. Clients will be assured of receiving necessary services.
8. Advocacy. Advocacy on behalf of clients is the responsibility of all staff.
9. Accountability and feedback. Services are evaluated on the basis of response to two basic questions: Were the services delivered? Did the services achieve the objectives specified in the service agreement?

Specifying the method of delivery might result in the development of a flow chart depicting client entry in the system, assessment of need, service planning, service delivery, monitoring, evaluation, termination, and exit from the system.

A third throughput element is the identification of *service tasks.* Use of the concept of service tasks is a relatively recent development; it was created primarily as a management tool for ensuring uniformity in the delivery and reporting of services. It also appears, however, to have value as a tool for bringing clarity to program design. Essentially service tasks itemize the steps of a service-delivery process. The specification of methods of delivery establishes the framework within which services will be delivered; service tasks delineate technical procedures. Service tasks have received some attention in the National Social Services Definition Project (Boston College Graduate School of Social Work, 1978).

Service tasks identify the major activities that go into each service. The service category "Adoption," for example, includes the following tasks:

- Study and evaluate the child's needs
- Arrange for care prior to adoptive placement
- Recruit, study, and select adoptive homes
- Supervise child until adoption is legal
- Provide advice, guidance, and postplacement services to adoptive parents
- Provide legal services, implement rights of adoptive parents
- Review nonagency cases at court request
- Provide financial services to meet the child's medical, emotional, mental, and developmental needs
- Provide services to natural parents

Descriptors such as these help clarify the tasks to be performed within the context of a particular method of delivery. Although the state of the art of program design generally has not reached this level of precision, trends appear to be in the direction of a specific identification of service tasks.

A fourth throughput element is the enumeration of *standards.* A standard has been defined as a specification accepted by recognized authorities, which is regularly and widely used, and which has a recognized and permanent status (Buck, Ealy, Haworth, Stanley, McClellan, & Vinson, 1973, p. I–4). Standards protect the consumer and ensure a minimum level of quality in the product or service. Standards affect all aspects of daily life, including health care, purchases of food, and the construction of buildings. A standard related to accessibility for handicapped persons to buildings reads as follows: "[All buildings shall provide] entrance ramps wide enough for use by individuals in wheelchairs, not exceeding a rise of one foot in twelve, with nonslip surfaces and with rails on both sides" (Accreditation Council for Services for Mentally Retarded and Other Developmentally Disabled Persons, 1980, p. 20).

Many accrediting bodies set standards for treatment, patient care, education, or other services. The Joint Commission on Accreditation of Hospitals or the National Council for the Accreditation of Services for Families and Children are examples. Development of acceptable standards has been a problem in many areas of human services, and much work remains to be done.

The final element of throughput is the identification of *units of service*. A unit of service is a common measure of effort expended. It is designed for management and accounting purposes and is the human service counterpart of quantification of products in business. Units, as used in a product-oriented business, would include such measures as the number of gallons of gas pumped, the number of pounds of meat processed, or the number of cars produced. Quantifying in this way provides a basis for meaningful comparisons. In the same way, human service enterprises need to compare productivity and to know what kinds of resources must be invested to achieve an expected result.

Bowers and Bowers (1976, p. 9) identify four basic types of units of service:

1. The time unit—for example, one hour of counseling or one day of day care
2. The episode or activity unit—for example, one counseling session, one referral
3. The material unit—for example, one meal, one article of clothing
4. The outcome unit—for example, one job placement

To this series we would add a fifth type—the output unit. The output unit is the number of clients who complete a service process, such as one graduate from a job-training program. Types 1, 2, and 3 are process units in the sense that they measure the effort or resources invested in the helping process. Type 4, the outcome unit, is qualitatively different in the sense that it measures achievement of an intended result. The measurement of process alone will always limit the usefulness of data collected in that it will describe only effort and resources expended without relation to the outcome achieved. In a commercial enterprise calculating a process unit would be analogous to counting the number of packages produced and sold without reference to profit. In the same way, the quantity of human service resources invested becomes meaningful only in relation to results achieved. Identification of units for each type of service completes the definition of throughput elements.

Output. In human service terms, output represents a "serviced population" (Abels & Murphy, 1981, p. 139). Outputs have also been defined as "those service products discharged from the system into the environment" (Rosenberg &. Brody, 1974a, p. 12). Outputs are the number of activities or units of service provided to clients who have passed through the system (for example, number of interviews) (p. 13). Specifically, output specifies what constitutes a completion of the service process. In some programs output is not defined, and so there is no basis for distinguishing between completions and partial completions. Those clients who drop out at different points in the process are categorized and enumerated, for accountability purposes, in the same way as those who have completed the process. Although this procedure may or may not hinder the service process, it has important implications for monitoring and evaluating the implementation process, effort, and efficiency. For example, completion of a job-training program may have been defined as successful completion of ten training sessions on fast-food preparation and service. If 50% of the trainees dropped out after five sessions, the program may need to be reevaluated. In addition, if effectiveness is to be measured, additional questions arise. If a trainee completes only five sessions of a ten-session training program and is unable to secure employment, should that failure reflect on the training program? In the absence of a clear definition of successful completion, that question cannot be addressed.

Outcome.   The final element of program design is specification of outcome measures—determination of the ways in which changes in the quality of life of clients will be measured. Specification of outcome is becoming an important component of program design as human service programs are being called on increasingly to justify expenditures based on observable and measurable effects on the quality of life of clients. Such criteria as improved self-esteem, improved housing, or improved home-management skills are used to measure outcomes. Because of the impact of outcome definitions on all other components of service design, it may be wise to specify outcome before specifying the remaining elements.

Techniques such as Goal Attainment Scaling (Kiresuk &. Garwick, 1979, p. 412) and a variety of other assessment scales are being used to test for progress through a preassessment, a midpoint assessment, and a post-assessment (Campbell &. Stanley, 1963, pp. 37–42). Although early measurements of outcome demonstrated little effect (and sometimes even deterioration) (Fischer, 1973, p. 5), recent measurements have been encouraging. Reid and Hanrahan (1982) state: "What can be said about outcomes for the experiments conducted since 1973? Perhaps the most striking point is that the outcomes of most of the studies were positive—that is, clients in experimental groups tended to show more gains than their counterparts did in the control groups" (p. 328).

The type of outcome measure used depends on the nature of the change opportunity, objectives, and services. Employment programs typically count the number of their graduates placed in jobs and still employed after three to six months. Certain substance abuse programs count the number of "clean" urinalyses during and after treatment.

Establishing clear outcome measures during the design phase can help avoid misunderstandings later between and among board members, executives, staff, clients, funding sources, and all those involved in bringing the program into existence. Programs that demonstrate effectiveness through the achievement of specified outcomes help strengthen the case for future funding and expansion of program resources.

Job Design

Job design refers to the ways in which tasks and responsibilities are arranged and assigned—"the grouping of tasks or functions into jobs and the relationships between these jobs. Particularly important here is the determination of the proper degree of specialization" (Filley et al., 1976, p. 337). A number of studies of organizations have demonstrated a relationship between effectiveness and job design. In their comparative study of research labs and container manufacturing plants, Morse and Lorsch (1970) concluded that employees, regardless of the type of setting in which they work, need to feel a sense of competence. To allow for achievement of this sense of competence, they found some jobs must be highly structured, while in others wide latitude should be permitted.

These are important considerations for those who design jobs in human service programs. Certain jobs (notably in child protective services) have been so broadly defined and have included such wide responsibilities that they cannot be accomplished as defined (Wasserman, 1970). Clearly such a situation does not lead to a sense of competence. Most often it leads to burnout and high turnover. At the other extreme, highly routinized jobs performed by people with advanced degrees also fail to lead to a sense of competence and represent a misallocation of resources.

Job design requires a high level of skill together with a thorough working knowledge of the program, the services, and the consumer population. Consumers can participate in job design in a number of ways. They bring an important perspective to the identification of needs to be met by the service provider. Consumers also can provide important feedback by evaluating performance.

The final product of this effort is a job description that lists the name, auspices, and description of the hiring organization, the tasks and responsibilities, the minimum qualifications, the salary or salary range, and the person who will accept applications. Box 7-2 is a sample job description.

Program Structure

In 1961, Burns and Stalker published their landmark study on organizational structure—a study that has had a significant impact on the question of the fit between structure and environmental demands. After collecting data from a variety of industrial firms, they developed a conceptual scheme that placed organizations on a continuum from a mechanistic type to an organic type.

Mechanistic organizations, considered appropriate under stable conditions, are characterized by the following features (Filley et al., 1976, pp. 274–275):

- Tasks are specialized and differentiated.
- Each task is more or less distinct from the whole.
- Tasks are reconciled or coordinated by immediate superiors.
- The rights, obligations, and technical methods attached to each functional role are carefully defined.
- The rights, obligations, and methods are written up as formal responsibilities of a job or position.
- Control, authority, and communication are maintained and supported by a hierarchical structure.

BOX 7-2   Sample job description

Job Description
Johnson County Personnel

Agency description
The Johnson County Child Welfare Department is responsible for serving all child-welfare needs in a county of 126,000 persons. Programs include adoption, foster care, child protective services, and day care.

Job title
Child Protective Services Worker II

General description
Under supervision, performs a variety of tasks in case management and in provision of direct and indirect assistance to families, children, and adults who are clients of the county child welfare program.

Example of duties

- Receives unusually difficult or complex cases requiring intensive or exceptional application of judgment and independent decision making in protective services for children
- Identifies services to be provided and establishes ongoing relationships with providers of services in the community
- Conducts a comprehensive assessment of client needs and level of functioning
- Establishes a case plan, schedule, and timetable for provision of services
- Monitors progress of ongoing cases; visits homes; confers with and counsels natural, adoptive, or foster parents, or guardians and conservators
- Effects termination of services when case objectives have been attained
- Investigates reports of abuse, neglect, or abandonment of children
- Makes recommendations on the need to remove children from residences and makes immediate decisions about such removals and about provision of supportive or emergency services
- Writes and dictates case notes, histories, narratives, and collateral materials

- Knowledge of organizational functioning is located at the top of the hierarchy, where the final reconciliation of distinct tasks and assessment of relevance is made.
- Interaction between members of the concern tends to be vertical—that is, between superior and subordinate.
- Loyalty to the concern and obedience to superiors are required as conditions of membership.
- Greater importance and prestige are attached to internal (local) than to general (cosmopolitan) knowledge, experience, and skill.

A large, bureaucratic state agency such as a department of mental health is an example of a mechanistic organization.

Knowledge, abilities, and skills
Knowledge of the policies, procedures, and practices of the agency and the program in which employed; knowledge of common human needs, growth, personality, and behavior, and sources of family conflict; knowledge of current state, federal, and local laws governing placement, custody, and treatment of children; knowledge of resources available in the community that may be utilized on behalf of applicants or clients; knowledge of the developmental and behavioral problems of children, their causes, symptoms, and treatment; knowledge of the effects and problems of foster care; knowledge of policies, procedures, and practices of courts with regard to cases involving custody and placement of children; knowledge of cultural, environmental, and community influences on behavior and development of individuals in specified client groups.

Skill in case management, in establishing and maintaining controls over case plans, schedules, timetables, priorities, and agendas; considerable skill in interviewing, eliciting information, and gaining insights into clients and families through the interview process; skill in counseling and interacting with families, children, and adults in the context of the program; skill in diagnosing case problems, assessing needs, and evaluating the usefulness or suitability of resources; skill in work management and work leadership; skill in oral and written communication; skill in interpersonal relations as applied to contacts with client families, children, and adults and with representatives of courts and various other agencies in the community.

Minimum qualifications
A master's degree in social work or a related field and two years' experience as a Child Protective Services Worker I

Salary range
$15,500 to $22,000

Contact person
Eileen Hall, Supervisor
Child Protective Services Unit
Johnson County Child Welfare Department

Organic structures, considered appropriate under changing conditions, are characterized by the following features (Filley et al., 1976, pp. 275–276):

- Specialized knowledge and experience contribute to the accomplishment of a common task.
- Individual tasks are adjusted and redefined through interaction with others.
- Responsibility for the whole is shared. Problems may not be passed off as being someone else's responsibility.
- Control, authority, and communication are built into a network of shared and interdependent relationships. Individuals tend to operate more from a presumed common interest with the rest of the organization and less from a contractual relationship between the individual and a nonpersonal corporation.
- Knowledge of organizational functioning is not located exclusively at the top but may be located anywhere in the network. This location becomes the ad hoc center of control, authority, and communication.
- Communication tends to proceed in a lateral rather than a vertical direction, including communication between people of different rank. Communication resembles consultation rather than command.
- Communication tends to consist of information and advice rather than instructions and decisions.
- Commitment to the concern's tasks and to material progress and expansion is more highly valued than loyalty and obedience.
- Importance and prestige are attached to affiliations and expertise valid outside the organization rather than to internal (local) knowledge, experience, and skill.

A research laboratory or university department is an example of an organic structure.

Burns and Stalker (1961) demonstrated that different environmental conditions call for different structures. The significance for human services is that, although most would agree that human service programs operate in a changing and even turbulent environment (therefore indicating the desirability of structures toward the organic end of the continuum), in practice human service programs are generally structured in accordance with mechanistic principles (Whittington, 1978, p. 81). Although structural alternatives are available, they are seldom used. Miles (1975) describes four alternatives to the traditional model; he calls these alternatives the linking pin, the project team, the mixed matrix, and the collegial (pp. 72–95).

The linking-pin structure allows an organization to make a transition from traditional hierarchical structures to interlocking groups. The interlocking feature is achieved by having designated positions perform dual functions. Instead of lines of responsibility that go only from a subordinate to a single superior, positions are linked into two or more units, thus permitting increased communications and lower-level decision making. The person filling the linking position has responsibility for carrying information back and forth to both units so that cooperation is improved and coordination is increased. Such a structure might be used, for example, in a mental health program where close cooperation of a screening and intake unit and a treatment unit was important to ensure continuity for clients. Under such a structure, one staff person, designated as having link-pin responsibilities, might carry a half-time work load in each unit. Figure 7-3 depicts the linking-pin model.

A second innovation described by Miles is called the project-team structure. All team members work toward a common set of goals. Each team focuses on a piece of the whole. Overall management is the responsibility of a top-level executive group or board. Decisions that affect the total project are made at the board level, while decisions on specific activities needed to achieve team objectives are left to the team. Such a structure might, for example, be used to design a new volunteer program. Representatives from several programs might serve on the board. Each board person would, in turn, head a team of staff and volunteers to develop a part of the new volunteer program. One team might work on recruitment, one on training, and one on job design. Figure 7-4 depicts the project-team structure.

A third structure Miles calls the mixed matrix; it is a combination of the linking pin with the project team. This design permits established agencies to experiment in new areas without restructuring the entire organization. A family service agency might, for example, take on a special project under a grant or contract to recruit and license adoptive homes for special-needs children. Although the adoption supervisor would be a liaison to the special

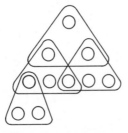

FIGURE 7-3. The linking-pin structure (From *Theories of Management* by R. E. Miles. Copyright © 1975 by McGraw-Hill Book Company. Reprinted by permission.)

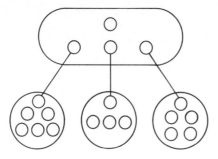

FIGURE 7-4. The project-team structure (From *Theories of Management* by R. E. Miles. Copyright © 1975 by McGraw-Hill Book Company. Reprinted by permission.)

team, the adoption unit would continue with business as usual. As new approaches are found to be successful, new skills and techniques could be taught to the regular adoption workers, thus gradually institutionalizing the successful practices of the special team. Staff from different levels within the regular adoption unit would carry special responsibilities within the team and would also be responsible for communication between unit and team. The mixed matrix is depicted in Figure 7-5.

The final model described by Miles is the collegial model, where everyone in the organization enjoys equal status. Each member is accountable for his or her behavior, and each has authority to make his or her own decisions. In essence, each person operates as an entrepreneur, with responsibility to others only on those matters that affect the group as a whole. To be utilized in human services, the collegial model would, in most cases, require modifications and adaptation to special situations. Clinicians or consultants in private practice, if each generated his or her own income, could utilize the model as described. For programs where communication and accountability are of concern, additional positions would have to be added to the model. Individuals would have to be designated as having special responsibility for communication, for linkage to other units, and for documentation and accountability. Figure 7-6 depicts the collegial model.

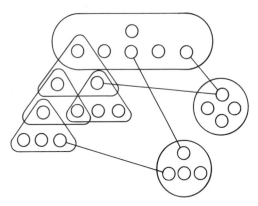

FIGURE 7-5. The mixed-matrix model (From *Theories of Management* by R. E. Miles. Copyright © 1975 by McGraw-Hill Book Company. Reprinted by permission)

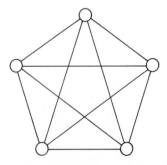

FIGURE 7-6. The collegial model (From *Theories of Management* by R. E. Miles. Copyright © 1975 by McGraw-Hill Book Company. Reprinted by permission.)

Miles (1975) includes all four structures in one illustration (Figure 7-7) to indicate the appropriateness of each structure for specific kinds of environment, goals, and technology.

These alternative designs raise important questions for those who plan and carry out human service programs. Much has been written about the problems encountered by professionals functioning in a bureaucratic structure (Mosher, 1968). Two concerns are raised. The first is the extent to which human needs can be met when services are delivered within a mechanistic structure that prescribes and limits the degrees of freedom for professional staff. The second is the extent to which programs can be accountable for results if degrees of freedom are increased. New structures must be developed and tried to discover a balance between flexibility and accountability in human service programs.

PROJECT APPROACH

The term *project* refers to a wide variety of activities, all of which have certain common characteristics. As defined in Chapter 2, a project is a set of short-term, result-oriented activities providing support services or direct services in response to unique conditions, problems, needs, or issues, in a community or organization. Time frames are typically one year or less. Client populations are highly specific, and planning tends to be carried out by persons who are closely involved with the change opportunity. Much of the work assigned to committees or task forces could be described as projects. An experimental effort to provide intensive casework services to juvenile first-offenders could also be described as a project. Similarly, a governor's blue-ribbon committee to study problems of relocation for families displaced by airport expansion would fit the definition of a project. These examples illustrate two different types of projects—the service project and the support project.

Service Projects

Many of the conditions, problems, needs, and issues dealt with in human services require unique approaches. Environmental conditions are constantly changing. New client populations are identified. New models of service are developed. Funding sources are often understandably reluctant to commit resources on a widespread, long-term, or permanent basis, given the many unknown variables presented by newly designed service efforts. A solution to this dilemma is the limited-scope, time-limited service project.

For service projects, many of the tasks are the same as those covered under the program approach. These tasks include the specification of design elements, the design of specific job responsibilities, and the development of an appropriate structure. For each task undertaken, however, participants must ask whether the short time frame will change the way it is conceptualized and carried out. For example, outcomes in a juvenile-offender project would most likely be indicators that can change in a short time, such as reduction of probation violations, rather than such indicators as positive adjustment to

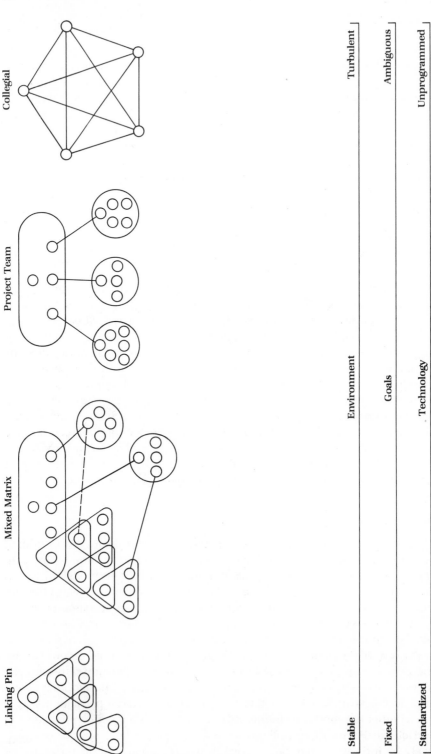

Collegial

Project Team

Mixed Matrix

Linking Pin

Stable	Environment	Turbulent
Fixed	Goals	Ambiguous
Standardized	Technology	Unprogrammed

FIGURE 7-7. Miles's depiction of four alternative models of organizational structure (From *Theories of Management* by R. E. Miles. Copyright © 1975 by McGraw-Hill Book Company. Reprinted by permission.)

school, family, or employment. The structure for consumer involvement may be direct participation on a policy-making committee or a review board rather than through the more time-consuming survey or communitywide participation techniques.

Precision in monitoring input, throughput, output, and outcomes of service projects is often critical to demonstrate effectiveness. Because the purpose of experimental or pilot projects is to determine whether such an effort should be considered for permanent or inclusive program funding, collection of reliable and valid data takes a high priority. A final report highlighting accomplishments in relation to stated objectives will usually be used to make decisions about continuation.

Service projects need not be experimental in nature. Some situations call for a one-time project to deal with an immediate or short-term problem. Permanent structures are not desirable or needed. Disaster relief is an example of such a project.

Support Projects

A second type of short-term change effort is the support project. Designed to support some aspect of the human service planning and delivery system, this type of project focuses on short-term efforts to meet specific needs. Its purpose is not to demonstrate the effectiveness of a particular service design but rather to raise funds, collect information, or make recommendations to deal with a specific change opportunity. Examples of support projects in human services might include developing or revising a training curriculum, designing a needs-assessment system, or streamlining data-collection forms. Characteristics of support projects are that they are typically nonroutine, tend to use teams (without hierarchy), require an active and involved leader, require decision making that can seldom rely on precedent, are adaptive to environmental changes, and utilize job descriptions that are flexible.

Outcomes expected from support projects are usually specific products, such as funds raised, a project report, or a training-curriculum outline. Participants are carefully selected for their experience, areas of expertise, and status. After convening a project team, those involved choose leaders, define the scope of the project, establish procedures, and assign responsibilities. Careful monitoring and rapid feedback are required. It is not unusual to make changes or adjustments in the process if monitoring and feedback indicate changes are needed.

Resources. Because of the highly flexible nature of support projects, a careful and detailed design is needed to achieve high-quality results within a limited time frame. In devising a design, the change agent has four resources available: time, skills, personnel resources, and operating resources (Matthies & Waalkes, 1974, p. 11). Each of these must be balanced against the others. If time is increased, personnel resources may have to be decreased. If the time frame must be compressed, then all other resources may have to be adjusted.

A project to develop a foster parent training program is an illustration. A time frame of six months is established for the design of a curriculum and the development of training materials. Skills needed include writing, illustrating, developing the curriculum, and preparing audiovisual materials. Personnel resources needed include people knowledgeable about foster care (professional staff, foster parents, foster children) and clerical personnel. Operating resources include supplies, training materials developed by others, duplicating services, and travel funds. If the change agent discovers an existing training curriculum and resource materials that are adaptable to the current need, the resources needed must be reevaluated and balanced. Time, skills, and personnel may be reduced, while operating resources to purchase or duplicate training materials will have to be increased.

The change agent should develop a project design using estimates that are as accurate as pooled knowledge and experience provide. The change agent should base the design on accepted norms for working time, including such considerations as five-day, 40-hour weeks, holidays, vacations, sick time, and other time away from the job. Thus, within a 90-day time frame, only 65 working days may be available for completion of a project. The change agent needs to be sure to add in less time for those who are working on the project only part time and to add in the time contributed by volunteers.

Design techniques.   One technique that has proved to be helpful in developing support-project designs is the Program Evaluation and Review Technique (PERT) (Federal Electric Corporation, 1963). PERT charting identifies the major activities to be undertaken, puts them in sequence, and estimates completion time for each activity. By calculating completion times for all activities, one can determine the time and other resources needed to complete the entire project.

PERT charting uses three basic concepts: event, activity, and time frame. An event is defined as follows: "(1) A PERT event must indicate a noteworthy or significant point in the project. (2) A PERT event is the start or completion of a task. (3) A PERT event does not consume time or resources" (Federal Electric Corporation, 1963, p. 13). A PERT activity is defined as "the actual performance of a task. It is a time-consuming portion of the PERT network and requires manpower, material, space, facilities, or other resources" (Federal Electric Corporation, 1963, p. 29). An event is depicted by a circle and designated by a number; an activity is depicted by an arrow or a line and is used to connect events (see Figure 7-8). For each activity there must be events that signify either the start or the completion of a task. Time is indicated by a number above the activity line, which signifies time units (days, weeks, or months). An example will illustrate the use of these elements in project planning.

The executive director of a large, metropolitan family-service agency has been approached by a group of citizens in a small town 100 miles away about the possibility of opening a branch office. The director appoints a project team headed by the assistant director and including a unit supervisor, two workers, the clerical supervisor, a board member, and two representatives from the small community. They have 90 days (65 working days) in which to develop a recommendation to the board. The project team decides on six major tasks: a study of community needs and problems, a study of existing resources, a study of community support, a study of financial support, a compilation of findings, and the development of recommendations. Some of these tasks can be conducted simultaneously, while others depend on the completion of prerequisite tasks. Figure 7-8 illustrates how this project might be charted. An accompanying work plan might be designed as in Table 7-1. In the illustration, working days are used to calculate time frames for activity completion. Any delays in the completion of prerequisite activities may require either an extension of the project completion date or a reduction of the time available for subsequent activities.

PERT charting offers several advantages as a technique for use in project design:

· It depicts the entire project graphically, permitting an overview at a glance.
· It facilitates coordination.
· It helps anticipate pitfalls.
· It can depict alternative paths to project completion.
· It establishes time frames.
· It provides a built-in monitoring system.

Disadvantages are that a well-done PERT chart is complicated and time consuming to construct and is of limited use when too much uncertainty exists. Some type of organizational tool invariably must be used, however, to keep track of all the activities involved in project design.

COORDINATING RESPONSIBILITIES AND INVOLVING ALL PARTICIPANTS

By this stage in the process, certain participants will have begun to emerge in leadership roles. The initiator raised the issue and then may have taken on the roles of monitor and advocate. The client system may have shifted from being passive and uninvolved to being outspoken and active. The targets of change

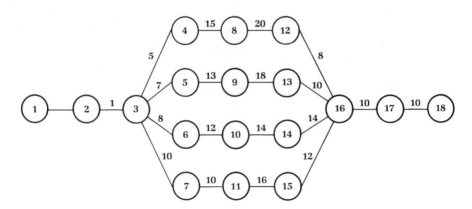

FIGURE 7-8. PERT chart

TABLE 7-1. Work plan

Activity Number	Activity Description	Event Number	Event Description	Staff Responsible	Completion Date
1–2	Convene project team	2	Project team convened	JS	5/31
2–3	Assign subcommittee responsibilities	3	Subcommittee responsibilities assigned	JS	6/1
3–4	Convene community needs committee	4	Committee convened	LM	6/6
3–5	Convene community resources committee	5	Committee convened	PD	6/8
3–6	Convene community support committee	6	Committee convened	FE	6/9
3–7	Convene financial support committee	7	Committee convened	JR	6/11
4–8	Design study for identification of community needs	8	Study designed	LM	6/23
5–9	Design study for identification of community resources	9	Study designed	PD	6/23
6–10	Design study to determine extent of community support for branch agency	10	Study designed	FE	6/23
7–11	Design study to determine extent of financial support for branch agency	11	Study designed	JR	6/23
8–12	Collect community needs data	12	Data collected	LM	7/19
9–13	Collect community resources data	13	Data collected	PD	7/17
10–14	Collect community support data	14	Data collected	FE	7/13
11–15	Collect financial support data	15	Data collected	JR	7/15
12–16	Compile and analyze community needs data				
13–16	Compile and analyze community resources data				
14–16	Compile and analyze community support data	16	Data compiled and analyzed	LM, PD, FE, JR	8/1
15–16	Compile and analyze financial support data				
16–17	Develop recommendations	17	Recommendations developed	JS	8/15
17–18	Write final report	18	Final report written	JS	9/1

may either have increased their resistance to change or have come to support the change objectives. The planners may have identified several alternative courses of action, while the implementers may have initiated exploration into the options most likely to yield results. The temptation for the change agent at this juncture is to allow the momentum developed by each of these participants to carry the change process through to completion. Careful planning, however, requires periodic checks on the involvement and commitment of participants in the change episode. The role of the change agent is to orchestrate the efforts of all individuals to ensure that all are working toward the same ends. Competing efforts should be minimized, with energies redirected toward a common purpose.

The change agent also needs to attend to the sequencing, coordinating, and timing of tasks and activities. Many change efforts have been rendered ineffective because they were poorly coordinated. One subcommittee may need information that is being produced by another group. If the information is not available on time, a meeting is wasted and enthusiasm is dampened. Another subcommittee may need to meet with a city council or school board member. A slip-up in planning this meeting may raise serious questions in the minds of others involved about the competence of the change agent. Details such as these can become critical incidents in the change process.

In assigning and keeping track of responsibilities, the change agent needs to be constantly aware of the issue of consumer participation. Meaningful change often requires that misrepresented or nonrepresented consumer groups increase and strengthen their participation as the change process progresses. Unfortunately, rhetoric about desired changes for clients has seldom been matched by results, either by change in the processes, redistribution of power, or reallocation of resources (Marris & Rein, 1973; Pilisuk & Pilisuk, 1973; Warren, Rose, & Bergunder, 1974). In the model presented here, consumer participation may bring about new power relationships between professionals and consumers, and consumers may take greater control over decisions that affect their lives. Outcomes may include the active involvement of clients in human service activities and issues, new designs for effective service delivery to clients, and reallocation of resources to underserved populations. Clearly, involving clients requires time and may, at times, produce decisions with which some professionals and other parties may not agree. However, only mutually planned and negotiated efforts can achieve the breadth of support needed to effect meaningful change in the organizations that provide consumers with services and in the communities in which consumers live.

In organizations, employees are often identified as members of the client system. In examining changes in organizations, Filley et al. (1976) explore two propositions related to participation: "(1) Providing opportunities for individuals to have influence over and participate in the change process will significantly lessen individual resistance to change. (2) Organizational development efforts which include as an objective the continuing involvement of employees will produce significant increases in motivation, satisfaction, and performance" (pp. 508–509). Although empirical support for these propositions is not clear and definitive, findings from other organizational and community efforts tend to support them (Rothman et al., 1976, p. 98).

The change agent must also build a political support base beyond professionals and consumers. A change effort, no matter how carefully planned and orchestrated, still must be accepted by decision makers. Policy proposals must be passed by a board of directors, state legislature, city council, or other body of elected or appointed officials. Proposals for new or modified programs or projects must be accepted by the agency board of directors, executives, staff, and, if additional funding is needed, by a funding source. A carefully developed plan in which thousands of hours have been invested can be defeated if such strategy considerations are ignored or are dealt with haphazardly. Proposals should be couched in terms that make them palatable and acceptable to decision makers. Widespread communication is helpful in building support. Careful selection of presenters and the method of presentation is also important.

Case Study

In a Midwestern county of 500,000 people, the human service system was on the verge of becoming seriously overloaded because of an economic recession. Unemployment was inching steadily toward 16%. The major employers were manufacturers of auto parts, and auto sales were at their lowest point in many years. Social service agencies in this county had provided a range of services for many years and had always been able to meet most of the needs of the people in the county. But economic hard times changed all that. Unemployment was up 11% over the previous year, incidents of family violence up 25%, crime up 18%, foreclosure on mortgages up 4%.

In the past, social service agencies would occasionally serve a transient or homeless person. Rarely would a family be destitute and in need of basic resources for survival. Food stamps and Aid to Families with Dependent Children generally provided a floor, permitting minimum standards of aid to be maintained. Now, however, all that had changed. The steady, small flow of destitute individuals and families had been replaced by a deluge of people with no remaining resources. Instead of a few families per month, 20 to 30 families were appealing daily for food, clothing, shelter, and medical care.

The staffs at the five emergency food and clothing centers were the first to recognize the problem. Their supplies were quickly exhausted, and they were turning away people they ordinarily would have served. In studying the situation, they began to realize that they were competing for donations from the same sources—grocery stores, restaurants, department stores, churches. Their publicity campaigns were not coordinated, nor were their collection and delivery systems. The directors of the five emergency centers formed a committee to explore solutions. Soon after, church leaders, United Way representatives, directors of the local emergency shelters, and local governmental representatives were added to the committee.

After collecting and compiling all the data available to them about the nature, size, and scope of the problem, they analyzed their findings and set the following goal: "to develop a coordinated network of emergency services for the provision of food, clothing, crisis shelter, and housing." Objectives were established for the design and development of networks to provide each of these necessities. The committee was now ready to proceed with the design phase and soon found its members were sharply divided on an approach, even though they agreed on the objectives.

Three proposals were developed. Plan A, using the policy approach, was to obtain agreement among major emergency-care providers that all public funding for emergency services in the county be coordinated by a central planning agency. This agency would act as an umbrella organization (not providing but coordinating services) and would develop policies and procedures for all emergency services in the county. The initial focus of this change effort would be to obtain formal agreement among major service providers for this model.

Plan B, using the program approach, was built around the redesign of existing programs. Four geographical sectors would be set up, and each sector of the county would include at least one center for the distribution of food and clothing as well as a crisis shelter and a program for the location of housing for displaced individuals and families. Funds and donations would be sought only within the boundaries of each sector, thereby eliminating competition. Publicity would be coordinated and sharing of resources to respond to local emergencies would be encouraged. This approach would require voluntary cooperation and redesign of existing programs.

Plan C, using the project approach, called for the creation of emergency-service centers. Each center would be responsible for providing all emergency services, and all programs would be under one administration. Each center would be strategically located according to need. This approach would be initiated through the creation and implementation of a pilot project to run for one year. If it proved successful, a second center would be initiated in the second year and so on until a complete transition had been effected to the new system.

These three options were developed by an ad hoc emergency-care planning committee. Plan A was supported by the United Way, which volunteered a staff member to organize the planning and resource-allocation process. Plan B and Plan C were supported by the two largest emergency-care providers. Each provider was willing to act as the core administrative structure for the new emergency-service system. Smaller emergency-service providers viewed all three plans as attempts to terminate their existence.

Case Study Discussion Questions

1. Three competing plans are proposed for consideration. As change agent, how would you go about developing consensus in support of one approach?

2. What participants would you involve in developing a consensus?
3. What are some ways you might involve consumers in the process?
4. If Plan A, the policy approach, were adopted, how might the following components be defined: those affected by the policy, what is to be provided by the policy, methods for carrying out the policy, a plan for financing the policy?
5. If Plan B, the program approach, were adopted, what might the following program elements be: target population, problem to be addressed, services to be delivered, method of delivery, service tasks, standards, units of service, outputs, outcomes?
6. If Plan C, the project approach, were adopted, how might the project be laid out in a PERT chart to ensure completion of all tasks within a year?
7. What criteria would you use to make the choice of plans?

SUMMARY OF PHASE IV

I. Definition

Designing and structuring involves the creation of a system capable of achieving the change effort objectives. Designing a change episode involves defining the purpose and nature of the change intended, creating a delivery system, and specifying overall responsibilities. Structuring a change effort involves defining specific jobs, positions, or responsibilities and specifying their relationships to each other.

II. Information needed

A. What goals and objectives were established in Phase III?

B. What approach will optimize chances for successful achievement of objectives?

1. If a policy approach is selected
   a. Who is affected by the policy?
   b. What is provided by the policy?
   c. How is the policy to be carried out?
   d. How is implementation of the policy to be financed?

2. If a program approach is selected
   a. Who will be included in the target population?
   b. What problems will be addressed?
   c. What services will be provided?
   d. What will the method of service delivery be?
   e. What service tasks will be performed?
   f. What standards will be established?
   g. What unit of service will be used?
   h. How will the output be defined?
   i. How will the outcome be defined?
   j. How will the program be structured?
   k. How will jobs be designed?

      3. If a project approach is selected
        a. What type of project is it?
        b. What type of design will ensure achievement of objectives?
   C. What strategy appears to maximize acceptance of the change effort?
III. Tasks to be accomplished
   A. Ensuring appropriate involvement of all participants, select an approach or combination of approaches
   B. Develop the details of design and structure, ensuring compatibility with goals, objectives, and action steps
   C. Coordinate responsibilities
IV. Products to be developed
   A. A complete policy, program, or project proposal
   B. A complete action plan for implementation, incorporating the elements of design and structure
 V. Next steps: transition to Phase V
Examine proposal and action plan and identify items that have implications for resource planning.

SUMMARY OF MAJOR POINTS

1. Objectives, although they are written in precise terms, do not determine the approach (policy, program, or project). This decision is made in the design and structure phase.
2. Designing a change effort includes defining the purpose and nature of the change intended, creating a delivery system, and specifying overall responsibilities. Structuring a change effort includes defining specific jobs, positions, or responsibilities and specifying their relationships to each other.
3. All appropriate participants should be involved in selection of a change approach.
4. Policy changes involve decisions about who is affected by the policy, what is provided, how the policy is to be carried out, and how implementation is to be financed.
5. Program changes involve decisions about input, throughput, output, and outcome; job design; and program structure.
6. Project changes require a decision about whether a service project or a support project will be used. If a service project is used, program design elements must be identified. If a support project is used, some type of management chart (such as a PERT chart or Gantt chart) should be developed.
7. Roles and responsibilities require careful coordination during the process of designing and structuring.
8. Sequencing and timing of tasks can be critical to the success of the change effort.

DISCUSSION OR SELF-STUDY QUESTIONS

A senior center offers a congregate meal and recreation program for the elderly. It is located in a community in which the elderly population (60 and over) is 46% Hispanic and 54% Anglo. A group of Hispanic participants has approached the program director (an Anglo male) and identified a number of problems. Their concern is that the senior center reflects exclusively Anglo culture, and there is little with which the Hispanic elderly can identify. They are asking that culture be considered a factor in planning meals, decor for the center, celebration of holidays, activities, and programs. The director responds that he had never really thought about it but welcomes their participation in redesigning the program and assigns you (the assistant program manager) chair of a task force. Please think through the following questions:

1. Who are the initiators, clients, change agent, targets, planners, and implementers? (Remember, there is often overlap in these roles.) What perspective will be represented by each and how will each be involved in the change process?

2. What agency policies may need to be changed to incorporate a new cultural perspective into program planning? Who will be affected? What will be provided? How will the policy be carried out? How will implementation be financed?

3. How might the meal program be redesigned to incorporate cultural perspectives? Identify the population to be served; the problems to be addressed; the services to be delivered; the method of delivery; the service tasks; the standards to be established; the units of service; the output; the outcome.

4. Assume a foundation is interested in developing a bicultural program and will provide funding for one year for redecorating and meal planning and for consultants with expertise in these areas. Develop a project design that will achieve the results within a year.

SUGGESTED READINGS

Filley, A. C., House, R. J., & Kerr, S. *Managerial process and organizational behaviors.* Glenview, Ill.: Scott, Foresman, 1976.

Gilbert, N., & Specht, H. *Dimensions of social welfare policy.* Englewood Cliffs, N.J.: Prentice-Hall, 1974.

Miles R. E. *Theories of management: Implications for organizational behavior and development.* New York: McGraw-Hill, 1975.

Morse, J. J., & Lorsch, J. W. Beyond theory Y. *Harvard Business Review*, 1970, *48*, 61–68.

Whittington, C. Organization research and social work. In S. Slavin (Ed.), *Social Administration: The management of the social services.* New York: Haworth Press, 1978.

CHAPTER
EIGHT

OVERVIEW
KINDS OF RESOURCE PLANS
TASKS OF RESOURCE PLANNING
RESOURCE PLANNING MODELS
THE USE OF RESOURCE PLANNING MODELS IN HUMAN SERVICES
RESOURCES FOR PLANNED CHANGE
 Options
 Trends
DEVELOPING THE RESOURCE PLAN
 Identify the kinds of resources needed
 Calculate or estimate the amount of each kind of resource needed
 Identify possible resource providers
 Acquire needed resources
 Adjust definition of change opportunity, change objectives, or action plan
DIFFERENTIAL RESOURCE PLANNING FOR POLICY, PROGRAM, AND PROJECT
APPROACHES

Resource Planning

OBJECTIVES

Studying the contents of this chapter should enable the reader to:

DEFINE AND DISCUSS KEY CONCEPTS:

> *Resource plan or budget*
>
> *Resource planning process*
>
> *Incremental resource planning*
>
> *Performance budgeting*
>
> *Program (or functional) budgeting*
>
> *Programming-planning-budgeting system*
>
> *Zero-base budgeting*
>
> *Redistributive change efforts*

IDENTIFY AND DEFINE FIVE RESOURCE PLANNING TASKS

SPECIFY THE PURPOSES OF RESOURCE PLANNING AND HOW RESOURCE
 PLANNING CONTRIBUTES TO EFFECTIVE ORGANIZATIONAL AND COMMUNITY
 CHANGE EPISODES

IDENTIFY COMMON AND UNCOMMON ASPECTS OF RESOURCE PLANNING FOR
 POLICY, PROGRAM, AND PROJECT APPROACHES TO CHANGE

LIST PUBLICATIONS AND IDENTIFY PERSONS CAPABLE OF ASSISTING IN THE
 IDENTIFICATION OF POTENTIAL RESOURCE PROVIDERS

GIVEN AN ACTION PLAN, DEVELOP A CORRESPONDING RESOURCE PLAN

In a real sense all planned change is resource planning. To consider any rational, conscious attempt to achieve an objective without considering the resources needed to pursue the proposed course of action is meaningless. Thus, in even the earliest phases of the change process, although they do not specifically or formally address the question of resources, one must consider the resources needed and expected to be available for the planned change episode. Informal notions or assumptions about the kind and quantity of these resources may change as the process develops, until formal estimates (or projections) and calculations are made during the resource planning phase.

The major product of resource planning is a document, often called a budget or resource plan, that reflects agreement among participants about how specific resources will be obtained and used to achieve the change-episode objectives (Lyden & Miller, 1972, p. 16). The resource plan serves several purposes. First, the matching of resources to the change objectives and the action plan is a final, formal check to ensure the feasibility of the proposed intervention (Hall, 1977, pp. 253–254). Second, when written action and resource plans are distributed, implementers know specifically what resources are available for carrying out the organizational or community change process. Third, the resource plan is a control document, providing resource projections for the change episode. Finally, as a quantitative statement, the resource plan provides data for monitoring and evaluating the fiscal aspects of the change epsiode.

KINDS OF RESOURCE PLANS

As used here, a resource plan (or budget) is a comprehensive statement of the monetary and nonmonetary goods (in-kind or donated personnel, supplies, equipment, and facilities) to be used in an episode of planned change. A resource plan is a document made up of paired words and numbers reflecting anticipated acquisition and use of resources for a given period of time (Lohmann, 1980, p. 120).

At times a program, project, or agency may have its budget allocation summarized as a single item in a larger budget or resource plan. The program, project, or agency is then considered a line item in the larger budget. For example, a county child welfare department may have its total annual budget summarized in the overall state budget with the following notation:

Child Welfare Department $1,588,150

In a second use of the term, a line-item budget is a budget statement or resource plan for a program, project, or agency that groups similar items into categories such as personnel and nonpersonnel or into even more detailed categories of wages and salaries, fringe benefits, and consultants' fees. A line-item budget for a county child welfare department might look like Box 8-1.

When a single agency carries out several programs, more detailed budget or resource plan information may be desirable than is found in a line-item budget. For example, a child welfare agency might be engaged in foster care, adoptions, and child protective services. The executive and board may want to examine the costs of each program. A program budget or resource plan is a document that specifies the allocations to each program within an agency. Box 8-2 illustrates a program budget for a child welfare agency. Functional (or program) budgets are most useful for constructing the resource plan. Their primary value is in relating specific resources, by cost category, to the implementation of the action plan. A still more detailed budget or resource plan identifies costs for each functional area within a program and can be used to

---

BOX 8-1   Sample line-item budget

Avocado County Child Welfare Department Budget

Personnel		$1,205,800
Employee-related expenses @ 20% (fringe benefits)		241,160
Operations		54,490
Supplies	12,500	
Telephone	6,350	
Equipment	12,240	
Rent	13,200	
Reproduction and printing	7,900	
Advertising	900	
Conferences	1,400	
Travel and per-diem expenses		86,700
In state	69,000	
Out of state	17,700	
Total		$1,588,150

BOX 8-2. Program budget for child welfare

Expense Category	Foster Care	Adoption	Child Protective Services	Totals
Salaries and wages	$522,800	$237,400	$445,600	$1,205,800
Employee-related expenses	104,560	47,480	89,120	241,160
Operations				
Supplies	2,500	4,500	5,500	12,500
Telephone	1,250	1,500	3,600	6,350
Equipment	4,500	4,540	3,200	12,240
Rent	3,800	4,600	4,800	13,200
Reproduction and printing	2,500	2,600	2,800	7,900
Advertising	500	100	300	900
Conferences	350	200	850	1,400
Travel and per-diem expenses				
In state	24,000	13,800	31,200	69,000
Out of state	7,000	2,200	8,500	17,700
Total program costs	$673,760	$318,920	$595,470	$1,588,150

calculate costs associated with the accomplishment of specific outcome objectives.

TASKS OF RESOURCE PLANNING

In resource planning, resources needed to achieve the change objective are identified, secured, and allocated in accordance with the objectives and action plan. Resource planning requires the accomplishment of a set of analytical (technical) and interactional (interpersonal and political) tasks (Lohmann, 1980, pp. 123–141).

Technical and analytical tasks for the initial drafting of the resource plan include listing the kinds of resources needed to achieve the change objectives, determining the quantity of each kind of resource needed (and the cost where appropriate), identifying potential resource providers, and obtaining commitment from contributors for each kind of needed resource. At this point the adjustment process begins. Often resources available will be inadequate to achieve the change objectives. The change agent must seek additional resources or modify the definition of the change opportunity, the change objectives, the action plan, or all three:

If resources needed > resources available	develop additional resources and/or modify definition of change opportunity, objectives, and/or action plan

Adjusting resources needed to match resources available requires great care by the change agent to ensure the integrity of the planned change process. Changes in one area require reconsideration of other decisions. For

example, if the resource base will support only ten of the 20 caseworkers
envisioned in the original action plan and the initial draft of the resource plan,
modifications may be necessary in the definition of the problems to be
addressed (an individual's alcoholism rather than family dysfunction), the
objectives of the counseling (fewer clients or a lower projected success rate),
or the means of service delivery (group counseling rather than individual, or
paraprofessional staff rather than professional). Once the needed resources
have been secured, the implementation phase can be started.

Resource planning as proposed in the present model is highly participatory. A frequently overlooked aspect of resource planning is the need to
develop a consensus among participants about the proposed plan. Human
service professionals frequently view resource planning, and especially
budget preparation, as a technical or even mystical procedure conducted by
experts—often people with no human service background or human service
values. However, if professionals filling various roles in programs and agencies
are to initiate organizational and community change they must participate in
the vital phase of resource planning. All participants must be involved if there
is to be widespread support for the overall change process. In a period when
human service programs are facing funding cutbacks and increasing pressures for accountability, close management of resources is needed (Lohmann,
1980, p. 7).

RESOURCE PLANNING MODELS

The experience of a family service agency illustrates the changing nature of
resource planning over the last two decades. As the 1960s began, the agency
received most of its financial support from the United Way, with client fees,
memberships, and fund-raising events contributing minor support. Funding
from the United Way was stable—everyone understood that if the United Way
campaign went as expected a small increase (over the then-modest inflation
rate) could be expected. If the campaign did not go well, a smaller increase or
even a modest decrease would be spread among member agencies.

When the family service agency decided to reach out to the poor and
minority communities in the mid- and late 1960s, governmental funds were
sought. The county and the local poverty program required annual proposals
from the agency, detailing what problems would be addressed, together with
objectives, action plans, and a budget. Family service found that, with each
passing year, these proposals became more elaborate and detailed. In one
instance, the poverty program required an evaluation to demonstrate that
counseling services helped the poor. Another time, the county cut funding for
counseling services, stating that although counseling was indeed producing
desired results, other programs produced more benefits for more citizens for
the same cost.

Even with increased evidence that family service counseling reached the
poor and helped them to strengthen their family relationships, the agency
found in the 1970s that levels of funding from governmental sources changed

(sometimes radically) from year to year. At the same time, the United Way tightened up its accountability system. Allocations remained relatively stable, but the United Way gave funds based on a given number of hours of service. Thus, in 15 years, this agency went from having a relatively stable relationship with one primary resource provider to having somewhat ambiguous relationships with multiple funding sources, each with its unique way of making budget decisions.

This brief history of one agency's experience illustrates a number of budget-allocation models. Models of budget making or resource plan development include incremental, performance, functional (or program), the programming-planning-budgeting system and zero-base budgeting. These models are not mutually exclusive. They represent general contrasting approaches to resource plan development as well as specific applications of the general approaches. We discuss each here briefly.

The *incremental model* uses some relatively firm base (frequently last year's allocation) as the starting point in considering current resource allocations. Current resource allocations include marginal additions to or deductions from this base, but the base itself is considered safe from reconsideration. Incremental changes may be based on history, politics, interpersonal relationships, or expected performance. In the family service illustration above, the early funding pattern of the United Way is incremental—each year allocation decisions began with the relatively safe base of the last year's allocation.

Marginal analysis is one form of incremental resource allocation (Lohmann, 1980, p. 137):

> From the vantage point of marginal analysis, a broad range of decisions, including budgetary ones, are made marginally, sequentially, and in successive incremental steps. Seldom, if ever, in the budget process of an agency can one expect to see the profoundest questions of purpose faced forthrightly, with a willingness to stick by the answer, no matter what. [This nonincremental] approach to decisions is suitable for philosophers and zealots but is demonstrably out of character with the fluid context of agency and program administration. Instead, we all generally tend to "satisfice"— considering only those factors and alternatives of which we are aware, by habit or choice, and those factors we cannot avoid.

Critics have challenged incremental decisions as essentially conservative in nature. This criticism is valid in the short term. However, an incremental strategy can be used to effect substantial changes through a series of directed and self-reinforcing changes over time. For example, a 5% to 10% annual change in allocations by the United Way to agencies specifically serving underserved populations (for example, the elderly, minorities, or the handicapped) can, if sustained over even a few years, produce a substantial redistribution of United Way funding.

Other models of resource planning favor past performance of the program or agency over historical, interpersonal, and political considerations. *Performance budgeting* relates current allocations to the past performance of an agency. Performance budgeting assesses outputs produced and the costs per unit of output, such as a cost per interview or cost per client-contact hour. Performance considerations may have been central to the budgeting decisions of all of the funding sources for the family service agency in the illustration. Even the United Way, using an apparently incremental model, might have made the past performance of family service one factor in its decisions. The performance approach to human service resource planning is limited because of problems encountered in finding common definitions for services and in developing a common base from which to evaluate performance. Nevertheless, a performance basis for allocations is necessary for any accountable method of human service planning. Other techniques that relate the costs of alternative interventions to the benefits or results expected to be derived, such as cost/benefit analysis, are based on this model of budgeting (Morris & Ozawa, 1981, pp. 150–157).

Program budgeting (or functional budgeting) also looks at performance but requires a further breakdown that relates specific costs to a specific activity rather than solely to a general category. In a program budget, items such as office supplies, rent, travel, or salaries are each related back to a particular program. If an employee spends time in more than one program, the percentages of time spent in each must be calculated or estimated. Program budgeting, therefore, yields a much more accurate and precise basis for calculating exact costs than does performance budgeting. This advantage is especially important in an era when program results are being carefully scrutinized to determine cost effectiveness. Within a multiservice agency, some programs may be effective and efficient and deserve future support, while others may not (Lohmann, 1980, pp. 142–144). In addition, a funding source may fund one service offered by an agency but not others. Program budgeting provides a method for identifying funds separately by program or function, and accounting for their use.

Perhaps the resource planning models most diametrically opposed to the incremental model are the programming-planning-budgeting system and zero-base budgeting. (For descriptions of the programming-planning-budgeting system, see Gruber, 1981, pp. 23–66; Miringoff, 1980, pp. 119–121; Turnbull, 1970. For a description of zero-base budgeting, see Pyhrr, 1970, pp. 111–121.) Each of these approaches begins the current resource planning cycle with a clean slate. Starting without the assumption of a safe base, each agency or program must justify its proposed budget on the merits of its current effectiveness and efficiency. Rather than the marginal analysis and change associated with the incremental model, both these approaches offer the opportunity for substantial changes in resource allocations from one resource planning period to the next.

The *programming-planning-budgeting system* (PPBS) was initiated by the Rand Corporation as a method of relating Defense Department expenditures to programs and was mandated by President Lyndon B. Johnson for the entire federal government in 1965 (Lohmann, 1980, p. 144). PPBS attempts to synthesize the techniques of long-range fiscal planning, program budgeting, and cost/benefit analysis in a manner that provides relevant information for decision making. The process begins with definitions of objectives for all programs, analysis of alternative strategies, adoption of preferred strategies, and the creation of a management information system to monitor performance.

Ultimately, however, PPBS proved to be too complex to implement, especially in human services with its inability to achieve consensus on clearly defined goals and objectives (Lohmann, 1980, p. 144). The primary legacy of this budgeting model for human services has been the wide array of economic-analysis tools available for use in dealing with financial problems.

Zero-base budgeting (ZBB), conceptualized by Peter A. Pyhrr, operates from the assumption that every budget request should be justified every year, that no programs are untouchable, that renewal of a program's or an agency's funding from year to year is not automatic. ZBB thus shifts the burden of proof to each manager to demonstrate that resources are consistent with current priorities and objectives rather than requiring the resource allocators to prove they are not. This seemingly minor shift of the burden of proof can be, in practice, a radical departure from traditional incremental budgeting, where past levels of funding are automatically assumed to be still valid.

President Jimmy Carter was a strong supporter of ZBB, both as governor of Georgia and as President. Like PPBS, ZBB was initiated for all government programs at the federal level and, like PPBS, was ultimately withdrawn. ZBB involves three steps and a feedback loop (Kreitner, 1983, p. 164):

1. Develop decision packages
   a. Managers analyze and describe specific activities in their areas of responsibility.
   b. Alternative ways of performing each activity are identified, weighted on the basis of cost versus benefit, and ranked.
   c. Recommended decision packages are forwarded to higher management.
2. Rank decision packages
   Department heads, with the help of a ZBB coordinator, rank recommended decision packages within each department. If necessary, department rankings are forwarded to top management for final ranking.
3. Allocate funds
   Available funds are allocated to decision packages according to final priority.
4. Feedback
   Results are used to improve the ZBB program and correct planning deficiencies.

In principle, ZBB offers a number of advantages. It involves lower-level staff and managers in the planning process, continually reexamines the validity of programs and services in the light of current priorities, and can lead to a significant reallocation of resources over a short period of time. Disadvantages in the human services include the high cost of involvement of already over-burdened staff, a lack of consensus on goals and priorities, and the relative inflexibility of many of the programs offered by public agencies. Again, however, like PPBS, ZBB provides a model and tools for thinking through the value of and benefits derived from existing programs and may lead to the short-term reallocation of resources.

THE USE OF RESOURCE PLANNING MODELS IN HUMAN SERVICES

How have these models for budgets or resource plans been used in planning for human services? Until the mid-1960s resource planning tended to be incremental. Marginal adjustments were made in levels of resources allocated to each policy area, agency, program, or project based on value, historical, political, interpersonal, and performance criteria (in descending order of importance) (Miringoff, 1980, pp. 33–40). This incremental approach to resource planning provided relative stability to human service programs and agencies.

Unfortunately, this incremental approach tended to serve poorly the needs of those elements of society underrepresented in existing power and influence structures and processes, as Cobb and Elder (1972), Gamson (1975), and Lowi (1971) observe. As nonrepresented or underrepresented people sought a share of resource allocations, the incremental approach was challenged both politically and technically. The poor, women, minorities, the handicapped, and emerging community groups and programs wanted to participate in resource allocation decisions.

The model of deliberately planned change proposed here views most organizational and community change (including resource allocations) as incremental in nature, with rational components operating within an essentially historical, political, and interpersonal context. Certainly the history of PPBS and ZZB attest to the power of the traditional, incremental budgeting model. The change agent may seek to strengthen the rational elements but realizes the neglect of historical, political, and interpersonal considerations can substantially limit the effectiveness of change efforts.

Yet the deliberate, professionally assisted model proposed here is intended to support the redistributive change efforts of oppressed people, groups, and communities. Can this redistribution be accomplished through traditional incremental budgeting practices? We believe it can. If properly used, a political base can direct an incremental adjustment of 5% to 10% a year toward the needs of underserved populations in a systematic and planned manner. In this way the radical or dramatic changes anticipated in PPBS and ZBB may still be accomplished within the framework of an incremental budgeting system. Thus, the model of change proposed here acknowledges the importance of both rational and political factors in a change process that supports the redistributive efforts of oppressed populations.

Might a performance-based resource allocation approach provide greater potential for social change and social justice than incremental budgeting? The limits of performance-based resource planning models have tended to be practical rather than theoretical. The assumptions of these models simply do not hold up in the real world (Braybrooke & Lindblom, 1963). Decision makers regularly act on incomplete information, seldom consider more than a few alternatives, and are subject to a strong array of historical, political, interpersonal, and informational constraints when making decisions. These constraints are significant as the context within which performance-based considerations operate (Mayer, Moroney, & Morris, 1974, p. 154). A further limit on the use of performance-based planning models is their imposition of time frames that may be unrealistic, or what Weiss (1972b) calls "premature evaluation." For example, the results of a long-term economic development program may be evaluated on an annual basis to satisfy the requirements of PPBS or ZBB. The demand for short-term, measurable results (for example, increased jobs or income) may preclude equal and fair consideration of long-range economic development strategies that might produce basic changes in the lives of oppressed people. However, dissatisfaction with performance-based models like PPBS and ZBB may well result from their overselling by zealous advocates. Recognition that change efforts are conducted within a strong historical, political, and interpersonal context may lead to selective use of performance models, increasing the usefulness of these models.

RESOURCES FOR PLANNED CHANGE

Resources for a change episode may be obtained from a variety of sources, using a variety of acquisition strategies and mechanisms. One frequently overlooked option is using existing resources in new and efficient ways. Recent challenges to human service programs suggest that traditional ways of operating need to be examined critically. The efficiency of any large social intervention can be increased, at least to some degree. For example, a network of employment-training services for the developmentally disabled initiated a comprehensive client-tracking system with clearly defined levels of progress. As a result, more clients were served better, at less cost per client; clients moved more rapidly from one service level to the next toward competitive employment (and therefore economic independence) at a lower cost to taxpayers. If human service professionals are willing to take a fresh look at how social interventions are implemented, other savings may be possible.

Options

If additional financial resources are needed for an episode of change, options include general revenues, earmarked taxes, user fees, employer/employee taxes, private and corporate philanthropic donations, in-kind contributions or volunteer time, fund-raising projects, and combinations of these sources.

General revenues come from local, state, and federal corporate and individual income taxes, sales taxes, and similar sources. They are channeled into a common pool for public spending on national security, human services, and other basic governmental functions. *Earmarked taxes* are special taxes or revenues, collected by any level of government, that are designed in advance for a specific purpose. They are kept in special trust funds and are disbursed for designated uses. An example is the federal gasoline tax to be used for highway construction, or a state lottery (a self-imposed tax) for education. *User fees* are payments by the consumers of a service or by the users of a facility. Such fees may cover only a portion of the actual costs or the total cost. They may be a flat rate ($10 for each child enrolled in a recreation program) or on a sliding scale according to income. Examples are water and sewer payments, tuition at a state university, and client fees for therapy at a community mental health center. *Employer/employee taxes* are special salary-based or payroll taxes. Like earmarked taxes, they are for a specific purpose—usually social insurance—and are held in trust. *Private and corporate philanthropic donations* are made by citizens and businesses to fight specific problems, meet the needs of specific populations, support human service programs, and further social, economic, and political causes. These resources may be obtained through a central campaign (for example, United Way) or through fund raising by the specific program or organization (for example, the Red Cross). *In-kind contributions or volunteer time* are nonfinancial goods (a van donated by an automobile dealer to transport the elderly, a plot of land donated by a community member for a community center, toys given by church members to a children's home). *Fund-raising projects* include charity bingo, telethons, golf tournaments and other exhibition sports events, dances, and raffles.

Frequently, *combinations of sources* are used in a single episode of planned change. For example, a women's group planning to open a shelter for battered women might obtain land from a local business, purchase building materials with funds from a charity dance and bake sale, have free building-trade services provided by local unions, obtain money for furnishings from a local corporate foundation, and use funding from the state mental health department, the United Way, and client fees to pay staff costs.

The sources chosen for an episode of change can have a substantial impact on the strategy of the episode and the objectives chosen. For example, a program financed by user fees is subject to less outside political and interest-group pressure than is one supported by general revenues. Similarly, although earmarked taxes are more palatable to the public than general revenues, there is less flexibility in how they may be spent and consequently less ability to respond to changing situations. Resource-acquisition options have wider implications than simply their impact on strategy and objectives. Sales taxes and payroll taxes are regressive, placing a heavier burden on low-income persons than on upper-income groups. Income taxes are somewhat progressive. Beyond the question of types of taxing, the question of the level of total taxes is significant. United States citizens pay among the lowest taxes of citizens in any industrialized country, yet the common perception that taxes are high is a factor inhibiting the development of an extensive and soundly financed system of human services in the United States. Any discussion of resource utilization, therefore, must consider that social values and preferences indicate the use of the voluntary sector and market economics, rather than government aid, to meet cultural, social, and economic needs.

In addition to knowing how resources may be obtained, the change agent should be aware of the mechanisms through which they are allocated. Government-assisted change episodes frequently involve federal and state or local partnerships. A planned change episode may be initiated at the federal level but be implemented locally or through the states. Anticipated costs may be shared and may involve the private as well as the public sector. Major resource-allocation or resource-utilization choices include purchase of service, third-party payments, general revenue sharing, block grants, and categorical grants.

Purchase of service is the practice of contracting for an authorized service with an already existing or newly created agency or program as an alternative to direct service delivery by the funding agency. An example is community residential care for developmentally disabled adults, where the state pays for care in existing or newly created public or private facilities as opposed to providing the service in a facility owned and managed by the state. Similarly, *third-party payments* of public funds for a given service are made to proprietary or not-for-profit individual providers or institutions (vendors) rather than to public agencies. Medicaid funding is through third-party payment. *General revenue sharing* involves unrestricted cash grants to state and local governments for whatever public programs they desire. The federal income tax generates substantially greater revenues than do the taxing programs of the states, so revenue sharing is a mechanism for providing states and localities with needed resources. *Block grants* are for a broad area of service, such as health or social services. *Categorical grants* are for narrow, restricted purposes— for example, to establish a specific program, such as a health-maintenance organization, or to establish services for a specific group of people, such as education for the handicapped.

Trends

Several trends and issues may be identified in examining resource allocation. In recent years there has been a shift from more to less restrictive federal funding mechanisms and from a lesser to a greater share of responsibility at the state and local levels for decision making. User fees are assuming increased importance in the human services. Use of multiple sources of funding is a common practice. Voluntary human service agencies that receive no governmental funding are rare. The consequences of these funding patterns include fewer total resources available for human services as human services compete with other private and public functions (for example, economic development, national defense, police and fire protection, and transportation); less federal initiative, regulation, and control, and greater state and local involvement in human service resource allocations; and probably a net redistribution of human service resources away from the most needy in society (Daley & Kettner, 1982, pp. 163–166).

DEVELOPING THE RESOURCE PLAN

This section explores participation in resource planning and describes and discusses the tasks to be accomplished while developing the resource plan. Tasks include identification of the kinds of resources needed, calculation or estimation of the amount of each kind of resource needed, identification of possible resource providers, acquisition of resources, and adjustments between resources available and the definition of the change opportunity, the objectives, the action plan, or all three.

Some professionals consider budget development or the more inclusive resource planning as essentially a technical task to be done by experts, perhaps with input from a limited number of significant participants. In our proposed model of change, resource planning is an integral component of the overall planned change process. Therefore, the resource planning process involves, at a minimum, members of the client, planning and implementing systems.

Professionals provide technical input for resource planning (for example, costing out the action plan and identifying potential resource providers). Involvement of clients ensures that the resources are used to achieve change objectives and that professionals do not allow other objectives to displace the original priorities.

Because resource decisions complete the action plan and match money and other resources with the change objectives, careful attention to the fit between objectives, action plan, and resources is crucial when modifications are made in one of these elements. It should be possible to visualize how objectives are to be achieved by reviewing the action plan and the resource plan. Care must therefore be taken to ensure that the narrative action plan and the resource plan are consistent. If paid consultants are included in the action plan, the resource plan must include payments to the consultants. Conversely, if the resource plan includes payments to consultants, the action plan must indicate how consultants will contribute to the change episode. Ultimately, if the process is carried through to conclusion, participants will use change objectives to monitor the implementation of the action plan and to conduct the evaluation. Like a sculptor or painter, the change agent must continuously go back over parts that are seemingly completed to ensure that, as new dimensions are added, they are consistent with those already in place.

When planning resources, the change agent must have what Lohmann (1980, pp. 146–147) calls "numerical imagination"—the ability to link conceptually the substantive tasks of the change episode to the abstract, numerical world of the resource plan. This talent is necessary both during the initial resource calculations and following completion of resource planning as adjustments are made in the level of resources, resource mixture, change opportunities addressed, objectives, and action plan. Although perhaps only a few professionals have a natural numerical imagination, most are at least capable of acquiring competence in resource planning with instruction and experience. Like walking, talking, or writing, resource planning is an acquired set of skills.

Identify the Kinds of Resources Needed

The first step in resource planning is the identification of the categories of resources needed to achieve the change episode objectives. The objectives and action plan developed earlier in the change process direct the change agent and the clients, planners, and implementers to the kinds of resources needed. In essence, the key question is: What categories of resources are needed to implement the action plan? Selection of categories to be used depends on the nature of the change episode, the financial information needs of possible funding sources, and existing resource accounts. If potential contributors request detailed accounting using specified categories or accounts, the change agent will use these categories (Hall, 1977, pp. 254–258).

Table 8-1 displays budget categories used by the U.S. Department of Education, the Grantsmanship Center, the United Way of America, and the Campaign for Human Development. Note that although no two sets of categories are identical, great similarity exists among the categories.

TABLE 8-1. Resource categories used by various sources

Federal (Department of Education)	Grantsmanship Center	United Way	Campaign for Human Development
Personnel	Personnel	Salaries	Personnel
Fringe benefits	Salaries and wages	Employee benefits	Salaries
Travel	Fringe benefits	Payroll taxes, etc.	Fringe benefits
Equipment	Consultants and	Professional fees	Office expenses
Supplies	contract services	Supplies	Consumable supplies
Contractual	Nonpersonnel	Telephone	Equipment purchased
Construction	Space costs	Postage and shipping	Equipment rental
Other	Rental, lease, or	Occupancy	Equipment
Indirect charges	purchase of	Rental and maintenance	maintenance and
	equipment	of equipment	repairs
	Consumable	Printing and	Reproduction and
	supplies	publications	printing
	Travel	Travel	Postage and freight
	Telephone	Conferences,	Telephone and
	Other costs	conventions, and	telegraph
		meetings	Travel expenses
		Specific assistance to	Staff
		individuals	Consultant
		Membership dues	Board or committee
		Awards and grants	Occupancy expenses
		Miscellaneous	Utilities
		Depreciation of building	Rent or lease
		and equipment	Repairs and
		Payment to affiliated	maintenance
		organizations	Program expenses
		Capital expenditures	Materials
		Current restricted fund	Stipends
		Land, building, and	Insurance
		equipment fund	Outside services
		depreciation	Consultants
		Other	Contractors
			Other

Calculate or Estimate the Amount of Each Kind of Resource Needed

Once the kinds of resources needed have been identified, the next question to be addressed is: How much or how many of each kind of resource is needed to implement the action plan? Few tasks during the planned change process produce more unjustified anxiety for inexperienced change agents. Fears of underestimating the true costs are understandable. How can the episode be successfully concluded if we run out of money before the work is finished? If we seriously overestimate the cost, will the funding source think we are padding the budget? Worse, if resource projections are off significantly in either direction (too much or too little) will the prospective contributors question our competence?

Cost projections. Preparing a resource plan requires a good working knowledge of the requirements of the action plan. The change agent attempts to develop a realistic budget that will allow successful completion of the change effort. Accurately anticipating the resources needed to achieve the objectives of the change effort is not easy, even with well-developed objectives and a precise action plan.

Cost projections are either calculated or estimated. Some costs (for example, local fixed-rate telephone service, salaries, and fringe benefits) can be and should be calculated with a high degree of precision. Other costs (for example, long-distance telephone charges, consumable supplies, and travel) require estimates. The change agent does not start from scratch when developing each budget. In calculating or estimating these expenses for a specific action plan, the change agent can obtain costs of similar programs or activities from personnel involved with these other programs and price quotes or estimates from individuals who presumably are knowledgeable (suppliers, consultants, and executives of similar programs). The change agent thus can consult others before making projections—considered, informed judgments.

The change agent uses the action plan as a starting point to identify the kinds and quantities of resources needed to implement the action plan and can then go on to estimate costs. If counseling and educational activities are in the action plan, the change agent must include in the resource plan personnel, materials, and other resources for counseling and education (for example, personnel costs for counselors and trainers and trainee expenses). Based on estimates of how many clients a counselor can work with in a year and the cost of a counselor for a year, the change agent can determine counselor personnel costs by calculating the number of clients to be served or the units of service to be delivered. For example, a full-time counselor might be able to carry 20 active cases at any given time. The program expects a complete client turnover every three months on average. Thus a counselor can handle an average of 80 cases annually ($20 \times 4 = 80$). If the program anticipates serving 320 cases annually, four full-time counselors are needed ($320 \div 80 = 4$). If the annual salary for a counselor is $16,000, the direct salary cost for counselors is $64,000 ($4 \times \$16,000 = \$64,000$). The change agent can make similar determinations for each kind of resource.

Budget adjustments. When making projections, even experienced budget developers or resource planners may make mistakes. In a given budget or resource plan, projections are made for several items (for example, travel, long-distance telephone, consumable supplies, and utilities). Travel may be underestimated by a few hundred dollars in a counseling agency, but consumable supplies and educational materials may not cost as much as anticipated. These individual calculations may individually be inexact but may balance each other. Although budget statements of projected costs for each kind of resource look exact ("consumable supplies—$25/month × 12 months × 3.5 employees = $1050"), as the action plan is implemented, adjustments among resource categories usually have to be made. The original estimates or calculations do not preclude transfer of resources from one use to another. Funding sources usually allow adjustments in resource use within some reasonable limits. A foundation may have a policy that up to 10% or $1000 (whichever is smaller) of the money estimated for any category may be transferred to other categories without notifying the funding source. A final means of adjusting the resource plan projections is to renegotiate with a funding source for substantial changes in use or for additional total resources. Legitimate underestimates are possible, especially in nonroutine, unique, or new activities. Renegotiations usually are acceptable under these conditions.

Budget justification or explanation. A separate section of the resource plan, usually called the budget-justification section, explains in detail the need for specific items and how and why costs were calculated or estimated as they were. The budget justification clarifies the thinking underlying budget decisions, prepares the change agent to discuss the possible impact of funding cuts, and, when implementation begins, acts as a guide in determining the appropriateness of expenditures. Box 8-3 illustrates a portion of a budget-justification page.

Identify Possible Resource Providers

Resources to implement the action plan may come from participants in the change process or from external sources. Internal sources include existing as well as new public appropriations, various program funds, contributions, volunteer services, contributed goods, and client donations and fees. Whenever possible, the use of existing resources controlled by or available to participants is preferable. Securing resources from external contributors takes time and money.

When external resources are needed, a wealth of published materials is available to assist the change agent in identifying potential contributors to the change effort. (See Daley, 1982; Hall, 1977; Kurzig, 1980; Lauffer, 1982; Tenbrunsel, 1982. See also *The Grantsmanship Center News*, published six times annually by the Grantsmanship Center, 1031 South Grand Avenue, Los Angeles, California 90015.)

In addition to these formal sources of information about potential resource

---

BOX 8-3 Budget explanation or justification

Line 1 ("Salary for executive director . . . . $30,000")

Full time × 12 months = $30,000/year

Line 2 ("Fringe benefits for executive director . . . . $ 7,900")
Sheltered retirement account
   7% of base salary $2,100
Medical insurance
   individual coverage—comprehensive
   Blue Cross and Blue Shield   2,400
Social Security   3,400
           Total executive fringe $7,900

Line 3 ("Travel for executive director . . . . $ 2,550")
Out-of-state agency-related conferences
   $750 each × 2 conferences = $1,500
Visits to agency branches
   1 visit/office/month × 12 months
   × 3 branches × 50 miles round trip
   (average) × 25¢/mile =   450
Miscellaneous agency travel
   200 miles/month × 12 months × 25¢/mile =   600
           Total executive travel $2,550

---

contributors, the change agent can use a number of informal sources. Participants in the change episode may provide valuable leads to resources. They may have personal, professional, organizational, or community relationships that can be useful in securing funding. *Similar change efforts* (programs, projects, agencies, groups) provide valuable resource information if sensitively approached. Often a direct appeal for assistance yields the best results. Local programs or programs outside the community may have been cited by funding sources, described in the professional literature, or reported at conferences as being effective. An appeal to pride in their program is both warranted and effective in seeking help. *Funding sources* can assist in identifying other potential resources and in developing a funding proposal. *Governmental agencies* (local, state, federal) have program officers whose responsibilities include assistance to community groups in identifying resources and developing proposals. *Universities* have specific personnel assigned to monitor funding availability and to assist university-related proposal writing. These university officials have information on a wide range of funding sources, only a small portion of which are used by the university. They might see assisting a community group as an appropriate university service to the community. Affiliation with a university through intern relationships may make available the expertise of the faculty in the area of proposal development. This list of resources is not exhaustive but is intended to motivate the reader to explore his or her own experiences and networks.

Acquire Needed Resources

Resource-development and grantsmanship literature identifies two types of tasks associated with effective resource identification and acquisition: the technical and the political or interpersonal. On the technical level, products of the earlier phases of the change process (the statement of the change opportunity, the objectives, and the action plan) can be used as components of the formal proposal required by many funding sources. Excellent guides are available to assist in preparing funding proposals (Hall, 1977; Kiritz, n.d.).

On the political or interpersonal level, resource allocators base their decisions in part on their assessment of the programs and the people requesting funding. Potential contributors prefer to invest resources in people and programs with a documented record of effectiveness in dealing with the situation to be changed or with similar situations. These preferences may result in conservative funding to the detriment of new, unusual, or nontraditional programs and agencies. The change agent working with new or nontraditional programs or agencies recognizes this conservative tendency of resource providers. To compensate, the change agent seeks to develop the strong and viable support of community leaders and groups, potential and actual clients or consumers, related professionals, and implementers. The groundwork for this support is established during the earlier phases of the change effort through the participation of these persons, groups, and organizations.

In helping the potential resource providers to decide to support the proposed change effort, the change agent can use a series of tactics. The change agent first identifies the resource decisions desired. Are new resources or existing resources to be used? Second, the change agent identifies resource allocators who can make the desired decisions. For example, in an attempt to initiate change in a human service agency using agency resources, the change agent identifies who in the agency can approve the use of the needed resources. Is approval of the board of directors needed? the executive director? a program director? At times more than one resource allocator might be capable of making the resource decision. In these situations, the selection of the allocator to be approached (or to be approached first) is a crucial tactical decision in the resource planning phase of the change effort. Third, the change agent focuses on how the desired resource decision can be made desirable, can be justified, or can be made to seem necessary to this resource allocator. In other words, the change agent tailors the strategy to the resource allocator (Daley, 1982; Fisher, 1969; Fisher & Ury, 1981).

Thus, the change agent must consider the appropriate and most effective interpersonal and political manner of engaging potential contributors as well as the technical specifications of the formal, written proposal. A well-written proposal that elicits the response desired from one funding source may or may not be an effective proposal for another. In light of the needs, preferences, or requirements of the selected resource provider, considerations of what constitutes a technically proper proposal may have to be subordinated to considerations of what will influence the allocator to make the desired decision. For example, a group seeking foundation funding for a project will have to construct its proposal within the constraints and according to the guidelines provided by the foundation. A large, professionally staffed foundation might ask for an elaborate proposal complete with sections containing descriptions of community need, program objectives, methods of implementation, sophisticated evaluation methodology, and a functional budget. However, for a small family foundation, the change agent might develop a proposal of a page or two in length, omitting entire sections found in the longer proposal and describing other sections in a paragraph or less.

In most cases, all resources do not come from the same provider. No single provider may have adequate resources or perhaps no single provider will fund all aspects of the change episode. For example, one source may not fund construction costs, and another, workers' salaries. Each provider may require different information on which to base allocation decisions, and each provider may prefer different kinds of interactions with applicants. For example, some funding sources prefer to conduct early communications in writing. Some require a site visit to the agency requesting funds before a final decision is made. Many prefer all communication to go through specific officials. The change agent tries to understand the needs and preferences of each potential resource provider. Whenever possible (and to the degree possible) the change agent is responsive to these needs and preferences.

A final consideration for the change agent is the presentation of the funding proposal. When a proposal is presented to a funding source, the impressions made by the presenters are important. Sometimes a crisp and efficient presentation of data is needed, while at other times an impassioned plea from a consumer or constituent is most persuasive. Recently many state legislatures, for example, have been persuaded to pass laws mandating strict and swift punishment for drunk drivers. Although statistical data have been available for many years, the presentations by parents of children killed by drunk drivers have, in some instances, provided the impetus for the deciding votes.

Thus, the change agent ensures that the funding proposal and presentation are developed in such a way as to generate the most support from the identified funding source. The change agent may write parts of the proposal and edit parts written by other participants. The political and interpersonal aspects of grantsmanship may necessitate the involvement of many diverse participants with the change agent coordinating the strategy. Often this strategy is integrated with the efforts to gain approval of the action plan.

This brief description of the considerations of the change agent when seeking approval for the action plan and funding proposal cannot do credit to the importance of this aspect of the change process nor to the rich literature dealing with this topic. A key point to remember here is that the involvement of participants (including potential resource contributors) during the planning phase can pay rich dividends when sanctioning and allocation decisions are made. If potential sanctioning bodies and resource contributors have been involved during the planning efforts, they have contributed to the proposed action plan and have become familiar and comfortable with the other participants. These contributions and relationships are crucial in their making positive sanctioning and allocating decisions.

Adjust Definition of Change Opportunity, Change Objectives, or Action Plan

Ideally, the resource requirements of the action plan provide the starting point for resource planning, Then, the total resources needed for implementing the action plan are secured. Unfortunately, the process is not always so neat and orderly. The resources available may not be the right kind or in the right amount. Adjustments may therefore be necessary to bring the action plan into conformity with the resource plan.

The change agent must make adjustments when the kinds and amounts of resources are not adequate to implement the proposed action plan—when desired and intended results of the change episode exceed the resource capacity. Adjustments bring into balance intentions and reality. Few episodes of change achieve resource levels adequate, for example, to move all persons evidencing a need (or a problem) into the desired future state of having the identified need fully met (or the identified problem fully solved).

A variety of adjustments are available to the change agent. Additional resources might be sought. Or the continuation of the change episode in the proposed form might be reconsidered. Perhaps inadequate resources doom the change effort, and the change system should be redirected toward feasible opportunities. Most likely however, the change agent faces a series of adjustments in the definition of the change opportunity, the change objectives, the action plan, or all three.

In adjusting the definition of the change opportunity, the change agent seeks a compromise between resources available and the nature of the situation to be changed. For example, an original definition of a community alcoholism problem might be narrowed to drunk driving (or, even narrower, teenage drunk driving). Adjustments in change objectives might entail restricting the population to be served, lowering the number of clients, or lowering or restricting expected outcome behaviors or status. For example, the drunk-driving program might serve only first offenders, persons willing to define themselves as problem drinkers, or teenage offenders. Or a lower level of success might be expected (30% rather than 50% of the clients will cease driving while intoxicated during the first six months after completing the program). Or the nature of the intervention (as reflected in the action plan) might be modified. In the example, because of inadequate resources for the originally conceived comprehensive alcoholism program (including law-enforcement enhancement, public education, and individual counseling components), the program might pursue enhanced law enforcement coupled with an aggressive public-awareness campaign.

Inadequate resources require precise planning so that those resources that are available are used to achieve the greatest good. Legitimate differences may

exist among professionals and other persons of good will as to what constitutes the greatest good (Banfield, 1970) or the best way to achieve it. With a
working consensus about what constitutes the greatest good, alternative
methods may be used. In this case, the change agent may roughly cost out a
limited number of alternatives in order to make quick and inexpensive
approximations of the kinds and amounts of resources necessary to achieve
the objectives. If resources available are adequate for more than one alternative, other factors, such as the probability of success using each alternative,
start-up time, start-up costs, and prospects for permanent funding, are considered in selecting the alternative to pursue. The change agent costs out each
alternative and provides planners with data on which to make decisions
about alternative methods.

Once completed, the proposed resource plan and the action plan should
be presented as one document to a variety of participants including clients,
planners, and implementers for feedback and discussion. If these plans can
withstand the scrutiny of these key parties, they stand a good chance of being
implemented. Both the action plan and the resource plan are sets of projections. Further adjustments are expected during implementation. The change
agent may explore the most probable adjustments and develop rough sets of
alternatives as contingency plans.

DIFFERENTIAL RESOURCE PLANNING FOR POLICY, PROGRAM, AND PROJECT APPROACHES

As one moves from policy through program to project approaches, resource
planning tends to become more specific and detailed in nature. Project
budgets are the most specific form of resource plan documentation, policy
budgets the least specific. For example, a federal initiative to establish local
child-abuse hotline services might begin with a national resource plan that
allocates "$100 million for projects in 200 local communities." The figures
"$100 million" and "200 local communities" might have been determined in
several ways. Possibly these numbers represent political judgments about the
amount of money Congress would be willing to commit if every state received
one or more local projects. Possibly, the cost of one average project might have
been calculated with some precision at $500,000, and the total amount availa-
ble ($100 million) divided by this figure to determine the approximate number
of community projects possible (200). Or the total amount available might have
been divided by the number of communities to be served to calculate the
average cost per project. Although such national initiatives must use approximations, the present change model suggests that even the roughest calculations are superior to incidental guesswork. In contrast to general calculations
(at best) at the national level, local projects and programs require precise and
detailed resource plans. The general resource plan becomes more specific as

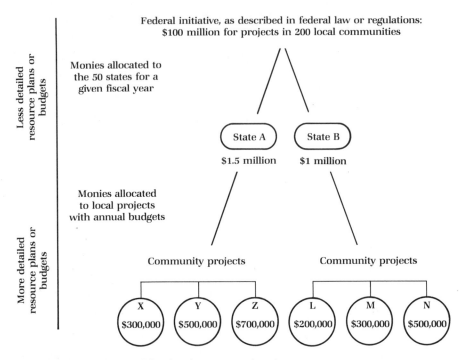

Federal initiative, as described in federal law or regulations:
$100 million for projects in 200 local communities

Less detailed resource plans or budgets

Monies allocated to the 50 states for a given fiscal year

State A — $1.5 million

State B — $1 million

Monies allocated to local projects with annual budgets

More detailed resource plans or budgets

Community projects

Community projects

X — $300,000

Y — $500,000

Z — $700,000

L — $200,000

M — $300,000

N — $500,000

FIGURE 8-1. Differential levels of resource planning

it approaches the local level—as the federal idea becomes a local project or program. Figure 8-1 depicts these differences.

Resource planning completes the planning phase of the organizational and community change process. Considered as a single document, the objectives, action plan, and resource plan will provide the blueprints for the implementation efforts to follow. The commitment of participants to these planning documents is vital to the successful implementation of the change effort.

Case Study

The program manager for child welfare services in Avocado County has just been fired because of inept resource planning and budget management. You have been serving as a unit supervisor and are asked to be acting program manager until the position is filled permanently. It is mid-August, and the board still has no report for the last fiscal year ending June 30. Your first assignment from the director is to reconstruct a program budget from the documentation left behind by your predecessor and to prepare a statement about comparative unit costs for the child welfare programs. A thorough search of the files turns up the document shown in Box 8-1 (earlier in this chapter).

In a file cabinet in one of the day care centers, you find the following documents: a contract for day-care space rental ($9600 per year); a contract for day care equipment rental ($7200 per year); an old memo stating that the supply budget for the day care program for the fiscal year just completed should be increased to $6000.

Budget-preparation guidelines state that in-state travel and per-diem expenses should be estimated as follows: "$100 per staff member per month, excluding clerical staff, with the exception that the day care program shall be allocated a fixed amount of $1800 per year." Out-of-state travel and per-diem funds shall be allocated to programs at the discretion of management.

The annual report for the fiscal year just completed is shown in Box 8-4. Personnel records indicate the staffing pattern illustrated in Table 8-2.

BOX 8-4   Annual report for case study

Avocado County Child Welfare Department
Annual Report

Foster care
Home studies for licensing = 1800
    Homes licensed = 1600
    Homes rejected =   200
Average number of interviews per home study = three 1-hour interviews
Average administrative time (recording, record keeping, etc.)
    per home study = 5 hours

Adoption
Home studies for adoption completed = 480
    Certified = 360
    Rejected = 120
Average number of interviews per home study = five 1-hour interviews
Average administrative time per home study = 3 hours

Child protective services
Total number of families served this fiscal year = 792
Average number of interviews per family = eight 1-hour interviews
    With family members   = four 1-hour interviews
    With collateral contacts = four 1-hour interviews
Average administrative time per family = 12 hours

Day care
Capacity = 180 children
Percentage of capacity this fiscal year = 100%
Days facility operated = 235
Child care days = 235 × 180 = 42,300
Average number of families = 90
Average number of social-work interviews per family = four 1-hour interviews
Average administrative time per family = 4 hours

TABLE 8-2. Staffing patterns for case study

	Foster Care	Adoption	Child Protective Services	Day Care	Management	Total
Clerical						
Secretary I	0	0	0	0	0	0
Secretary II	3	1	3	2	0	9
Secretary III	0	0	0	0	0	0
Administrative Assistant	0	0	0	0	3	3
Paraprofessional						
Child-Care Worker	2	0	0	10	0	12
Home Worker	0	0	5	0	0	5
Professional						
Social Worker I	0	0	0	0	0	0
Social Worker II	15	5	18	1	0	39
Social Worker III	0	0	0	0	0	0
Supervisory						
Supervisor I	0	0	0	0	0	0
Supervisor II	3	1	3	1	1	9
Supervisor III	0	0	0	0	0	0
Management						
Manager I	0	0	0	0	0	0
Manager II	0	0	0	0	0	0
Manager III	0	0	0	0	3	3

The department fiscal officer has furnished you with the salary schedule in Box 8-5.

BOX 8-5 Salary schedule for case study

Clerical staff
Secretary I	$ 8,400
Secretary II	9,200
Secretary III	10,000
Administrative Assistant	10,400

Paraprofessional staff
| Child-Care Worker | 10,400 |
| Home Worker | 10,400 |

Professional staff
Social Worker I	15,500
Social Worker II	17,000
Social Worker III	18,500

Supervisory staff
Supervisor I	19,000
Supervisor II	20,000
Supervisor III	22,000

Management
Manager I	20,000
Manager II	22,000
Manager III	24,000

Case Study Discussion Questions

1. Using a sheet of accounting paper with at least six columns, set up the framework for your program budget as follows:

   For the six column headings list:
   Foster care
   Adoption
   Child protective services
   Day care
   Management
   Totals

   Down the left column list:
   Personnel
      Clerical
      Paraprofessional
      Social workers
      Supervisors
      Management
   Employment-related expenses
   Operations
      Supplies
      Telephone
      Equipment
      Rent
      Reproduction and printing
      Advertising
      Conferences
   Travel and per-diem expenses
      In state
      Out of state
   Total Program Costs

2. Using the information provided, set up a functional (program) budget for Avocado County child welfare programs by filling in the correct amounts as indicated for foster care, adoption, child protective services, day care, and management. *Not all information has been given to you. You will have to make some decisions on your own about specific allocations to programs.*

3. Calculate the following: total cost per program; cost per home study in foster care and adoption (total program cost ÷ homes studied); cost per family in protective services; cost per child-care day for day care; cost per interview for foster care, adoption, child protective services, and day care; percentage of social worker time spent in home study or family service, including interview time and administrative time, by program (use a base of 235 workdays per year).

4. Comment on the appropriate use of resources by each program and its efficiency, based on your findings. Did you find any glaring discrepancies or unexplained allocations that appear to need reevaluation before the next budget cycle?

5. If outcomes were measured and data available, how might you use data on successful outcomes to compare program effectiveness?

SUMMARY OF PHASE V

I. Definition

Resource planning identifies the kinds and quantities of resources needed to implement the action plan, identifies potential contributors, secures resources from providers, and, if necessary, makes adjustments between resources available and the change opportunity definition, the change objectives, and the action plan. With the successful completion of resource planning, the participants agree on the use of available resources to implement the action plan.

II. Information needed
   A. What resource needs are anticipated during the life of the project, the first program year, or the first year and duration of the policy?
   B. For each type of resource, what contributors are certain, probable, or possible?
   C. What kinds of resources (including money) and what quantities can be secured from each provider?
   D. What additional money or other resources are needed?
   E. What resources can be used in place of other resources, under what conditions, and at what exchange ratio?
   F. When and where will cuts be made if budgeted expenses exceed all available resources? If more resources are not obtained, what changes will be necessary in the definition of the change opportunity, in the objectives of the change episode, and in the action plan?

III. Tasks to be accomplished
   A. Identify kinds of resources needed to implement the action plan
   B. Calculate or estimate the amounts or quantities of each kind of resource needed
   C. For each kind of resource, identify and contact potential contributors
   D. Secure resources
   E. Match available and needed resources
   F. Adjust definition of change opportunity objectives, methods, or resources, or seek other resources
   G. Write out a draft of a resource plan including an explanation (justification) sheet
   H. Distribute draft and seek feedback from clients, planners, and implementers
   I. Revise the plan based on feedback and additional information
   J. Secure final approval of revised plan from appropriate participants

IV. Products to be developed

A resource plan, including resources available (secured), proposed use of resources (a budget), and justification or explanation of use (a budget-justification sheet).

V. Next steps: transition to Phase VI

The change objectives, action plan, and resource plan, considered as one blueprint, are the basis for the implementing activities to follow.

SUMMARY OF MAJOR POINTS

1. The major product of resource planning is called a resource plan or a budget. This document reflects the agreement of participants about how specific resources will be obtained and used to implement the action plan.
2. Models for human service resource planning include incremental, performance, program, zero-base budgeting, and the programming-planning-budgeting system. A single human service agency may be funded by several sources, each using a different resource-allocation model.
3. Resources for organizational and community change efforts may be obtained from a variety of sources, using a range of strategies and funding mechanisms.
4. The initial draft of the resource plan is constructed by listing the kinds of resources needed, determining the quantity of each kind of resource needed, identifying potential resource providers, and obtaining commitments from contributors for each kind of resource needed.
5. Resources available may be inadequate to implement the action plan as originally conceived. If so, adjustments are made to arrive at a feasible compromise between resources available for the change effort and the definition of the change opportunity, the change objectives, the action plan, or all three.
6. Resource planning involves members of the client, planning and implementing systems as well as potential resource providers. Participation of these diverse participants enhances the technical merits of the resource plan while at the same time developing commitment to the plan.
7. Resource planning tends to be more specific and detailed in nature as it moves from policy to program or project approaches, as a change effort is translated from a national initiative through state to local levels for implementation, and for change episodes of shorter duration.

DISCUSSION OR SELF-STUDY QUESTIONS

1. What tasks must be completed to develop an initial draft of a resource plan?

2. Based on the action plan developed in Chapter 7, develop a resource plan.

3. What contribution to resource planning should be expected from the change agent, clients, planners, implementers, potential resource providers?

4. How do the technical tasks associated with budget development relate to the interpersonal and political tasks?

5. What does the change agent use to identify the kinds and quantities of

resources needed to implement the action plan? What sources of consultation are available?

6. How have the various models of resource planning and allocation affected oppressed populations (women, the elderly, minorities, the handicapped)? In your opinion, what model or models offer the best hope for oppressed populations to achieve a just distribution of resources? Why?

SUGGESTED READINGS

Fisher, R., & Ury, W. *Getting to yes: Negotiating agreement without giving in.* Boston: Houghton Mifflin, 1981.

Hall, M. *Developing skills in proposal writing* (2nd ed.). Portland, Ore.: Continuing Education Publications, 1977.

Lauffer, A. *Getting the resources you need.* Beverly Hills, Calif.: Sage, 1982.

Lohmann, R. A. *Breaking even: Financial management in human service organizations.* Philadelphia: Temple University Press, 1980.

CHAPTER NINE

Implementing Change

OBJECTIVES

Studying the contents of this chapter should enable to reader to:

DEFINE THESE KEY CONCEPTS

Implementation

Compliance

Performance

Bargaining

Negotiation

Prescription

Enabling

Incentives

Deterrence

DESCRIBE OR EXPLAIN

The interplay between compliance and performance

The impact of change residue on implementation

The importance of overlap between planners and implementers

Four technical activities in implementation

Three types of interpersonal activities in implementation

The process of principled negotiation

Distinctive aspects of policy, program, and project implementation

$\mathbf{T}$he implementation phase is a major transition in the change process. Implementation marks movement from planning to doing, from preparation to action. Up to this point, the change agent has been involved in exploratory and developmental tasks. Energies have been directed toward explicating and shaping the framework for action. The focus of the change effort has been defined, explored, and refined. The change agent has mobilized and involved the participants. A blueprint for the construction of the policy, program, or project is now in hand. At the point of implementation, the locus of responsibility shifts from the planners to the implementers. The adequacy, thoroughness, and effectiveness of the planning effort are about to be tested.

Many texts on problem solving fail to mention the implementation phase or devote little attention to it. The major emphasis tends to be on advance planning, with the expectation that implementation will take care of itself. Yet many have discovered that even the best-laid plans go astray. Bardach (1979, p. 36) comments:

> Whether we are talking about simple or complex cases, the fundamental implementation question remains whether or not what has been decided actually can be carried out in a manner consonant with [the] underlying decision. More and more, we are finding, at least in the case of complex social programs, that the answer is "no." So it is crucial that we attend to implementation.

A body of literature on the problematical aspects of policy and program implementation has emerged (Bardach, 1979; Williams, 1980; Williams & Elmore, 1976). Various scholars and practitioners using retrospective research designs have provided evidence of frequent substantive discrepancies between what is planned and what is done. This research has directed attention to the demands of the implementation phase and to the analysis of implementation problems so that they might be prevented or reduced.

ROLE OF THE CHANGE AGENT

Implementers test the projections and expectations of earlier phases against reality. As barriers and gaps are encountered, they modify or revise plans. The implementation process thus is frequently not routine but rather is dynamic, changing, and adaptive. No change agent can possibly anticipate all contingencies or control all responses. Implementers are guided by plans, but they must also be responsive to immediate environmental conditions and interrelationships. Thus, the process of implementation is not merely a mechanical one of starting up a machine, but it is an active period in which the change agent directs, motivates, rewards, communicates, and maximizes control.

Facilitating implementation is a complex process. Organizations and communities are open systems made up of interdependent internal parts in constant interaction with the external environment. Majone and Wildavsky (1979) point out that implementation difficulties may be encountered not only when the original plan turns out to be infeasible but under almost any circumstances. Implementers must try to respond to the dynamics of the change context: "Many, perhaps most, constraints disappear or are overcome (e.g., through learning), while new ones emerge. The solution space undergoes continuous transformation, shrinking in one direction, expanding in another. Consequently, the implementer's left hand must be probing constantly the feasibility boundary, while his right hand tries to assemble the various program components" (p. 180).

The importance of the implementation phase is clear. As projections become reality, the change agent must take an active role in encouraging and guiding participants, affirming goals and objectives, realigning roles, and revising plans. Implementation demands close attention to plans, to the interactions between planners and implementers, and to outcomes. The success of implementation depends on vigilance, attention to detail, recognition of the meaning of experiences with implementation, and skillful facilitation by the change agent.

Two criteria for effective implementation are compliance and performance. *Compliance* refers to following the blueprint and adhering to agreed-on processes and intentions. To be in compliance, implementation activities must correspond to the plans that have been developed. *Performance* refers to assuring planned outcomes and products. To demonstrate performance, implementation must achieve stated objectives.

Both compliance and performance are important. Stressing only compliance in implementation may produce faithful follow-through of plans but an inappropriate, unintended, or undesired result. It fails to take into account the possibility of unanticipated consequences or errors in judgment in developing the action plan. Emphasizing only performance, however, may negate the involvement, preferences, and commitments of those who have engaged in the planning phases.

Compliance and performance can be illustrated by a project designed to expose juvenile first-offenders to the realities of prison life. The plan is to have them spend a day in a state prison under the supervision of a prisoner who has been specially trained for the project. The desired outcome is to motivate the young people to take some specific actions toward constructive behaviors. If, however, some of the participants experience serious negative side effects, the issues of compliance and performance have to be addressed. Compliance (perhaps even contract compliance) may require that all juveniles referred to the program be accepted and complete the planned agenda. Performance considerations, however, dictate that a thorough screening system be established and that only selected juveniles complete the program. Both standards must guide implementation as it proceeds. Action plans designed with an eye to flexibility and to the maintenance of a balance between compliance and performance are most likely to succeed.

PREPARING FOR IMPLEMENTATION

The best preparation for smooth and effective implementation is thorough work on the first five phases of the change effort, as described in Chapters 4 through 8, together with extensive communication among all participants about the intent and the direction of the change effort. Assuring that all participants know the expectations and parameters of the change episode enhances clarity and control. Concrete and specific objectives, planned design and structure, and resource commitments provide the basic blueprint for implementation.

Also helpful in preparing for implementation is attention to two facets of the context: change residue and overlap between planning and implementing systems. The change agent will find analysis of residue helpful in anticipating possible obstacles to the transition from planning to operation. Assessment of overlap—or the absence of it—will contribute to understanding communication needs.

Reassessment of Change Residue

Although the residue, or aftereffects, of earlier planned change efforts was considered as early as the preplanning stage, it is worthy of reconsideration also at the point of implementation. Earlier negative experiences with attempts at change in an organization or community can affect perceptions of and support for the present change effort. People within the organization or community or implementers may be predisposed to look favorably or unfavorably on the initiation of another change process depending on the consequences of, experiences with, or perceptions of earlier efforts.

Some negative residue may not be the result of inadequate planning or unforeseen side effects but of value conflicts or opposition to the intent of the change. Some persons who lost power or resources or who perceive the prior change as threatening important values will try to discredit it and will continue to oppose new changes that move in similar directions. Exploration of the extent and location of this opposition enables implementers to develop strategies to address it.

In addition to the residue from prior change efforts, the change agent also faces the effects of or carry-over from the planning phases of the current change effort. Any inadequacies in the quality of planning or failure to involve significant participants can have serious consequences at the point of implementation. Acknowledgment and analysis of the residue are necessary in order to respond to it. Strategies discussed in the section on interpersonal activities later in this chapter include ways to address change residue. Not all residue is negative. It is clearly, however, the negative residue that is problematical for the change effort.

Provision of Overlap between Planning and Implementing Systems

The degree of overlap between planners and implementers can be seen as points on a continuum. At one extreme, the planners and implementers are the same actors. At the other extreme, they are totally different groups of people who have no contact and no communication other than the written plan. The situation will dictate the degree of overlap in most cases, but efforts should always be directed toward establishment of face-to-face contact and an ongoing relationship between the two groups. With overlap, those who are to be involved in the implementation process are able to participate in its design. They have a chance to anticipate its impact and study its requirements. Their understanding of new roles and responsibilities is good. They have an investment in seeing the plans on which they have spent time implemented.

Overlap may also contribute to effective resistance to change if some actors do not agree with the goals, objectives, and methods that have been adopted. Brager and Holloway (1978, p. 221) caution:

> One could also argue that participation in making a decision with which a member disagrees or which he perceives as contrary to his interests will not bind him to the decision. It could instead strengthen his resistance precisely because he understands the meaning of the goal's impact on him or because he carries a reservoir of negative feeling from having lost on the issue.

If among the implementers there are those who opposed and continue to oppose decisions made in the planning process, the change agent may choose to return to an earlier phase of the process or to change the make-up of the implementing group. Further work on building consensus and commitment wherever the basic disagreement started—whether in the definition and analysis of the change opportunity or in setting goals and objectives—enhances the chances of successful implementation.

In some instances, despite overlap of planning and implementing systems, consensus is impossible to secure. The change agent may nonetheless choose to proceed, attempting to reinforce support and neutralize opposition. Several actions will help. The change agent may restate and publicize the process that was used in planning, reminding actors of opportunities provided for input and participation. The change agent can clearly restate and review the rationale for the change and affirm widespread backing by the majority. The change agent can try to negotiate compliance if not agreement. Ultimately, however, if the change agent is unable to secure a minimally acceptable level of support, the change agent must consider a change in implementers. Even with good support, change is difficult to implement. Lack of support or, worse, sabotage by the implementers can destroy the change effort and leave a long-lasting negative residue.

The crucial role of overlap may be illustrated by two examples. In the first, a volunteer worked with two professional staff members and a member of agency administration to set up a lending library for clients. It included novels about families and individuals facing crises, as well as self-help books. The group solicited donations, purchased bookshelves, and established a circulation system. When the volunteer returned to visit the agency a year later, she found the library unused. One of the professional staff who had helped secure it had been transferred to another unit, and the other had taken maternity leave. No training or orientation about the use of the library had been provided to other workers. They did not see the value of literature as a therapeutic tool and therefore had not made use of the lending library as a resource.

In the second case, two social work practicum students on the pediatric ward of a teaching hospital worked with permanent nursing staff and attending physicians to change the standard hospital rounds procedure. They found many children upset after an entourage of physicians and students had swept into the room, examined a child, discussed among themselves the child's medical history and condition, and left. The child often felt frightened or overwhelmed. The new procedure entailed discussing the history and condition in a conference room and limiting the size of the groups that would interact with the child during the examination period. Information about the rationale for and operation of this policy was built into the head nurse's orientation lecture, which was given to all new personnel and interns rotating through this service. On a visit three years later, one of the former social work students observed the policy still in effect.

Where overlap is minimal, opportunities for communication between planners and implementers become essential. The change agent needs to establish mechanisms for interchange between planners and implementers on a regular basis. These may be meetings, conference calls, site visits, or monitoring reports. The absence of built-in overlap is compensated for by the creation of such processes during the implementation phase.

THE IMPLEMENTATION PROCESS

Putting plans into action is a complex, multifaceted process. A policy, program, or project is about to move from being an abstract idea to being a concrete reality. Uncertainty may be evident. Will the change really address the identified opportunity? How well will objectives be met? How much will implementation disrupt or alter the status quo? Will all the elements fit together as planned? In some ways, planning a change episode is similar to designing and assembling a large piece of machinery or equipment. At this point, all the parts are in place and the power is connected. It is time to turn on the switch. Will it run? Will it run effectively and efficiently? Will it produce up to expectations? No one will know until the implementation process begins.

Implementation is the initiation, management, and administration of the action plan. As such, it involves a series of technical and interpersonal tasks, the handling of which will be dictated largely by the nature of the change effort. Technical tasks include initiating activities necessary to begin the implementation phase, orienting all personnel, coordinating activities, and adapting to the realities of the situation as needed. Interpersonal activities include managing resistance and conflict, developing self-regulation and self-control, and strengthening the support base.

Technical and interpersonal activities continue simultaneously throughout the change process. Although we discuss them separately in the following sections, change agents carry them out in a dynamic and interactive manner, utilizing techniques and skills as needed without regard for a "correct" or "appropriate" implementation process. The following sections explore these implementation activities briefly. Those readers interested in complete coverage of implementation processes and techniques should refer to the literature on human service management and administration.

TECHNICAL ACTIVITIES

By following the blueprint developed in the planning phases, implementers now set the action plan into motion. Component parts must be assembled, and activities must be coordinated and monitored.

Initiating the Action Plan

Early tasks often involve locating space, hiring, purchasing, and other activities associated with implementation of the resource plan. As indicated above, in many change efforts those people who will carry out the plan are already selected and have had some degree of participation in the planning. In some cases, however, this overlap will not be possible. Funds to hire new staff may not be available until the complete plan is approved. If so, the change agent must now implement the whole series of personnel processes including recruitment, screening, selection, hiring, orienting, and training. The change agent must secure space and purchase equipment and supplies. The change agent must carefully attend to all the details of the start-up process.

Initiating the action plan entails designating people to carry out responsibilities, watching schedules, clarifying expectations, and monitoring activities. Although a director may have been hired or designated to head the change effort, the change agent still needs to be aware of implementation activities, always keeping the purpose of the change effort in mind. Flexibility is a crucial quality to cultivate because the environment in which implementation takes place has unpredictable aspects.

Orienting Participants

Once settled in at an established location, implementers should have a comprehensive orientation to the overall philosophy, purpose, and thrust of the change effort. Orientation sessions have several functions. They bring together those who will be entering into implementation activities to allow them to begin to form relationships. They assure that everyone receives basic information and has an opportunity to raise questions and clarify roles and responsibilities. They promote an *esprit de corps* among those engaging in the change effort.

When possible, it is advisable to involve planners in the orientation process. Not only does their inclusion give them visibility and support, but it can also establish links and help ensure consistency about the intent and expectations of the change effort. The orientation, in addition to including a clear message about philosophy, values, and intent, should provide specific information about performance expectations; it should clarify how the plan will be implemented and monitored, specific job expectations, performance evaluation, and the support resources available.

The change agent should be aware of the mixed emotions that accompany the initiation of action plans. Those deeply committed to the change are likely to be eager to start. Some may be anxious about the expectation for new behaviors and new relationships. Some may be confused or at least uncertain about how the plan will work in action. Sensitivity to these feelings and acknowledgement of their legitimacy are important.

Coordinating Activities

The task of coordinating the implementation activities has several aspects. One part of coordination is *integrating component parts* of the change effort. The initiation of a shelter for battered women requires coordination among those who are locating, equipping, and furnishing the house; those who are developing the eligibility criteria, fee structure, and referral system; and those who are developing a public-relations program to acquaint the community with the service. Any delays or unforeseen obstacles in one area may have an impact on other parts of the effort. A term that has come into recent use to describe this role is *orchestrate*: to combine in a harmonious way.

Harmony results from a number of factors, a major one being consistency. For example, job design should be consistent with structure. People hired because of their ability to create and work independently should not be placed into a rigid, bureaucratic structure. Reward systems should be consistent with performance. Often those who perform most competently are rewarded simply by being assigned more work, while those who perform poorly receive fewer and fewer assignments. This type of inconsistency leads to low motivation and morale.

An important tool for effective coordination is *communication*. In addition to the previously discussed communication links between planners and implementers, the change agent must establish other communication lines. Accurate information is critical to appropriate performance. Extensive use of staff meetings, memos, conferences, and other techniques ensures that implementation is consistent with the plan. As data are generated through a monitoring system, feedback to staff on all aspects of performance can help effect necessary corrective actions.

A third aspect of coordination is *time issues*. Three time factors affect the technical task of creating and sustaining an implementing group capable of carrying out the action plan effectively and efficiently. One is the time that elapses between planning and implementing a change. The second is the total time framework for a change episode. The third is the timing of the intervention in relation to the timing of interacting systems.

A relatively short time period between the completion of the planning phase and the initiation of the implementation phase strengthens control. Participants have the plans fresh in their minds. Unanticipated environmental factors have less opportunity to intervene, and committed resources are more likely to be available. There may be less turnover in personnel as well. The energy created by involvement in planning gives momentum to the change effort. Proximity of implementation enhances this momentum, while delays allow it to lose force.

Sometimes long gaps between planning and implementation are difficult to avoid. The plan may have to proceed through several complex bureaucratic channels before approval is secured and personnel decisions and other design decisions are made. Implementation of a new public program may be held up while regulations are proposed and adopted. If funding from external sources is needed, implementation may be deferred or delayed until resources are authorized and allocated. A possible consequence of such time gaps is that they provide an opportunity for opposition to mobilize and express resistance or for supporters to lose interest and enthusiasm. The change agent should try to minimize the time lapse between planning and implementation whenever possible.

However, the change agent should allow sufficient time to carry out the first five phases of the planned change process in a comprehensive and thorough manner. If the time frame is too short and the planning is rushed or cut short, the quality of implementation will be diminished. McLaughlin (1976) discusses two innovative educational projects, one successful and one unsuccessful, that illustrate the point. The successful project "had extensive and ongoing staff training, spent a lot of time and energy on materials development, arranged for staff to meet regularly, and engaged in regular formative evaluation" (p. 176). The second fared less well (p. 176):

> Because of late funding notifications, there was little time for advance planning or preservice training. Project teachers were asked to implement a

concept they supported, but few had seen in operation. The planning that was done subsequently was mainly administrative in nature. . . . In our view, implementation of this project was only pro forma, largely because of the absence of implementation strategies that would allow learning, growth and development, or mutual adaptation to take place.

A short time frame often requires substantial compression of early phases of the change process. The change agent must use professional judgment in such cases to decide whether to proceed. The change agent may decide to abort the change effort if its integrity and success are questionable because of insufficient time. An unsuccessful episode will leave a negative residue that will affect future efforts to work for community or organizational change.

The third time issue in the implementation phase is coordination with the cycles of other organizational and community systems. The integrity or effectiveness of some change efforts depends on having implementation begin during a particular time period. A compensatory program in the public schools to teach reading skills to slow learners was delayed. Implementation occurred in November instead of September, and the staff encountered great difficulty in securing the release of children from the classroom. Teachers and students had established schedules and commenced activities that made inclusion of this program disruptive or inconvenient. The change agent should be aware of program cycles and synchronize the implementation phase accordingly.

In summary, coordination is a critical ingredient of successful implementation. Managing integration activities, communicating, and attending to time considerations all contribute to an implementation process that maximizes its opportunities to meet or exceed expectations.

Facilitating Adaptations and Adjustments

A final technical task in the implementation phase is facilitating adaptations and adjustments. The need to change aspects of the plan comes from two sources. First, some elements of the plan itself may fail to develop exactly as expected. For example, income from fees for services may be substantially lower than projected, and the budget may have to be adjusted accordingly. A second source of changes may be defects in the original intervention plan. Defects may reflect inadequate information available to the original planners, flawed planning, or simply new conditions that affect implementation. Even change in another system—such as a change in the administration of a referring agency—can have an impact on implementation, especially if that change was not known in advance. In short, all organizations and communities operate in a large system that includes other organizations and communities. Changes in any part of the large system can affect the target system.

Adapting to environmental factors is complex because many external variables are unexpected or unpredictable. As Majone and Wildavsky (1979) note, "Because of cognitive limitations and the dynamic quality of our environment, . . . there is no way for us to understand at first all the relevant constraints on resources. We can discover and then incorporate them only as the implementation process unfolds" (p. 183). Two techniques for controlling and responding to the environment are to systematically review environmental factors and to build as much flexibility as possible into the design. Techniques for review of the environment include use of environmental impact statements, force-field analysis, environmental scanning, and trend data for forecasting. Building in flexibility might include developing contingency plans for aspects of the implementation when environmental conditions appear ambiguous or when predictors indicate the possibility of substantial change. A plan to develop a child sexual-abuse treatment unit within a child protective services program might have two alternative staffing plans. One would be based on the accepted budget figure, and the other would accommodate a rumored freeze on hiring and a 10% budget cut. Such adaptability allows implementers to maintain their momentum despite environmental change.

The task of the change agent and the actors is regularly to monitor and assess the implementation process. We cover techniques for monitoring in the following chapter. Problems or opportunities may arise that affect the availability of resources or the demand for services: changes in funding, personnel, priorities, climate of opinion, referral sources, or other relevant factors. Adaptation must be timely and must address the problem or opportunity and its implications systematically.

This process of making adjustments during the implementation phase of organizational or community change is similar to the phenomenon of change orders in the construction industry. When the contractors begin to erect the building designed by architects, they are in constant communication with those who commissioned the building as well as the designers. If some building material is unavailable as specified or if one of the two initiating parties sees a way to improve the design, they execute a change order to modify the construction. Although they make an effort to minimize the number and scope of such change orders, they recognize the necessity for and the inevitability of some changes. It is better to expend some energy, time, and money altering the building during construction than to have to change the way the building is used or to remodel after construction is complete.

Making necessary adjustments depends on continuous monitoring and interpretation of progress. The objectives give direction and provide standards for these assessments. Interaction between planners and implementers facilitates the identification of deviations from plans, exploration of their possible consequences, and determination of whether modifications are needed.

INTERPERSONAL ACTIVITIES

Making the action plan operational requires the support and interaction of many persons. Typically, the implementers must develop new working relationships and learn new policies and procedures, roles and responsibilities.

Proposed changes may threaten existing territorial prerogatives or patterns of resource distribution.

Managing Resistance and Conflict

Change disturbs the equilibrium of a person, group, organization, or community. It requires alterations in behavior, in interactions, or in both. The change agent can expect people to resist change because it moves them from the realm of the known and comfortable into the realm of the unfamiliar and risky.

Warren (1977b), in his discussion of resistance to change, cautions change agents about potential bias. He points out that some resistance may come from rational conviction, from plausible reasons for opposing a proposed change (p. 52):

> But it is important to guard against the naive presumption that whatever any change agent cares to have as a change objective is *ipso facto* desirable and that any opposition to it must be considered not rationally defensible. If the point seems belabored here, it is simply because there is so little recognition of it in the literature, and so much of the naive assumption that "change" is *ipso facto* desirable, along with its partial synonym, "innovation."

The key to managing resistance to change is to expect it and to approach it analytically and directly. Although the degree of resistance to change may be affected by personality factors, change agents should expect a certain level of resistance from all workers at both the individual and group levels because of the investment these people have in the status quo. This resistance to change is often referred to as a "sunk cost." Filley, House, & Kerr (1976, p. 468) state:

> While "sunk cost" is ordinarily thought of as relating to tangible assets, when considered in broader terms it can help to explain opposition to change in a great many instances. People's time, energy, and experience may all be considered to be investments, and any loss or reduction in their value may be felt as keenly as if actual money or property were involved. Considered from this standpoint the introduction of a new invention or a new procedure may threaten individuals' investments in their own experiences, and may perhaps even jeopardize their careers.

In other words, any change involves potential for loss; it may appear to devalue knowledge and experience built up over years. Awareness of this dynamic sensitizes the change agent to the need to demonstrate that benefits will outweigh costs. A certain amount of marketing—determining the interests and preferences of participants and demonstrating how the proposed changes can satisfy those interests and preferences—is important to gain support for the change. The change agent may also develop incentives such as assurances that new skills or procedures will be used for a considerable period or are marketable if the worker changes jobs. When one community mental health center adopted the SOAP (Subjective-Objective Assessment and Planning) method of case recording, the administration informed staff that 23 other human service agencies in the community used this system. This system would thus facilitate interagency research and referral, and workers could list skills in using this method on their resumes.

Change also requires energy and effort to break old habits and learn new ones. It disrupts established working relationships and alters the functioning of systems. The potential for negative unanticipated consequences is high. Extensive discussion and sharing of information about the meaning, the parameters, and the requirements of the change tend to reduce anxiety and resistance.

Mager and Pipe (1970) propose a model for approaching resistance to change analytically and constructively. They suggest examining those situations where an employee is not performing as expected to determine whether the problem is related to skill deficiency (need for training, practice, or feedback), absence of incentive (need to remove punishment or arrange positive consequences), or external obstacles. Once the reason for a performance problem has been analyzed, an appropriate solution can be determined and put into effect.

A change effort is likely to engender not only resistance but conflicts as well because it often involves scarce resources, divergent interests, or unclear expectations. The change agent must therefore utilize conflict resolution skills to facilitate implementation. Several approaches are possible. One is the use of force or authority (through coercion, policy or executive order, railroading, dominance, majority rule). Another is agreement to give and take (through standard adversarial negotiating and bargaining, bribery, arbitration, compromise). Filley and associates (1976) label these methods "win-lose" or "lose-lose" because they result in dominance of one side over the other or concessions by both, with all parties losing something (pp. 165-166). The awareness or perception of losing may diminish participants' energy, commitment, interest, or creativity.

Integrative problem solving is, by contrast, a "win-win" method (Filley et al., 1976, p. 167). It consists of defining the problem to clearly identify the goals, objectives, and values of the parties; generating a variety of alternatives for examination; and evaluating all possible solutions and arriving at an agreement acceptable to all parties. *Defining the problem* entails looking at needs, interests, and desires, rather than starting with solutions. It is a participatory process in which the viewpoint of each party must be acknowledged and accepted by the other as the starting point for problem resolution. *Generating alternatives* requires creating many possible solutions in order to provide a wide range of choices. Approaches such as brain-storming, nominal group technique, Delphi, and surveys are useful at this point (Delbecq et al., 1975). *Evaluating solutions and deciding* is a process of making judgments and coming to agreement. In addition to seeking and applying acceptable standards or criteria, participants may use the process of consensus decision making. In consensus decision making, without using voting or tradeoffs, parties seek a solution that is agreed to by all members of the group. If any person disagrees, participants must rework the solution and discuss it further. Experiments with consensus decision making have shown it to be effective (Filley et al., 1976). Time constraints, limited expertise, irreconcilable value perspectives, or personality differences can, however, limit the opportunities for achieving consensus and may necessitate individual or small-group decision making.

Ultimately, effective implementation may call for an ongoing process of bargaining and negotiation. As defined by Daley and Kettner (1981, pp.29-30), bargaining is a process between two or more actors that is intended to produce agreement. It is a long-term process that involves the use of a variety of strategies designed to secure a favorable agreement. In negotiation, an explicit or formalized relationship is established in the form of face-to-face interaction. Here, parties present positions, seek common grounds, make concessions, and achieve agreements.

In some contexts, such as labor disputes, negotiation is frequently an adversarial process in which each side uses its power and resources to gain advantage and secure an agreement that maximizes its interests. Such an approach creates a win-lose situation, which leaves some participants dissatisfied, alienated, or angry. Negotiating and bargaining can be conducted differently, however.

The Harvard Negotiation Project has developed an approach called *principled negotiations, or negotiation on the merits* (Fisher & Ury, 1981). The four rules basic to this approach are to separate the people from the problem, to focus on interests not positions, to invent options for mutual gain, and to insist on objective criteria.

1. *Separate the people from the problem.*

If negotiation is conducted as positional bargaining, the emphasis is on gaining advantage; the identity and self-esteem of parties are tied to their success or failure in securing their demands. By *separating the people from the problem,* the parties identify the problem rather than positions. In order to focus on solving the problem, parties must build a positive working relationship based on "accurate perceptions, clear communication, and appropriate emotions" (p. 22). Wherever problems with the relationship arise, the parties need to address these problems. The parties in negotiation should thus think of themselves as partners in a problem-solving effort, not as adversaries.

2. *Focus on interests, not positions.*

Taking a position is like proposing a solution without allowing for mutual exploration of the problem. In a conflict situation, each party has certain interests based on needs, values, preferences, goals, or concerns. The two parties in a bargaining situation will have some common interests as well as divergent ones. They will also have multiple interests. Being clear and firm about interests and *focusing on interests rather than positions* enables both parties to understand the elements that must be reflected in an acceptable solution.

3. *Invent options for mutual gain.*

Parties typically enter negotiations with an idea of what they want and a desire to secure its acceptance. Successful principled negotiation depends on giving up the commitment to a single answer and the orientation toward one's own problems only. After gaining an accurate perception of each others' interests, parties need to engage in the creative *generation of new options* that build on shared interests or dovetail differing interests. Producing a number of possible options that might satisfy both sides facilitates ultimate agreement.

4. *Insist on objective criteria.*

The existence of some conflicting interests is unavoidable. Rather than resolving them by a contest of wills, participants can *use objective criteria.* Doing so makes the negotiation legitimate and reasonable. Objective criteria may be legal precedents, market values, professional standards, costs, equal treatment, and scientific judgment. Fair procedures include drawing lots, letting one party make the division while allowing the other party first choice, taking turns, and letting a third party decide. The search for objective criteria needs to be a joint one, guided by reason and principle.

Inevitably conflicts will arise over decisions that must be made in the implementation phase. Approaching the varying perspectives analytically greatly increases the chance of positive resolution. The conflict-resolution techniques described here can be profitably employed if lines of communication can be kept open and the development of adversarial relationships can be prevented.

Developing Self-Regulation and Self-Control

Human service professionals often express discomfort with the whole notion of control, preferring instead to place trust in professional performance based on ethics and values. However, ensuring compliance and performance requires control, and control is an essential part of the implementation process. Control implies an exercise of power. If this exercise of power comes from outside, implementers may develop some resistance or resentment. To the extent that the control comes from within, resistance and resentment can be minimized. Internalized controls produce an independent system as well. A task for this phase of the planned change process therefore is to develop in implementers a system of self-control or self-regulation.

Bardach (1979) identifies four commonly utilized instruments of control that promote self-regulation: prescription, enabling, incentives, and deterrence. *Prescription* entails following orders and requirements because of acceptance of the authority of the source or because of a sense of moral obligation. Legitimate power (affirmation of the right of the wielder of power) and referent power (identification with the person wielding power) undergird prescription. Prescriptions are a basis for self-control only if the recipient accepts their legitimacy and authority. Prescription, Bardach notes, "is characteristically backed up by deterrence or incentives" (p. 112).

Enabling consists of giving needed resources to another to promote some undertaking. The assumption is that the provider of resources and the recipient share congruent goals and that some benefit will be received, perhaps in the form of status or recognition. This utilitarian or remunerative source of control has a quality of mutuality and exchange.

Incentives are promises of rewards based on future performance. An incentive offers benefits in order to elicit specific behavior. For an incentive system to be effective as a form of control, payment needs to be based on evidence of performance. If the amount of the award is proportionate to the degree of performance, there is a disincentive or punishment for the nonperformer. The major challenge in devising incentive systems is to design performance measures that are suitable, meaningful, and measurable. Too often process or outputs are rewarded rather than outcomes. As a result of a weakness in this regard in the Medicaid system, for example, in some clinics physicians process and are reimbursed for as many as 20 patients per hour per doctor. No proof of outcomes (improvement of health) is ever demanded or offered.

Deterrence is a form of control based on the threat of future punishments for noncompliance. It is coercive in that it threatens negative consequences if behavior is not appropriate. It assumes a conflict of interest or incongruity of goals between the controller and the controlled. Punishment is generally a last resort, used sparingly because of the resentment it generates. Yet deterrence becomes a weak method of control if those controlled do not expect the proposed sanctions to be exercised.

The most effective instruments for self-control are those built on remunerative power. If implementers gain prestige, self-esteem, or material resources or rewards as a result of compliance and performance, they are likely to continue those behaviors.

Strengthening the Support Base

The change agent needs a support base to provide sanction, give advice and encouragement, and exert influence when needed. The support base typically includes people both within and outside the planning and implementing groups. It may be organized in formal groups and entities such as advisory committees, boards of directors, and consultants, and it may also include informal groups or networks of staff or volunteers working on planning or implementing. Although the change agent initiated the development of a support base in the preplanning and early planning stages, its active engagement is crucial in the implementation stage. If support groups are to be called on, the change agent must inform them about and orient them to the philosophical as well as the technical aspects of the change effort. This informing and orienting should be ongoing, not just at those points where support is needed.

Orienting and informing members of the support base enables them to maintain a connection to the change effort and to offer technical and other assistance at appropriate moments. The support base is a sounding board and a source of constructive criticism. Internal members can provide feedback on problems and questions that might be emerging as the implementation moves forward. External members can provide the same kind of input but from the community perspective. Regular and comprehensive communication through minutes, newsletters, meetings, media, and other methods helps to maintain and strengthen the support base.

Enlisting the assistance of the support base may be desirable when public relations, expanded resources, or technical advice is needed. Members of the support base have access to different kinds of resources—tangible and intangible—to facilitate the change effort. Their knowledge of the political system, interpersonal relations, and other resources augments the resources of the planners and implementers. In addition, one should not underestimate the value of moral support. Change agents often feel somewhat isolated and alone. The existence of a support base demonstrates that the vision is shared and that there is a broad base of commitment to the change (Bryan, 1981).

POLICY, PROGRAM, AND PROJECT IMPLEMENTATION

The major differences between policy, program, and project implementation are in the areas of time lag after planning is complete, clarity of intent, and overlap and communication between planners and implementers. Social policy typically requires a longer time between planning and implementation, tends to be less clear, and involves little if any overlap as compared with program and project planning. Possibilities for problems in compliance and performance are therefore greater with social policy change than with projects and programs. Moreover, social policy is often complex. It moves from a statement of intent to a program to implement the intent. The intent may be somewhat ambiguous, and, if so, the ambiguity may contaminate the subsequent change process. Unclear policy is functional and politically expedient, according to Gates (1980, p. 65):

> The legislative adoption of written policy often requires the establishment of coalitions with different and conflicting interests; vague written policies offer the advantage of allowing each actor in the coalition to "interpret" the policy (both individually and on behalf of his constituents) as promoting his own interests.

A second aspect of the social policy process that affects implementation is the many systems involved and the subsequent separation between planners and implementers. One institution may control the finances (for example, the legislature), another the administration (a program delivery agency), another the evaluation and oversight (a state agency). Bardach (1979) notes that the fact that elements are in the hands of many different parties leads to implementation politics (p. 37):

> It is a form of politics in which the very existence of an already defined policy mandate, legally and legitimately authorized in some prior political process, affects the strategy and tactics of the struggle. The dominant effect is to make the politics of the implementation process highly defensive. A great deal of energy goes into maneuvering to avoid responsibility, scrutiny, and blame.

Bardach identifies four major problems likely to be encountered in policy implementation: diversion of resources, deflection of goals, dilemmas of administration, and dissipation of energies. All these problems complicate the implementation of social policy and make expectations difficult to achieve without careful attention to a strategy for implementation.

With organizational policy, especially in small agencies, these problems are much less likely to emerge. Often the same actors participate in both the planning and implementation. The expectations of organizational policy are typically expressed in specific terms, and time lag between planning and implementation is minimal.

Program implementation varies considerably in time lag, clarity of intent, and overlap and communication between planners and implementers. Major variables include the complexity, size, and scope of the program. Planning, designing, and implementing a new parent-education program in a small family service agency can be accomplished in a relatively short period of time with clear objectives and good communication. Initiating a highly complex program such as a new community information system presents more problems in timing, clarity, and communication than does the parent-education program. Many individuals and organizations throughout the community must be involved. Service definitions must be written and agreed on. Data-collection and data-processing systems must be designed. Such complexity may necessitate years of planning prior to implementation. The many unknowns involved will cause vagueness in some components. Overlap between planners and implementers will be limited. In short, the nature of the program will, to a great extent, dictate the type of implementation problems that will be experienced.

Projects have short time frames and limited objectives and, therefore, should pose the fewest problems in implementation. Time lag between planning and implementation typically is short, although waiting for decisions on funding can considerably lengthen the time lag. Objectives are highly specific, thus minimizing any lack of clarity about intent. Utilizing many of the same personnel for planning and implementation typically maximizes overlap in projects.

Although these descriptions of similarities and differences among policy, program, and project implementation attempt to depict some common experiences with these approaches, wide variations occur in implementing change efforts. Experiences will not always mirror these descriptions. There will always be exceptions. Careful planning and attention to the details of implementation can often help minimize time lag and vagueness, while maximizing overlap and communication. Probably the dominant theme in the literature on implementation is to avoid assumptions. Simply because a change effort has been well planned, one should not assume that implementation will proceed smoothly and without complications. Careful attention to the process and to the technical and interpersonal considerations of implementation can help ensure an orderly, efficient, and successful transition from planning to implementation.

_____ *Case Study*

The staff in the psychiatric unit of a county hospital identified a problem related to chronic mentally ill (CMI) patients. Many CMIs who would formerly have resided in state mental hospitals were returning to the community because of an emphasis on deinstitutionalization and living in the least restrictive environment. The community, however, had made few supportive arrangements for CMIs. Outpatient therapists at the county hospital were seeing more and more of these people, which contributed to unrealistically large caseloads and poor treatment as well as to staff overwork and burnout. CMI patients need ongoing services. Their improvement usually is minimal but they need support to prevent deterioration and the development of behavior dangerous to themselves or others.

Numerous meetings of public and private groups concerned about the problem resulted in a plan that included the establishment of several day-care facilities. Commitments for funding came from the city council, county board of supervisors, and state mental health agency. The centers were set up through purchase-of-service contracting with a community family service agency (FSA).

The FSA established a planning committee including a caseworker from the county hospital, two family members of CMI patients, a supervisor from a community mental health center, a faculty member from the university, three FSA staff members, and an FSA board member. They developed a plan for locating the programs in three different geographical areas—downtown in a store front, mid-town in a church recreation hall, and at the edge of town in an unused warehouse. Activities were to be primarily recreational in nature.

The first implementation problem they encountered was caused by residue from an earlier episode of change. The mid-town church had previously provided space for a drug-counseling program, and neighbors had had many unpleasant interchanges with clients following group sessions. This time they were determined to keep the program out of their neighborhood, and they circulated a petition to prevent its implementation. Considerable delay ensued while the zoning board heard the case. The decision eventually favored the FSA. The agency sent workers to neighborhood schools and churches to provide educational seminars on the nature of mental illness and the needs of the CMI population. The downtown program was immediately overcrowded and was unable to comply with contract requirements to accept all referrals. The police actively referred CMI vagrants, and the downtown area had many cheap boardinghouses where CMIs often settled. The outlying center, however, was underused because of the inadequate transportation system.

Case Study Discussion Questions

1. Part of the FSA contract specified that all referrals, including self-referrals, would be accepted into the program. Overcrowding raised problems relative to performance. Closing intake would raise problems relative to com-

pliance. Identify at least three options that would be responsive to both compliance and performance issues.

2. How does a change agent find out about change residue prior to implementation? Identify several types of residue that might have been problematical in this situation, and indicate how the change agent might have known about the issues prior to implementation.

3. Design a system that will ensure overlap and maximum communication between planners and implementers.

4. Describe the technical and interpersonal tasks necessary for successful implementation at one of the centers.

SUMMARY OF PHASE VI

I. Definition

Implementation is carrying out what has been planned, or putting the action plan into effect. It involves activating the policy, program, or project and adapting and adjusting the plan to assure compliance and performance.

II. Information needed

A. What change residue has been carried over from earlier change efforts?

B. What negative carry-over exists, if any, from earlier phases of this change effort?

C. How much overlap is there between planners and implementers?

D. What factors should be considered in carrying out implementation?

1. What activities will promote compliance?

2. What activities will promote performance?

E. What specifically are the technical tasks to be accomplished and by whom?

F. What specifically are the interpersonal tasks to be accomplished and by whom?

III. Tasks to be accomplished

A. Identify and address change residue

B. Identify issues of compliance and performance

C. Identify overlap and gaps between planners and implementers

D. Engage in technical activities to promote effective implementation

1. Initiate the action plan

2. Orient the implementers

3. Integrate component parts of the change effort

4. Ensure communication and interaction between planners and implementers

5. Address problems in timing

6. Facilitate adaptation and adjustment of the action plan

E. Establish and maintain the interpersonal relations needed to promote effective implementation

1. Expect and address resistance to change

    2. Develop an analytical approach to the resolution of conflict

    3. Utilize negotiating on the merits or integrative problem solving to resolve disputes and difficulties

    4. Develop mechanisms of self-regulation and self-control

    5. Engage the participation of those who make up the support base for the change

IV. Products to be developed

The further development or activation (or both) of the action plan, highlighting the tasks detailed in III above.

V. Next steps: transition to Phase VII

Identify components of the action plan that should be included in the management information system.

SUMMARY OF MAJOR POINTS

1. Implementation requires active guidance by the change agent to assure compliance and performance.

2. Analysis of change residue and of overlap between planners and implementers provides needed background information before initiation of implementation.

3. Technical activities in the implementation phase include initiating the action plan, orienting participants to the philosophical as well as the technical aspects of the change effort, coordinating the change effort, and facilitating adaptations and adjustments.

4. Interpersonal activities in the implementation phase include managing resistance and conflict, developing self-regulation and self-control, and strengthening the support base.

5. There are some differences in and distinctive aspects of implementation depending on whether it is of a policy, program, or project. Primary differences relate to time lag, clarity of intent, and overlap and communication between planners and implementers.

DISCUSSION OR SELF-STUDY QUESTIONS

1. You have been assigned the responsibility of designing a development and training program for staff members for the upcoming year in an agency of about 100 people. After a thorough planning process including a training-needs assessment, design of the program, selection of training courses and instructors, and scheduling, you are ready to implement the program. After the first two sessions you discover that absenteeism is running about 50%. Informal feedback indicates that the staff has never taken training seriously. Throughout the planning process they gave you polite responses, but they never intended to treat this program any differently from previous programs. You have already made a commitment, in your objectives, to effect a whole series of behavioral changes in staff performance, based on your belief that all

would complete the training. Outline a plan for dealing with residue, overlap, performance, and compliance.

2. This year's graduating class developed a plan for orienting new students. The program is to be implemented by the faculty and officers of next year's student association. What specific implementation considerations and activities need to be incorporated in initiating the action plan; orienting participants; coordinating activities and time frames; facilitating adaptations and adjustments?

3. The board, director, and selected staff of an alcohol counseling program have been working with consultants to redesign the program. The new approach will include 12 group education and counseling sessions. One-to-one casework is to be phased out. In general, long-time employees are opposed and newer employees are in favor of the change. As director, how would you go about marketing the change and bargaining around major points of disagreement?

4. Explain how implementation of a federal policy (such as block-grants legislation) differs from implementation of a program (such as one for job-skills training) or a project (such as the distribution of surplus commodities to the homeless) as each relates to time lag, clarity of intent, and overlap between planners and implementers.

SUGGESTED READINGS

Bardach, E. *The implementation game: What happens after a bill becomes a law.* Cambridge, Mass.: MIT Press, 1979.

Fisher, R., & Ury, W. *Getting to yes: Negotiating agreement without giving in.* Boston: Houghton Mifflin, 1981.

Pressman, J. L., & Wildavsky, A. (Eds.). *Implementation* (2nd ed.). Berkeley: University of California Press, 1979.

Williams, W. *The implementation perspective: A guide for managing social service delivery programs.* Berkeley: University of California Press, 1980.

Williams, W., & Elmore, R. (Eds.). *Social program implementation.* New York: Academic Press, 1976.

CHAPTER TEN

Monitoring the Change Effort

OBJECTIVES

Studying the contents of this chapter should enable the reader to:

DEFINE THESE KEY CONCEPTS

> *Monitoring*
>
> *Evaluation*
>
> *Data*
>
> *Information*
>
> *Inputs*
>
> *Throughputs*
>
> *Outputs*
>
> *Outcomes*
>
> *Output tables*
>
> *Input documents*
>
> *Data processing system*

DESCRIBE OR EXPLAIN

> *Four major uses of management information*
>
> *Six considerations in developing an information system*
>
> *Elements included in the input, throughput, output, and outcome components of the system*
>
> *The relationship between objectives and monitoring*
>
> *Five steps in developing an information system*
>
> *The benefits of computerization*
>
> *Different types of information needed in organizations and in communities*

The term *monitor* comes from the Latin word *monere*, which means "to warn." Monitoring systems are essentially early-warning systems designed to provide information that is useful in keeping a change effort on course. Collecting data and information about the implementation process can be one of the most challenging and rewarding phases of the change episode if handled thoughtfully and sensitively. Data collected and analyzed during this phase will help to determine whether the change effort was worthwhile—whether the changes were implemented as planned and whether they are having the anticipated impact. How sterile the whole process would be without knowing the answers to these questions!

DIFFERENCES BETWEEN MONITORING AND EVALUATION

Various authors have defined the terms *monitoring* and *evaluation* with slightly different shades of meaning. Rossi, Freeman, and Wright (1979) define monitoring as "assessment of whether or not a program is (1) operating in conformity to its design, and (2) reaching its specified target population" (p. 16). They define impact evaluation as "assessment of the extent to which a program causes changes in desired directions in the target population" (p. 16). These definitions imply that monitoring deals with process and impact evaluation with outcomes. They ask two monitoring questions: "Is the program reaching the persons, households, or other target units to which it is addressed? Is the program providing the resources, services, or other benefits that were intended in the project design?" (p. 33). Impact assessment questions are: "Is the program effective in achieving its intended goals? Can the results of the program be explained by some alternative process that does not include the program? Is the program having some effects that were not intended?" (p. 33).

Wholey, Scanlon, Duffy, Fukumoto, and Vogt (1970) state that evaluation has three distinguishing characteristics: "Evaluation (1) assesses the effectiveness of an ongoing program in achieving its objectives, (2) relies on the principles of research design to distinguish a program's effects from those of other forces working in a situation, and (3) aims at program improvement through a modification of current operations" (p. 23). Monitoring, they state, is "the assessment of managerial and operational efficiency of programs or projects through periodic site visits and other management techniques" (p. 27). As with the previous definitions, these imply that the focus of monitoring is internal—on functions of the organization or program—while evaluation looks at both internal functioning and client outcomes.

Suchman (1967) discusses five types of evaluation: effort, performance, adequacy of performance, efficiency, and process. Effort, efficiency, and process are clearly components of program or organizational functioning. Performance and adequacy of performance are related to client outcomes or impact on a client population. Moroney and Grubb (1981), utilizing Suchman's five types of evaluation, illustrate how each type can be useful in providing different kinds of information about program functioning (pp. 612–616). They define monitoring as addressing the question "Who is getting what, from whom, at what cost?" Again, evaluation is defined as focusing on both process and outcome, while monitoring is limited to process.

The Urban Institute has published a series of monographs that focus on monitoring client outcomes (Millar, Hatry, & Koss, 1977a, 1977b; Millar & Millar, 1981). The authors define monitoring, as used in their own context, as "the regular collection and analysis of outcome information" (Millar & Millar, 1981, p. 2). The emphasis seems to be on the term *regular.* "Ad hoc, one time only, special studies of outcomes," they state, "are not monitoring as defined in this manual" (p. 2). Client outcome monitoring, therefore, is the regular collection and analysis of data related to the condition or satisfaction of clients after receiving a service. Although they do not specifically define evaluation, the authors state that "outcome monitoring and in-depth program evaluations are complementary activities" (p. 6).

It appears, then, that some authors distinguish monitoring and evaluation by limiting monitoring to analysis of inputs and throughputs, while others distinguish the two by depth of analysis. As used in the model presented in this text, both monitoring and evaluation are defined by the content and intent of the function. Although we see monitoring and evaluation as complementary functions, each has a different purpose. Both focus on the process of implementation as well as the outcomes of a planned change effort. *Monitoring* attempts to determine whether the implementation system is proceeding as planned and what outcomes are achieved. *Evaluation* attempts to determine the effectiveness of the process and the value of the outcomes. In other words, monitoring keeps track of implementation and outcomes, while evaluation places a value on their usefulness and effectiveness. (The degree of rigor applied to the evaluation process determines whether evaluation or evaluation research is being conducted; we discuss evaluation in the following chapter.) Whenever positive or negative values are placed on interpretation of data, whether through impressionistic observation or rigorous statistical analysis, the change agent has, by our definition, moved beyond monitoring to evaluation.

If, for example, a special project provides intensive counseling to parents who abuse and neglect their children, both monitoring and evaluation are carried out. Monitoring, among other things, keeps track of the extent and type of counseling and other services received. It answers questions about the characteristics of clients, number of sessions and hours of counseling received, type of counseling, cost, types of problems identified, services needed, client status following service, and other process and outcome considerations. Evaluation, however, places a value on the process and outcomes. The focus of evaluation is on the extent to which abuse and neglect are reduced and the value or significance of the intervention. There are some important links between the monitoring system and the evaluation system. By examining different types of interventions and comparing different outcomes, one can continually refine treatment approaches to make them increasingly effective. Similarly, by looking at cost factors, one can determine which services are having the most beneficial effects for the resources invested and which appear to be too costly to continue as designed.

Data collected in the monitoring and evaluation phases of the change process can answer these and many more questions. These data are fed into an overall collection and processing system called a *management information system*. Most management information systems today in human services are computerized. The volume of data needed for decision making in most change efforts has moved beyond the point where manual tabulation and record keeping are practical.

USES OF MANAGEMENT INFORMATION

Although each discrete piece of data will not, by itself, be useful for decision making, data when aggregated and analyzed can yield information. Information is useful to many different individuals and systems who examine it from a variety of perspectives. Weiner (1982) notes: "One needs to differentiate 'data' from 'information.' The former is meaning free; the latter is data to which humans apply a referent to provide a meaning....Computers can process data; human beings take data and convert it into information" (p. 267).

In general, management information systems aid decision making. How is the effort proceeding when compared with the plan? Where are the points of breakdown? Are they significant enough to warrant a change now, or can that wait until all problems have been identified? Are all the data necessary for decision making being collected? What is the time lag between collection and use by management?

Slavin (1978, pp. 477–478) identifies specific appropriate uses of an information system as follows:

General
· Planning and policy development
· Decision making
· Coordination of client services

Institutional management
· Budgeting
· Program development
· Program monitoring
· Public relations
· Evaluation
· Cost analysis
· Social and legislative action
Service delivery
· Referral and follow-up
· Continuity of service
· Service integration and coordination
· Tracking clients
· Recording
· Staff evaluation
Research
· Knowledge building
· Social problem analysis
· Program evaluation
· Practice testing

Development of a sound and reliable information system that can be of help in answering relevant questions is a time consuming and costly undertaking. It is, therefore, critical that those who design such systems examine carefully the specific purposes for which information will be used. Once information has been developed, some organizations tend to shroud the findings in secrecy. Management information becomes a tool for the exercise of power, for writing reports, or for rewarding and punishing staff. Any of these uses alone misses the spirit of a sound and effective use of data and information.

Many individuals and systems are involved in change efforts and need data and information for decision making. Management and the board of directors, for example, need to know whether activities have been implemented as planned, the costs of implementation, and the effectiveness of services. Staff need to know something about the effectiveness of different intervention approaches, the effectiveness of their own interventions, and the extent to which units or programs are meeting objectives. Likewise clients, key actors, initiators, advocacy groups, and the general public may all need information about the change effort, its implementation, its costs, and its effectiveness. Information thus serves important functions internal to the change effort as well as the external functions of developing positive public relations and support. Without open communication, avenues of potential support and corrective action may be cut off. Two change efforts, making different uses of data and information, will illustrate this point.

One of these projects was designed to deal with the problem of teenage drug abuse, the other to meet crisis needs of the poor and unemployed. The drug program received widespread publicity when first proposed. Space was donated for a meeting place, a board of directors was created, and fund raising began. The response from the community was enthusiastic, and $50,000 in start-up funds was raised quickly from corporate and individual donations. Once the money was raised, no further information was forthcoming about the program. After about six months, program supporters came back to the public for additional donations. The donated space was inadequate, and new space had to be rented. This time the response was not enthusiastic, and the fund-raising goal was not reached. Although the organizers were certainly well intentioned, they neglected to keep others informed about the progress of the project. People who initially supported the program raised questions about accountability and the appropriate use of funds. Even though there was no basis for concern about mismanagement, the lack of dissemination of data and information about the project led directly to declining support.

The support project for the unemployed began within an existing agency set up to provide emergency food and clothing. As unemployment figures rose sharply, the agency's resoures became inadequate. The agency made arrangements with the local newspaper to run a series of stories about the kinds of problems people were bringing to the agency, using fictitious names. People needed money, for example, to turn on the utilities, to repair a car, to install a telephone. The response was overwhelming. Within days the overall fund-raising goal was reached. The agency continued the newspaper series by reporting what was done with the money and what effect it had on the families helped. Donations continued, and what had been intended as a temporary project became an ongoing, self-supporting program. In this case the simple sharing of information—letting donors and the general public know how the money was used—led to increasing support for the project.

Not every change effort can have extensive media coverage, but openness and the sharing of information are important. When data and information are not shared, staff, community interests, funding sources, the board, and other interested individuals and groups will most likely become alienated from the change effort or, at best, simply continue past performance. With information sharing, these individuals and groups can make many constructive contributions that may enhance the change effort.

CONSIDERATIONS IN DEVELOPING AN INFORMATION SYSTEM

Good information can strengthen a change effort, but good information is difficult to develop. Collection of data usually involves paperwork—one of the least attractive tasks for most human service professionals. The collection of good, reliable data, therefore, often depends to a large extent on *acceptance of the information system by staff.* If they believe the system provides meaningful information, receive feedback from it, find the feedback useful in adjusting performance, and are rewarded for superior performance, then they will support sound data collection procedures. Staff input into the conceptualization, development, implementation, and use of the information system is therefore critical.

A second consideration is *cost*. Systems that must be newly designed and programmed, where new hardware must be purchased and new forms developed, may cost many thousands of dollars. For initiating and implementing the change episodes we envision with our model, such a major effort is unlikely. A related concern, however, is *compatibility with existing systems*. Perhaps the insertion of a few additional items into an existing system, together with some reprogramming of the ways in which the data are processed, will meet the information needs for the change effort.

A fourth consideration is the *safeguarding of information*. The integrity of a system is judged on its ability to protect confidential information. One method of protecting client identity is through the use of a client identification number rather than a name. A second is to limit access to individually identifiable recorded information. Much of the information needed can be displayed in the form of tables as aggregated data. This information is generally not individually identifiable and therefore is acceptable for limited distribution. Specifically identifiable client material should be needed only by workers and supervisors or for professional use in a case conference. All other access to identifiable client data should be limited by policy statements and security measures.

Aggregated data, too, should be protected from unplanned distribution. Statistics that indicate, for a given community, high crime rates, poor education, or high levels of alcohol and drug abuse can be used in different ways. From a sociological perspective, these data can indicate structural constraints and oppression of selected population groups. From a political perspective, the data can be used to stereotype and to make a case for strengthening what may be already oppressive approaches in law enforcement, education, and other public programs. To the general public, such data may stigmatize residents of a neighborhood or members of a group.

In short, the safeguarding of information is a matter to be considered carefully. Policy statements should spell out appropriate uses of data and procedures for gaining access. Security measures include administrative controls over the system, user identification systems, locked storage of material, and controlled distribution mechanisms. In addition, measures that control access to confidential information can be programmed into a computer.

If the system is to be used appropriately, *training of staff* is critical to ensure understanding and gain support. Each level of staff—managers, supervisors, workers, fiscal support staff, clerical staff, and others—plays an important role in implementing the information system. Each must have a clear understanding of expectations, be trained to relate to the system appropriately, and receive feedback on correct and incorrect performance.

A final task in developing an information system is *assuring the information is used*. Many organizations have found that even well-conceptualized and soundly designed systems have not been used by those who could benefit from the information. Reasons for low utilization include resistance to a new system, lack of awareness that information is available, lack of knowledge of how to use it, slow availability of information, and lack of feedback or consequences for poor data collection procedures. With the proper supports, data can strengthen and enhance the change effort and its impact. As indicated earlier, thorough training of all levels of staff is one method of support. Another is active utilization by management of the information generated. If supervisors meet regularly with their units to analyze and discuss the implications of last month's data, staff members will become familiar with the information system. In addition, if funding patterns and reward systems demonstrate respect for the data generated, staff will show an interest in the system. However, if the data are seldom used and there is little feedback to staff, they will not use the information system as a resource for making adjustments in performance.

COMPONENTS OF THE SYSTEM

The specific variables used in constructing a management information system depend on whether the change involves services to clients or whether the change effort is a specific project such as fund raising or innovations in the planning and delivery system. In both cases, however, the variables are part of inputs, throughputs, outputs, or outcomes. Abels and Murphy (1981, p. 139) describe each of these components as follows

- inputs (needs, demands, constraints, resources)
- throughputs (assignment of resources, modes of intervention, personnel allocation, time frame and so forth)
- outputs (serviced population)
- outcomes (impact of service over a period of time)

One might classify each of these design components as developed in Chapter 7 for information system purposes. Table 10-1 illustrates this classification.

When a project, program, or policy provides services, input data include, at a minimum, the characteristics of clients at the point of intake. These data give a profile of clients who use the services and the types of problems brought to the agency. Workers can also make a preservice assessment of problem severity when clients enter the system. Using these data elements permits a later cross-tabulation with service and outcome data to determine whether particular types of clients (young, old, male, female) respond better to particular types of programs. Throughput data reveal types and costs of the services provided, as well as effectiveness, when cross-tabulated with outcome data. Output data can aid in determining the number and types of clients completing the program, and outcome data can be used to determine which services are most and least effective for which types of clients.

Supportive projects, programs, and policies are designed to strengthen or support some component of the planning and delivery system. Data collection, therefore, concentrates on the characteristics of the system, its problem-

TABLE 10-1. Classification of design components

Service Project, Program, Policy	Supportive Project, Program, Policy
Inputs	*Inputs*
Target population characteristics	Target system characteristics of planning or
Age	delivery system
Sex	Type of project, program, or policy
Ethnicity	Problematical features
Education	Effects on overall program
Income	Indicators used to illustrate existing
Census tract	strengths and weaknesses
Etc.	Characteristics of other participants—client,
Presenting problem classification	action, change agent system
Type	*Throughputs*
Severity	Intervention activities
Worker characteristics	Individuals or units involved
Throughputs	Types of activities
Services provided	Time spent on intervention activities
Method of delivery	Costs associated with intervention
Service tasks	*Outputs*
Standards	Completed activities
Costs	*Outcomes*
Outputs	Changes effected as a result of intervention
Units of service delivered	
Number of clients completing the program	
Outcomes	
Client progress or improvement in measur-able terms	
Specific aspects of client's status or ability to cope with environment	

atical features, and the effects of change. Characteristics of the system vary depending on the focus of change. If, for example, a project is designed to develop a new performance evaluation system, one set of characteristics will be identified. If, however, it is designed to develop a public relations campaign, a different set of characteristics will be identified. The guiding principle is to select indicators that, if changed, will give evidence of effectiveness and will aid in understanding success or failure. This same principle guides the selection of throughputs, outputs, and outcomes.

Two examples will help illustrate the type of components to be included in a management information system. A service project designed to serve meals to the elderly might require these components:

Input
1. Characteristics of clients
   a. Age
   b. Sex
   c. Ethnicity
   d. Census tract
   e. Income
   f. Employment status

g. Nutrition-related problems
2. Data on community nutrition-related health problems
3. Revenues
   a. Direct payment (fees, contributions)
   b. Subsidy

Throughput
1. Number of meals served
   a. Per person
   b. Overall
2. Any factors that vary from meal to meal, such as nutritional value, hot or cold meal, quantities per person
3. Meal site or location
4. Supportive services provided, if any
5. Costs
   a. Per person
   b. Overall

Output
1. Number of participants who complete the program within a given time frame

Outcome
1. Level of nutritional health as compared with preproject level
2. Client satisfaction data

Client characteristics indicate the types of people participating in the program and, at a later point, whether the program is meeting needs. Data on community nutrition related health problems reveal whether the population served is the population in need. Concern often arises over whether those most in need are actually receiving services. These data provide a basis for responding to that concern. Throughput data indicate, in a precise manner, what is being provided. If attendance patterns vary significantly, for example, data about the types of meals served may provide reasons for that variation. Data on supportive services and costs help determine what services are most needed and overall program costs. Output data are important because programs such as this one are often designed to demonstrate improvement in those who take full advantage of it. If a person who is assessed as severely malnourished comes only once a week, that attendance pattern may have an important effect on how much that person is helped by the program. Outcome data measure program effectiveness and achievement of outcome objectives.

For monitoring purposes, the project might use Tables 10-2 and 10-3 to display some of the data collected. Many other options, of course, are available. In this simulation, 100 clients are participating in the meal program. Table 10-2 is a monthly report showing each client (from 001 through 100) with selected descriptive characteristics, number of meals served, and the total cost for that client for that month. Table 10-3 then aggregates this individual client data by age, sex, ethnicity, and health status. Costs can then be calculated for each of these subgroups. Data about supportive services used,

TABLE 10-2. Sample individual output table for a service project

Senior Center Meal Program Individual Client Profile
Report for the Month of _____

Client Number	Age	Sex	Ethnicity	Census Tract	Health Status	Number of Meals This Month	Total Cost (at $1.75 per meal)
001	55	M	B	1275	1	18	$31.50
002	61	F	B	1275	2	20	35.00
003	57	F	C	1283	1	14	24.50
.	.	.	.	.	.	.	.
.	.	.	.	.	.	.	.
.	.	.	.	.	.	.	.
100	72	M	C	1285	3	9	15.75

TABLE 10-3. Sample aggregated output table for a service project

Senior Center Meal Program Aggregated Client Profile
Report for the Month of _____

Characteristics of Participants	Total Registered Participants Number	Percent	Meals Served This Month Number	Percent	Total Cost (at $1.75 per meal)
Age					
55–59	30	30	940	47	$1645
60–64	29	29	640	32	1120
65–69	26	26	260	13	455
70 and over	15	15	160	8	280
Sex					
M	41	41	720	36	1260
F	59	59	1280	64	2240
Ethnicity					
A. Asian	2	2	0	0	0
B. Black	18	18	460	23	805
C. Caucasian	73	73	1400	70	2450
D. Hispanic	6	6	120	6	210
E. Native American	1	1	20	1	35
Health status					
1. No nutrition problems	68	68	1200	60	2100
2. Slightly malnourished	26	26	580	29	1015
3. Severely malnourished	6	6	220	11	385

improved nutrition, or client satisfaction could be displayed in the same manner.

A supportive project designed to reduce the size of caseloads would require different types of data to determine project effectiveness. The important point here is that any organization can simply reduce caseloads and put clients on a waiting list. That in itself is not a complex problem. But what will the cost of this reduction be in types, quality, and quantity of services provided? Will complex problems be screened out? How much will the cost per case go up? Will outcomes for those served improve? Will the change achieve the desired effect of reducing stress on staff and permitting time for improving the quality of services? Only collection of data can provide a basis for answering these questions. Some of the following variables may provide useful information:

Input
1. Existing caseload characteristics
   a. Size of caseload
   b. Problem types
   c. Types of services provided
   d. Units of service per case
   e. Cost of service per case
   f. Outcomes with existing caseloads

Throughput
1. Changed caseload characteristics
   a. Size of caseload
   b. Problem types
   c. Types of services provided
   d. Units of service per case
   e. Cost of service per case
   f. Outcomes with reduced caseloads

Output
1. Difference in the number of clients completing a service within a given time frame
2. Difference in cost per client within a given time frame

Outcome
1. Difference in outcome scores within a given time frame
2. Difference in quality of work life for staff

Tables 10-4 and 10-5 provide examples of how the data collected might be displayed. These two tables illustrate selected features of the caseload for each worker. Jackson's caseload is illustrated at the point of change and again six months after the reduction in caseload size. For each type of service, the number of cases is reduced at the postchange point. Also, for each type of service, the amount of service provided goes up, the cost goes up, and the outcome scores go up. One might conclude, then, that the amount and quality of service are improved by the changes, at least for this worker. Determining whether the change is cost effective requires analysis of other factors including available program resources and objectives.

TABLE 10-4. Sample prechange output table for a supportive project

Family Counseling Center
Caseload Profile by Worker at the Point of Change

Worker	Service Types	Number of Cases	Mean Units per Case (1 unit = 1 hour)	Mean Cost per Case	Mean Outcome Scores (range = 0–100)
Jackson	Individual counseling	9	30.3	$757.50	72.0
	Marriage counseling	12	23.1	577.50	77.3
	Parent Effectiveness Training	10	12.6	315.00	80.1
	Family therapy	5	39.0	975.00	80.5
	Group counseling	6	26.5	662.50	82.7
Franklin Etc.					

TABLE 10-5. Sample postchange output table for a supportive project

Family Counseling Center
Caseload Profile by Worker Six Months After Change

Worker	Service Types	Number of Cases	Mean Units per Case (1 unit = 1 hour)	Mean Cost per Case	Mean Outcome Scores (range = 0–100)
Jackson	Individual counseling	7	39.8	$995.00	88.1
	Marriage counseling	9	29.9	747.50	89.7
	Parent Effectiveness Training	8	17.8	445.00	86.6
	Family therapy	4	48.8	1220.00	92.2
	Group counseling	4	36.1	902.50	89.0
Franklin Etc.					

NEED TO MONITOR THE ENTIRE CHANGE PROCESS

Monitoring and evaluation are directed primarily to the implementation phase of the change process. However, work done in other phases can influence the effectiveness of change, and this work, too, must be monitored. Identifying and analyzing the need for change, establishing goals and objectives, planning design and structure, and resource planning all require monitoring. If any type of breakdown occurs in the implementation phase, participants need to know whether it is a design failure, resulting from problems in earlier stages of planning, or whether it is an implementation failure.

Problems in the change process can emerge for various reasons. An inadequate data base, failure to involve the appropriate people, poor conceptualization of the need for change, improper use of theoretical frameworks, faulty analysis, poorly conceptualized goals and objectives, bad design or resource planning can all contribute to the failure of a change effort to have the desired impact. Monitoring only the implementation phase will not necessarily detect these flaws. Each of these decisions requires careful study while it is being made, constant reevaluation during the implementation stage, and a postimplementation analysis.

Monitoring implementation will, however, help to determine whether tasks, activities, and agreements are carried out as planned. Throughout the process the use of some type of formal tracking system will ensure that all activities are completed within the agreed time frame. The Gantt and PERT charts described in Chapters 6 and 7 provide techniques for monitoring implementation.

Monitoring objectives requires special attention. Setting objectives (as described in Chapter 6) is a long, deliberate, and time-consuming process. Both process and outcome objectives guide the change effort and help determine the appropriateness of activities. It is, therefore, important to monitor the implementation of process objectives and progress toward achievement of outcome objectives carefully. Implementation of process objectives, like other activities, can be monitored through formal tracking techniques like Gantt and PERT charting.

Progress toward achievement of outcome objectives, however, should be a part of the management information system. Each component of an outcome objective becomes a focus for data collection. As discussed in Chapter 6 the four components are time frame (By when will the objective be achieved?), target group (On whom will the change effort have an impact?), result (What changes should be expected?), and criteria (How will the changes be measured?). Examining the time frame should highlight the degree of progress compared with the total time allowed for achievement. If the effort is one third of the way toward accomplishment but two thirds of the time has elapsed, the information system should be used to warn those affected of this problem. Client group characteristics must be included to determine whether the appropriate people are being served. The expected results and the measurement criteria reveal the impact of the change effort. Identifying responsible parties may or may not be a part of a formal management information system, but keeping track of those responsible will save time if they have to be contacted when problems or opportunities emerge.

BUILDING A MANAGEMENT INFORMATION SYSTEM

Often in the past data collection systems have been constructed much the way one would design a simple survey questionnaire. Management would organize a task force made up of representatives of each level of staff who were interacting with the system, typically a supervisor, a worker, a manager, a clerical person, a data-entry person, and a data processing person. This task force would pool information needs, design forms for data collection, and design a system for data processing. All too frequently this approach produced reams of printouts that had limited use. Consider that even a simple system using ten variables can yield several hundred comparisons if each item is cross-tabulated with every other item. Although the data elements may have been carefully and wisely selected, too often little attention was paid to the ways in which data would be aggregated and used for decision making.

As an alternative to beginning with the data collection (input) documents, Burian (1977, p. 11) proposes the following steps for developing a management information system:

1. Sketch out goals and objectives—that is, spell out what the system is to produce
2. Rough out dummy output reports—tables of the type one would expect to come out of the system
3. Design the input documents—the forms for collecting the data
4. Test the input documents
5. Design the processing system
6. Conduct a trial run of the system

King and Clelland (1981, p. 277) propose essentially the same approach in a series of eight steps. Early steps specify who will use the data produced, what kinds of decisions must be made, and how the data will be used. The next series of steps involves the development of a model of the data collection system and achievement of consensus around the model to be adopted. The final step is determining what information will be needed to make the decisions specified in the model. Both approaches essentially turn the process around, beginning with output considerations or decisions to be made and then working backward to develop information requirements, input reports, and a processing system.

Designing rough drafts of possible output tables helps to identify which data elements will be used for decision making and which ones fall into the category of "nice to know." Information overload can render a system ineffective for many potential users, and it may be wise to eliminate those items that are simply nice to know and to concentrate on those that will be used for decision making. As indicated earlier, data used for decision making include those needed to determine progress on objectives as well as those needed to identify important client characteristics, to determine service and cost effectiveness, and to identify outputs and outcomes.

Given these requirements, the following steps are useful in designing a system: identifying the decisions that must be made once the change effort has been implemented; selecting the data elements needed to make these decisions; determining how the data should be displayed in order to make them useful for decision making; designing data collection forms (the input documents); and organizing the data processing system.

Identifying the Decisions to Be Made

Implementation of a change effort requires various decisions. Such decisions as whether to continue or discontinue, to stay on course or change direction, to increase or decrease resources to specific parts of the change effort, or to freeze spending for certain items can all be made based on data generated by the information system. The system can also be used for making decisions about scheduling and assigning work, managing resources, monitoring and measuring work, and evaluating individual and program performance. As indicated, objectives are important in identifying the decisions to be made.

Selecting Data Elements

Identifying subunits or modules can aid in the selection of data elements. A client identification module that clusters client identification items, for example, would include all descriptive information needed for decision making about the effects of the change effort on clients. A worker identification module would include names or identification numbers, work unit and location, and other necessary descriptors. A problem identification module would include a checklist of problems or needs. Other data elements might include fiscal data, service data, disposition or termination data, and evaluation or follow-up data.

Determining Data Display

Designing a user oriented information system is a critical step in the process. Two reasons frequently cited for low utilization of management information are lack of awareness of how to use information and gaps between information and implications for action (Cotter, 1981, p. 145). Data, to be useful for decision making, should be comparative preintervention and postintervention, unit A and unit B, outcomes for clients of worker 1 and outcomes for clients of worker 2, dropout rate of one ethnic group of clients and dropout rate of another. The possibilities are almost limitless. Decisions about output reports should be based on the information needs of the organizations, groups, and individuals to whom reports will be directed. These may include change agents, clients, planners, implementers, political bodies, funding sources, the board of directors, the general public, and management.

Designing Data Collection Forms

User involvement is again important at this stage in the development of a workable system. The design of data collection forms (input documents) must allow for their efficient and accurate completion. Input documents include face sheets, staff activity reports, client tracking reports, and evaluation reports. The arrangement of items is important. In addition to being designed for ease in completion, forms should be designed to facilitate efficient processing of the data. A thorough field testing of forms is advisable before they are adopted on a permanent basis.

Organizing the Data Processing System

A formal design of the processing system includes a flow chart that depicts the process—the points at which documents are completed, the distribution of documents, the processing of data on the documents, the generation of output reports, the distribution of output reports, and provisions for feedback and correction based on output reports.

An example will illustrate the ways in which these five steps for building an information system are applied. An objective of a change effort is as follows: "By June 30, to increase the job placement rate for trainees at least 75% as indicated in the monthly placement report." The action plan focused on training unit supervisors in job placement resources and techniques. Following training, placement rates were to be tracked for all workers and supervisors to determine whether the training of unit supervisors made any difference in job placement for clients.

As the first step, the change agent examines the decisions to be made. The change agent needs to decide, for example, whether the training of supervisors is having the desired impact—that is, whether the placement rate is being increased. One should also be able to decide whether the pace of placement increase is acceptable since a time limit has been set. Finally, one should be able to decide whether the combination of training and feedback is the critical variable in increasing the rate of job placement and, if not, what the important variables are.

Moving to identification of data elements, the change agent might decide that these elements will include worker data (What worker is responsible for each client?), supervisor data (What supervisor is responsible for each worker?), caseload data (What types of cases are in each worker's caseload?), service-provision data (What job training and services were given to each job applicant?), and placement rate data (How many clients were placed in jobs?).

From these data elements, output reports or tables can be constructed. Table 10-6 is an example of an output report. When the data are collected and

TABLE 10-6. Sample output report

Report for the Month of _____

Monthly Report of Unit and Worker Activity and Placement

Unit and Worker	Number of Applications Processed This Month	Total Units of Job Training Prescribed for Applicants	Mean Units of Job Training Prescribed for Applicants	Total Units of Service to Applicants	Mean Units of Service to Applicants	Number of Applicants Completing Training This Month	Number of Applicants Placed in Jobs This Month	Placement Rate
Unit A								
Worker 1								
2								
3								
4								
5								
Total Unit A								
Unit B								
Worker 1								
2								
3								
4								
5								
Total Unit B								
Unit C								
Worker 1								
2								
3								
4								
5								
Total Unit C								
Total program								

inserted, this table will provide some helpful comparisons. It will show how many job applicants per month are processed by each worker and unit, how much job training is prescribed, how much total service is given in addition to job training, how many applicants are completing training each month, and the number and percentage of those completing training who are placed in jobs.

This table, by itself, will not help the change agent to know whether the change effort (training of supervisors) is effective in increasing the placement rate. By examining comparable data from before supervisory training and after supervisory training, however, the change agent can determine whether the training made any difference and in what directions. Examination of the data can also help to identify other factors that might possibly have influenced changes.

From this output report, the data collection forms can be designed. The change agent might determine that a daily report of worker activity (Table 10-7) is needed in order to compile the monthly report. The worker activity (input) forms must contain all the data needed for the monthly (output) report. This simple daily report will provide all the data needed to identify worker, the supervisor (from unit identification number), the types of cases (by matching client identification number to client application form), service provision (units of training and other services provided), and placement rate (number completing training and number placed in jobs).

Finally, the last step in building an information system requires the charting of a data processing system (Figure 10-1). The illustration is simplified and liberties have been taken with flow charting principles for the sake of clarity. The document symbol indicates the points in the process where documents are completed. All documents go to data processing for production of output reports.

When designing such a system, even the novice realizes that a good deal of testing and experimenting is necessary to identify and eliminate problems. Planning for implementation of the system should include a period of testing, with rapid feedback to facilitate prompt adjustments. When the data and information flow is working as needed and producing accurate and reliable reports on which decisions can be based with some degree of confidence, the system is ready for permanent installation.

THE USE OF COMPUTERS

By now it should be clear that we assume the use of computers in managing information. As Weiner (1982) states: "There are probably no areas of human services that have not been touched by the computer. . . . Some of this use has been for financial and administrative processes; other applications have been patient and client care; still others have been for planning and evaluation purposes" (p. 300).

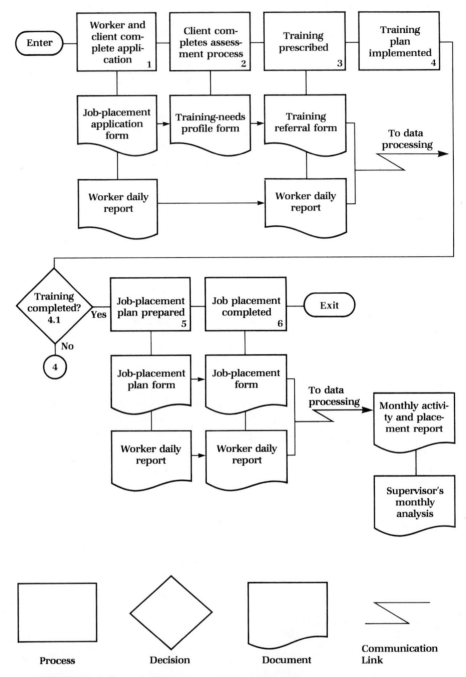

FIGURE 10-1. Sample flow chart of a data-processing system

Although some may question the use of computers for initiating relatively small-scale changes in organizations and communities, one should carefully weigh the implications of the alternatives. Any alternative to electronic data processing will involve some hand tabulation of data, possibly including

TABLE 10-7. Sample input document

Daily Report of Worker Activity

Worker identification number	Unit identification number	Date

Please indicate all client related work activity for the day in the columns below.

Client Identification Number	Enter 1 if New Application	Units of Training Prescribed (1 unit = 1 training day)	Units of Service Provided (1 unit = 15 minutes)	Enter 1 if Training Completed	Enter 1 if Placed in a Job

Totals

hundreds of hours of clerical time. On balance, it may well be less expensive to consider either adding data to an existing system or developing a special program.

Computer program designers have dealt with many of the fears of the past to the satisfaction of human service professionals. They have designed security systems to protect the confidentiality of the client. Human service professionals have developed problem and service taxonomies that reflect client needs, and they have created evaluation scales that quantify client progress and outcomes. Of course, data always provide only a basis for making both management and casework decisions. Those interpreting the data must carefully weigh values.

One should view seemingly negative results with any client population from the perspective of the entire system and structure within which that population lives and functions. Characterizing individuals, groups, or whole communities in negative ways, such as "high crime areas" or "poor training and education risks," can stigmatize individuals and result in oppressive and discriminatory practices. Responsible use of data requires interpretation in context, considering a wide range of influencing factors. With careful collection, processing, analysis, and use of data and information, the potential exists for services to become increasingly relevant to individual needs and to contribute to improved functioning for clients.

COMMUNITY INFORMATION SYSTEMS

For the purpose of monitoring project, program, or policy changes in the organizational arena, a management information system will suffice. When the change effort goes beyond the limits of an organization, however, a communitywide monitoring and evaluation effort is needed. A community information system for human services collects data about all human service processes and outcomes within specific geographical or functional boundaries.

Although the process for creating a community information system is similar to that for creating a management information system, the undertaking is considerably more complex. Many individuals, organizations, and systems must reach agreement on a range of variables. A common taxonomy or classification system for problems and services is basic. Standards for similar services must be uniform. Common service tasks and units of service must be defined. Outcomes must be measured in a uniform manner for all similar service programs and projects. A common set of client characteristics, service characteristics, and outcome indicators must be established. Creation of a community information system typically requires many years of effort together with extensive communication and trust building before it can be ready for implementation.

The benefits of a community information system, however, can be substantial. Utilization of common definitions and a common data base can help to identify the size and scope of community conditions, problems, and needs. It can aid in identifying priorities, both for types of service and for client populations. It can help in making decisions about service effectiveness and in allocating resources. In short, a community information system can be an invaluable tool for monitoring and evaluating human services in a community.

In summary, a data collection and information system is vital to the successful monitoring and evaluation of a change effort. Selection of data elements should be undertaken with great care to ensure that data collected will be limited to those items that will be used for monitoring and evaluation purposes. Information systems should be designed to ensure that they will contribute to decision making. During monitoring participants track both the process and outcomes of a change effort, while during evaluation they make judgments about the quality and usefulness of the change process and outcomes. Ultimately the basis for judging the success or failure of a change episode is the data generated by the information system. Careful attention to the quality of indicators, to extensive input, and to system design is therefore indispensable.

Case Study

At a staff meeting of a community information and referral service center, both management and staff expressed dissatisfaction with the current system for evaluating performance. Staff members who provided direct face-to-face service to clients felt they were being evaluated primarily on a subjective basis, while supervisors and management pointed out that poor documentation of activities by workers did not provide adequate information for an objective evaluation. Both groups agreed, therefore, that they would attempt to build an information system that would help in the assessment of performance. The project was assigned to a task force.

Services provided included intake, short-term counseling, referral, development and maintenance of a community resources file, follow-up, and telephone contact only. In designing the system, they agreed that evaluation of performance for face-to-face services should be based on the quality and quantity of work done; that quality of work was difficult to measure in an information and referral agency, but that data on problem type, number of cases, and follow-up activities would help; and that cost prevented the measurement of outcomes for clients, so they would judge a successful completion to be either satisfactory termination following short-term counseling or client engagement with a referring agency (or both).

After much deliberation, the task force agreed that the system should provide a data base on which to make the following decisions: Which workers had the highest numbers and highest percentages of successful completions? For the successful completions, what were the problem types, mean units of service per case, and cost per unit of service? In the interest of keeping the system simple and efficient, they felt that if they knew at least which workers were dealing effectively with what types of problems and at what cost, they would have created the basis for fair and equitable performance evaluation.

Figure 10-2 is a flow chart of the intake, counseling, and referral process. The intake unit completed a face sheet that identified, among other things,

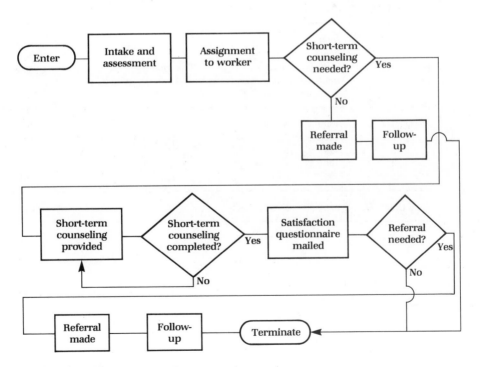

FIGURE 10-2. Flow chart for case study

the problem types presented by the client. The client was then seen by a worker who provided short-term counseling or referral or both. Short-term counseling was followed by a client satisfaction questionnaire, and referral was followed by contact with the referring agency to determine whether the client initiated contact.

The task force, using the variables identified as indicators of performance, constructed the output table illustrated in Table 10-8 in rough draft form. They submitted it to staff for review and comment.

Case Study Discussion Questions

1. List these six variables: Total clients assigned, units of service by problem type, mean units of service per client, total units of service this month, total program costs per worker, and cost per unit of service per worker. Next to each variable, indicate what value that variable has in evaluating performance and what limitations or possible misuses you might anticipate in using that variable.
2. What are some of the reasons why each of these variables differs from worker to worker as indicated in Table 10-8?
3. The task force indicated that successful completions were important. They defined successful completions as follows: for short-term counseling, an overall mean score of at least 75 on client satisfaction forms; for referral, at

TABLE 10-8. Output table for case study

Workers and Units	Total Clients Assigned this Month	Total Units of Service by Problem Type (1 unit = 15 minutes)				Total Units of Service This Month	Mean Units per Client	Total Program Costs	Cost per Unit of Service
		1	2	3	. . N				
Worker 1	120	16	47	33	. .	420	3.5	$ 3,723	$ 8.86
2	138	2	27	66	. .	345	2.5	2,410	6.98
3	113	19	32	51	. .	305	2.7	3,355	11.00
4	106	33	55	21	. .	435	4.1	3,534	8.12
5	99	25	16	91	. .	317	3.2	2,866	9.04
Total Unit 1	576	95	177	262	. .	1,822	3.2	$15,888	$ 8.72
Worker 6									
7									
8									
9									
10									
Total unit 2									
Total program									

least 75% of clients referred for services initiate contact with the referral agency and either engage in the service process or are placed on a waiting list (as determined in follow-up procedures). Design an output table that indicates the numbers and percentages of successful completions.

4. What variables are completely missing from this system that you think could affect the performance of workers?

SUMMARY OF PHASE VII

I. Definition

Monitoring the change effort involves keeping track of implementation. Although closely related to evaluation, monitoring places emphasis on whether activities have been implemented without placing a value on the quality of that implementation.

II. Information needed

  A. What uses will be made of management information?

  B. What individuals and systems will use the data and information?

  C. How can data and information best be communicated to those who should have access to it?

  D. What factors should be considered in developing a management information system?

    1. How can staff be persuaded to accept and use the system?

    2. How much will it cost?

    3. How can it be designed to fit with an existing system?

    4. How can data and information be safeguarded?

    5. What training will be needed?

    6. How can we assure use of the data and information generated?

  E. What are the components of the system?

    1. Input components

    2. Throughput components

    3. Output components

    4. Outcome components

  F. How can we ensure that progress toward achievement of objectives will be monitored?

III. Tasks to be accomplished

  A. Identify and list purposes of management information

  B. Identify and list individuals and systems who will make use of management information

  C. Plan for staff participation in system design

  D. Plan for location of system

    1. Calculate costs of adding to an existing system

    2. Calculate costs of a separate system

  E. Plan for safeguarding data and information

  F. Plan for training users

  G. Plan for building supports for using the data generated into the ongoing change process

H. Identify and list components, including indicators used to monitor objectives
I. Build the management information system
   1. Identify decisions to be made
   2. Select data elements needed to make decisions
   3. Determine how data should be displayed
   4. Design data collection forms
   5. Organize the data processing system
   6. Implement a trial run
   7. Correct problems
   8. Install permanently
IV. Products to be developed
   A plan for development of a management information system that includes the tasks in III above.
V. Next steps: transition to Phase VIII
   Separate those indicators to be used for monitoring purposes from those to be used for evaluation.

SUMMARY OF MAJOR POINTS

1. Monitoring systems keep track of implementation, ensure that activities are proceeding according to plan, and provide a data base for use in decision making.
2. Monitoring and evaluation data form the basis of an overall collection and processing system called a management information system.
3. Because many different people and groups use management information systems, they should be designed to serve many different purposes.
4. Considerations in developing an information system include acceptance by staff, cost, compatibility with existing systems, ethics regarding the safeguarding and use of information, training of staff, and assurance of utilization of the information.
5. The specific variables used in constructing a management information system are inputs, throughputs, outputs, and outcomes of the project, program, or policy.
6. Change agents should refer back to objectives to ensure that monitoring of progress toward their achievement occurs.
7. Building a management information system consists of five major steps: identify decisions to be made, select data elements needed to make decisions, determine how data should be displayed to be useful in decision making, design data collection forms, and organize the data processing system.
8. To make the most efficient and effective use of data and information, the use of computers will probably be necessary.
9. Information needs change depending on the arena (organization or community). Data collection systems should be adapted accordingly.

DISCUSSION OR SELF-STUDY QUESTIONS

1. You have taken a job as director of a special one-year project to increase awareness of different cultures among preschool children. No monitoring system was designed for the project. How can you be sure that everything is proceeding according to plan?
2. Give some examples of how a management information system can meet these needs: public relations, staff development and training, and identification of the least expensive or most effective methods of treatment for clients.
3. You have designed an information system that records the progress of each client served by an agency. You would like workers and supervisors to use the data, including selected demographic characteristics, to analyze effectiveness patterns. Write out your instructions in a way that will ensure that this analysis takes place.
4. A new short-term family treatment project is designed to improve communication among family members by teaching six communication techniques. List the input, throughput, output, and outcome variables.
5. Using the five steps in building a management information system, design a system to determine whether a new affirmative action policy on recruitment and selection of minority students is having the desired effect of increasing minority student enrollment in your program.
6. The state legislature has passed a law creating a new special education program designed to prepare developmentally disabled children for mainstreaming in regular classrooms. How would the data needs of the state senate research department differ from those of the special education director of a local school district?

SUGGESTED READINGS

Cotter, B. *Planning and implementing social service information systems.* Washington, D.C.: Project SHARE, U.S. Department of Health and Human Services, 1981.

Millar, A., Hatry, H., & Koss, M. *Monitoring the outcomes of social services.* Vol. 1, *Preliminary suggestions.* Vol. 2, *A review of past research and test activities.* Washington, D.C.: The Urban Institute, 1977.

Millar, R., & Millar, A. (Eds.). *Developing client outcome monitoring systems.* Washington, D.C.: The Urban Institute, 1981.

Moroney, R. M., & Grubb, C. T. Research and evaluation: Contributions to social work practice. In N. Gilbert & H. Specht, *Handbook of the social services.* Englewood Cliffs, N.J.: Prentice-Hall, 1981.

Rossi, P. H., Freeman, H. E., & Wright, S. R. *Evaluation: A systematic approach.* Beverly Hills, Calif.: Sage, 1979.

Suchman, E. A. *Evaluative research.* New York: Russell Sage Foundation, 1967.

CHAPTER ELEVEN

Evaluating the Change Effort

OBJECTIVES

Studying the contents of this chapter should enable the reader to:

DEFINE AND DISCUSS THESE KEY CONCEPTS

> *Evaluation*
>
> *Evaluation research*
>
> *Research*
>
> *Types of evaluation*
>> *Effort or activities*
>>
>> *Performance or outcomes*
>>
>> *Adequacy of performance*
>>
>> *Efficiency*
>>
>> *Implementation process*
>
> *Validity*
>
> *Reliability*
>
> *User oriented evaluation*

LIST AND DISCUSS TASKS IN EVALUATING AN EPISODE OF CHANGE

DESCRIBE AND EXPLAIN

> *How to evaluate the progress of an episode of change*
>
> *How to evaluate the implementation of an organizational or community change effort*
>
> *How to evaluate the outcomes of an organizational or community change effort*

While monitoring keeps track of activities, events, and outcomes, evaluation makes a judgment about or attaches a value to the phenomena monitored. The purpose of evaluation is to develop information that will lead to effective and efficient interventions. The model of organizational and community change proposed in this book uses evaluation as a means to improve the effectiveness and efficiency of the change episode during each phase of the process. This critical and analytical approach to change thus provides information for ongoing assessment and refinement of the change process itself as well as of the outcomes of the change episode. For example, based on the evaluation of a new service program implemented in an agency, the change agent may refine the intervention at any point in the process to make it more effective, less costly, or both. Data generated during monitoring and evaluation thus provide the basis for subsequent decisions that guide the change effort.

When a change agent initially considers a change opportunity, he or she makes key decisions that lay the foundation for evaluation by tentatively structuring the situation. Participants collect and analyze data related to presumably significant factors. They choose objectives that reflect variables hypothesized to be important. They formulate an action plan that identifies activities and events crucial to the accomplishment of the objectives. The frameworks they utilize during identification and analysis of the change opportunity and during objective setting, together with the events and activities identified in the action plan, provide the content for the monitoring and evaluation systems. For an evaluation system to maximize its contribution to a change effort, therefore, earlier phases of the change episode must have a clear conceptual framework. Data collection for evaluation purposes follows logically within the same framework.

If, for example, a change opportunity is viewed as a need for improvement in housing, sanitary facilities, and nutrition, data on these needs will have been collected and analyzed during the early phases of the change episode. Objectives will focus on improving the quality of housing, sanitation, and nutrition for a specific client population. The action plan will identify activities and events contributing to improvements in housing, sanitary conditions, and nutrition. The information system will monitor changes in housing, sanitation, and nutrition, and evaluation will indicate improvement or progress in these areas.

The change agent is responsible for ensuring that the evaluation contributes information for decision making during the change episode. The change agent may actually conduct the evaluation, may coordinate the evaluation efforts of others, or may act as a catalyst. The terms *evaluator* and *change agent/evaluator* will be used interchangeably in this chapter to denote the change agent's primary responsibilities and multiple roles. Our proposed model of organizational and community change does not anticipate the use of external evaluators during a change episode.

DEFINITIONS

Evaluation is a social process of making judgments about the merit, worth, or value of a change. Evaluation makes judgments about those change episode inputs, throughputs, outputs, and outcomes that have been monitored. The information collected about these components has a value or degree of merit attached during evaluation and then becomes the basis for decisions (Suchman, 1967, pp. 7–11; Weiss, 1972b, pp. 1–6, 10–18). Evaluation covers a wide variety of activities, from fleeting judgments made on the basis of a single, impressionistic observation or piece of data to thoroughly considered conclusions drawn from rigorous scientific experiments. Suchman (1967, p. 83) identifies distinct levels of information or types of measurement, ranging from expressions of consumer satisfaction to experts' judgments to information generated by scientific measurement. The use of scientific methods and techniques to collect and analyze data on which judgments are made is called *evaluative research* or *evaluation research*. Carrying out evaluation research increases the probability that the evaluator can with confidence prove rather than assert the value of a change (Suchman, 1967, pp. 7–8).

During a change episode, both evaluation and evaluation research may be appropriate, depending on the intended use of the information. If the change agent needs to know whether an experimental program causes clients to reduce their drug use, evaluation research may be indicated. If less powerful information (such as the number of clients who complete a treatment program) is needed, less rigorous methods may be adequate. An example of highly useful but less powerful information would be a survey of clients' satisfaction with the drug-counseling program.

Suchman (1967, pp. 81–82) draws a useful distinction between research and evaluation research.

> Evaluative research has no special methodology of its own. As "research" it adheres to the basic logic and rules of scientific methods as closely as possible .... [Evaluative research] utilizes all available techniques for the collection and analysis of data and employs a wide variety of research designs. It may be carried out under experimental laboratory conditions or in the natural community. In other words, evaluative research is still research, and it differs

from nonevaluative research more in objective or purpose than in design or execution.

(See also Perkins, 1983, p. 315.) The purpose of nonevaluative research is to produce information that can be generalized beyond the time and place of its genesis. In contrast evaluative research is limited largely to a given time and place or a specific change episode. In evaluation research, the evaluator describes the conditions under which a specific intervention can be said to produce a measurable outcome (Suchman, 1967, pp. 77–83).

Evaluators conduct *formative evaluation* during implementation and use it for improving the intervention. *Summative evaluation* occurs after the intervention. Evaluators use information produced by a summative evaluation to determine the ultimate value or worth of the process and outcomes. They might use the results of a summative evaluation to decide whether to continue an intervention after a trial period, whether to expand an intervention, or whether to use a similar intervention strategy in other settings. Although summative evaluations tend to generate more powerful information than formative evaluations, implementers more frequently find data generated by formative evaluations to be more useful (Weiss, 1972b, pp. 16–18).

TYPES OF EVALUATION

Evaluation may cover five different areas: effort or activities, performance or outcomes, adequacy of performance, efficiency, and the implementation process (Suchman, 1967, pp. 60–73). Each type of evaluation offers a particular perspective on a change effort and is part of a complete evaluation system. Information developed by all five types of evaluation is used to assess the total change episode, including both outcomes and process. Relating evaluation to specific objectives and budget items allows the change agent to identify which components of an intervention are effective and efficient and to understand how and why some intervention elements were successful while others were not.

Effort or Activities

Evaluation of effort or activities concerns the quantity and quality of change activities. This most basic form of evaluation simply measures activities or throughput without concern for the results of the activities. Effort measures assure that something is being done but not necessarily that anything is being accomplished. Effort data reflect contacts with the clients or the targets or both. The number of organizational or community meetings held, the number of casework interviews conducted, or the hours of homemaker service provided are all measures of effort. Many service units are defined by effort: a therapy session, a day of child care, or a meal delivered to an elderly person's home. Unit costs are calculated using these effort measures together with financial data. Effort evaluation fulfills a vital accountability function. It provides evidence that change implementers are doing what they are supposed to do. Effort information compares anticipated and actual levels of activity and forms the basis for activity controls and resource allocation (Moroney & Grubb, 1981, p. 616).

Performance or Outcomes

Although effort measures are vital indicators that participants are engaged in the prescribed change activities, they fall short of answering the central question in evaluation: Do the activities produce the desired and predicted positive effects or outcomes or results or impacts? "What happened as the result of this program that would not have happened in its absence?" (Moroney & Grubb, 1981, p. 614). Performance or outcome evaluation concerns improvements in the quality of life of the clients or targets or both as a result of the change efforts.

Caseworkers are expected to interview clients (effort), but, more importantly, by use of interviews and other techniques, to improve the life situation of clients in some specific way (performance). Similar expectations exist for change efforts at the group, organizational, and community levels. The neighborhood community worker is expected to meet with residents (effort) in order to produce specific improvements in the quality of neighborhood life (performance) (Brody & Krailo, 1978, pp. 226–236). If a reduction of child sexual abuse is the objective in a change episode, the incidence or prevalence of child sexual abuse will be the content of the performance evaluation. If increasing the number of minority police officers is the change objective, the racial composition of the police force will be the content of the performance evaluation. Performance or outcome evaluation provides the basis for justifying the use of resources for the intervention—the accomplishment of intended and desired results.

Adequacy of Performance

Adequacy evaluation concerns the relationship between the outcome and the total need as identified early in the change process (Suchman, 1967, pp. 63–64). If a change agent identifies 300 families with inadequate housing, evaluation of the adequacy of performance would examine the results of the change effort as compared with this total need. Perhaps the original change objective was to construct new public housing for 100 families and to make self-help housing improvements for the remaining 200 families. If, during the change episode, it becomes apparent that insufficient resources are available to provide both the new public housing and the housing improvements at the anticipated levels, plans have to be modified. Perhaps 30 families are placed in new public housing, and the housing improvements are abandoned as an intervention option. Ultimately, this choice of attaining adequate new public housing for 30 families must be assessed against the continuing housing needs of the unaffected 270 families. Making this assessment does not denigrate the tangible and desirable gains for the 30 relocated families but rather puts those gains in perspective. Thus, at a minimum, gains for 30 families cannot be evaluated as meeting the identified housing need. Evaluation of the adequacy of performance "is simply a comparison measure of need satisfied by the program intervention relative to the existing need for that service as identified in the needs assessment phase of the planning process" (Moroney & Grubb, 1981, p. 615).

Efficiency

Efficiency evaluation makes judgments about the ratio between the inputs of an intervention (resources) and the outputs and outcomes of that intervention (products and performance). *Cost efficiency* relates the costs of inputs to unit outputs of services—without concern for the results of the intervention. Two counseling agencies might calculate their costs for delivering an hour of individual therapy at $25 and $50 per hour. All other things being equal, the $25 unit cost appears to be the more efficient use of resources.

$$\text{Agency A} = \frac{\$100,000 \text{ program costs}}{4000 \text{ interviews}} = \$25 \text{ unit output cost}$$

$$\text{Agency B} = \frac{\$200,000 \text{ program costs}}{4000 \text{ interviews}} = \$50 \text{ unit output cost}$$

A second type of efficiency evaluation, *cost effectiveness*, relates inputs of an intervention (resources) to outcomes. Holding interviews with clients in a counseling agency is not an end in itself but a means to effect changes in the client's status, behavior, or life situation. If in the two counseling agencies all variables are comparable (clientele, problems, types and length of intervention, types of client outcomes), but the agency with a $25 unit output cost is effective in producing desired changes in only 20% of its clients, while the agency with the $50 unit output cost is effective with 50% of its clients, the more expensive unit output cost is a better buy.

$$\text{Agency A} = \frac{\text{unit output cost (hour of counseling)}}{\text{outcome efficiency factor}} = \frac{\$25}{0.2} = \$125 \text{ unit output cost}$$

$$\text{Agency B} = \frac{\text{unit output cost (hour of counseling)}}{\text{outcome efficiency factor}} = \frac{\$50}{0.5} = \$100 \text{ unit output cost}$$

Thus, the program with the lowest unit output cost may not have the lowest unit outcome cost. In evaluating the efficiency of an episode of organizational or community change, the change agent needs to assess progress by both the cost of a unit of output and the cost of a unit of outcome or results (Moroney & Grubb, 1981, p. 615; Suchman, 1967, pp. 64–66).

Implementation Process

Recent emphasis on documenting the outcomes of professional interventions does not detract from the attention that needs to be directed at understanding "how and why a program works or does not work" (Suchman, 1967, p. 66; see also Chommie & Hudson, 1974). Process evaluation concerns the manner in which an intervention is implemented. Implementation plans specify who is to do what, with whom, when, and how, but during implementation even carefully developed plans may need to be modified based on experience. Formative process evaluation uses data on the implementation activities as a basis for refining the implementation. At the completion of a change episode, summative process evaluation, using complete data, including ultimate outcome data, provides a vital understanding of how and why the intervention was successful or not successful.

Although the change agent is concerned with determining whether or to what degree a completed intervention is successful, the change agent also needs ongoing information that can be used to make the change process itself effective and efficient. Formative process evaluation provides this needed information. The change agent constantly seeks this "during-during-during" (Weiss, 1972b) evaluation data as a tool to improve the quality of the implementation process.

Formative process evaluation identifies, measures, and assesses what happens as an intervention is implemented (Chommie & Hudson, 1974, pp. 684–686). Intervention plans are statements of predicted and expected activities, events, and results. Formative process evaluation compares the predicted and expected with the actual activities, events, and results. If the intervention is not being implemented as planned but the desired results are being obtained, perhaps some other factors are causing the results. In other situations, if the plans are being implemented as developed but the predicted results are not being achieved, the planned intervention model can be said to have been tested and failed. If, however, process evaluation indicates that the intervention model explicated in the plan has not in fact been implemented, the intervention model cannot be said to have been tested and failed. Rather, the implementation process itself is flawed. This distinction is important as can be seen from the following example.

A minority youth employment program predicted that, through peer counseling and intensive job skills training, a minimum of 200 minority youths would complete a job training program and be regularly employed for at least six consecutive months after completing the program. After the program ended, summative performance evaluation indicated that fewer than 50 minority youths actually met this standard of success. The funding source was ready to conclude that this demonstration project of peer counseling and job skills training was ineffective in achieving employment objectives with this population. Then the evaluators presented a second set of findings about how this program was implemented. Peer counseling was not provided to most program participants because the job skills training took up all the trainees' time. Thus, the traditional job skills approach displaced the proposed peer counseling. The funding source then understood that the intended approach had not been tried and failed. It was never tried.

Process evaluation uses subjective measurement devices, including participant observation and diverse quantitative and qualitative methods. This type of measurement is of a low order but with a wide-angle view of the context of the focal behaviors (Chommie & Hudson, 1974, p. 686).

Process evaluation often requires that the evaluator interact with the implementation process, or at least with the implementer's targets and clients, rather than relying primarily on official and formal records and measurements. During the ongoing evaluation process, the evaluator may interact with implementers and others, eliciting their response to the evaluator's initial findings.

Process evaluation provides valuable information on why an intervention works or does not work and may suggest new approaches, interventions, or modifications of current intervention strategies or procedures. Process evaluation also provides a valuable check that the intervention actually follows the proposed model (Moroney & Grubb, 1981, p. 617).

Each type of evaluation provides a different kind of potentially useful information about the change episode. None is essentially better or more preferred than the others. To maximize the effectiveness and efficiency of a change effort, the change agent might use all five types of evaluation. As we discuss below, needs for specific information determine which types of evaluation are necessary.

PROBLEMS WITH EVALUATION

Role Conflicts

Historically, evaluators and practitioners have received different training and education, have had different reference groups, and may have harbored negative stereotypes about each other. They have tended to begin from different perspectives. Implementers, planners, change agents, and clients (consumers) have an investment in the view that the change process (intervention) is proceeding nicely and has value. In contrast, the evaluator enters the picture to make judgments about the worth of the intervention (Aronson & Sherwood, 1972, pp. 283–293; Banner, Doctors, & Gordon, 1975, pp. 24–45; Rothman, 1974, chap. 11; Suchman, 1967, p. 155).

Evaluators extol the virtues of a pharmacological model, where implementers test an experimental intervention and delight in making refinements in the original intervention model. (Aronson & Sherwood, 1972, p. 290, suggest the pharmacological model; see also Banner, Doctors, & Gordon, 1975, p. 32.) Implementers, however, consider the evaluation to be a measure of their own worth or effectiveness not that of the model (Newman & Turem, 1974, pp. 5–11). Although some authors contend that evaluation is an ethical requirement of professional practice (Rosenberg & Brody, 1974b, p. 349), often professionals present obstacles to evaluation activities. This may be changing as more practitioner/evaluators are prepared for practice.

Political Issues

Implementers may not want to run the risk of having their work judged, especially if their work serves clients, groups, organizations, or communities stigmatized by society. When faced with politically motivated challenges, effective social interventions might not benefit from positive findings but might be vulnerable to negative ones (Banner et al., 1975, p. 42; Meld, 1974, pp. 451–452; Suchman, 1967, pp. 132–151; Weiss, 1972b, pp. 2–3).

Evaluation is a social and technical process conducted within a political context. Considerations of resource allocations (who gets what) influence the evaluation process. Change implementers often assume that an intervention (policy, program, or project) is effective because they are actively involved and are observing firsthand what they perceive to be positive results. To risk measuring whether the intervention is in fact effective in achieving predicted outcomes is to become politically vulnerable (Campbell, 1972, p. 188). In short, if a program keeps score, it might lose.

Although much literature on the politics of evaluation stresses the defensiveness of the implementers based on perceived threats associated with negative findings, the positive function of evaluation findings is relatively underplayed. Evaluation in the proposed model serves three functions. Essentially unproductive, no-win functions and activities can be terminated with the least cost to the change effort if identified early. Problematical, but potentially productive, win-able elements of the change process can be adjusted to produce positive results if identified during the process. Finally, productive, winning components, if identified and given high visibility early in the process, can become powerful reinforcers to participants in the change effort. Alinsky (1972) notes the utility of selecting change objectives that are win-able, significant to participants, and visible. Evaluation is a means of making positive results known to change system members.

Evaluation Design Issues

A perceptive observer has noted that when a little boy is armed with a hammer, everything that the little boy encounters "needs" hammering—nails as well as good china. Similarly, evaluators trained in the use of the classic, experimental evaluation research design may at times advocate the use of this valuable design in situations where less costly and less time-consuming quasi-experimental designs would generate perfectly adequate, although less powerful, information. The use of more rigorous designs when less rigorous designs will yield adequate data contributes to excessively costly evaluations, to results reaching decision makers too late to be used, and even to the wrong kind of information being provided to decision makers.

Further, inappropriate use of the experimental design disregards the realities of many social interventions. The conditions necessary for a good experimental design may be absent. Interventions may not allow for random assignment of clients to control and experimental groups. The intervention may change through time. Goals and objectives may be missing, vague, conflicting, or may change. Data (especially on the outcomes clients expect and on the outcomes achieved) may be inadequate or missing (Voth, 1975; Weiss, 1972a, pp. 7–14).

Validity and Reliability

Problems with validity and reliability are particularly significant in performance evaluation, although they may occur with other types of evaluation. *Validity* is "the degree to which any measure or procedure succeeds in doing what it purports to do" (Suchman, 1967, p. 120; see also Tripodi, 1983, pp. 47–48). The evaluator expects to use a variety of means to test the validity of the evaluation results (Suchman, 1967, p. 124):

> Since validity is judged in terms of purpose, it is important in any test of validity to indicate some criterion of utility against which validity can be appraised. There is no single test of validity which can serve this purpose. Rather validity is built up through a series of tests or arguments. These tests range from the face validity of logical reasoning to the predictive validity of a specific future event. (See also Epstein & Tripodi, 1977, pp. 33–35.)

Several methods are available to assess validity. In evaluating a program dealing with child sexual abuse, for example, a direct measure of the sexual activity of victim children has *face validity*—it appears to measure what it claims to measure (the undesirable sexual activity with the children). Similarly a measure of the sexual activity of victim children has *content validity*—it addresses the kinds of things about which conclusions will be drawn. *Consensual validity* is established by agreement of a panel of experts. *Correlational validity* exists when a relationship between two phenomena is established— for example, when it is known that sexual activity with an appropriate partner is inversely related to sexual activity with the child partner. *Predictive validity* exists when data on one behavior or status can be used to predict a second behavior or status—for example, when it is known that if the perpetrator is sexually active with appropriate partners during a given time period, then during that time period sexual activity with the child is reduced or eliminated (Bloom & Fischer, 1982, pp. 39–44; Suchman, 1967, pp. 120–121).

Validity is a problem in all phases of the evaluation process, including the initial conceptualization of the change opportunity and selection of change objectives, sample selection, and data collection, analysis, and interpretation (Campbell, 1972, pp. 190–192; Campbell & Stanley, 1963, pp. 5–6; Epstein & Tripodi, 1977, pp. 117–118; Suchman, 1967, pp. 116–126; Webb, Campbell, Schwartz, Sechrest, & Grove, 1981, pp. 1–34; Weiss, 1972b, pp. 62–63). The careful reasoning that went into the change opportunity definition and analysis, objective setting, action and resource planning, and information system design represents an investment in a valid evaluation. During the planning phases of the change episode, the change agent developed a theoretical base for understanding the nature of the change opportunity, including factors contributing to its existence. The intervention is guided by an implicit or explicit hypothesis generated from this theory. Process evaluation tests this hypothesized relationship: when the prescribed intervention is implemented, do desired results occur?

Reliability is the "probability of obtaining the same results upon repeated use of the same measuring instrument, whether this be an objective test or a subjective judgment. This criterion represents the dependability or stability aspect of an evaluation" (Suchman, 1967, p. 116). The evaluator seeks measures that will be consistent; if what is being measured does not change, future measurements should show no change. "If a measure is reliable, then the results obtained will be the same if the measure is used with the same person at two different (but reasonably spaced) periods of time, if two versions of the same measure are used, or if the same measure is used (or scored) by two different observers" (Bloom & Fischer, 1982, p. 36; see also Suchman, 1967, pp. 116–120).

Reliability is related to validity in important ways (Suchman, 1967, p. 117):

> Reliability is a necessary condition for validity. An evaluative measure which cannot be depended upon to give the same results upon repetition because of large random errors obviously cannot be used to measure anything and therefore cannot have any validity. However, a reliable measure may still have low validity; that is, although the measures are consistent, they do not deal with the "right" criterion.

Thus, if the evaluator selects the weight of the therapist as an indicator of therapeutic success, evaluation results of these measures might be reliable but probably totally without validity. They measure a characteristic of the therapist that is irrelevant to therapeutic success.

Taken together, the degrees of validity and reliability provide a sense of the soundness of the evaluation findings. A high degree of validity and reliability indicates findings may be used with confidence as the basis for decisions.

Each of the problems identified in this section may constitute a serious obstacle to the evaluation of change episodes. The change agent as evaluator must be aware of these problems. Yet each of the identified problems is, to a large extent, capable of being addressed if the change agent is disciplined and careful in conducting the evaluation and takes steps to avoid or minimize their effects. The following section outlines an evaluation model that minimizes the effects of the problems historically associated with evaluation.

THE CHANGE EPISODE EVALUATION MODEL

The Change Episode Evaluation Model (CEEM) produces useful information for specific decisions by identified decision makers. *Useful information* means information that is intended to be applied to a specific future decision (Bloom & Fischer, 1982, pp. 3–27; Moroney & Grubb, 1981, p. 611; Suchman, 1972, pp. 55–56; Weiss, 1972a, pp. 1–7; Weiss, 1974, p. 675). *Decisions* are choices that direct future actions. *Decision makers* are people who make these choices. Thus, this model provides a specific decision maker with the right information at the right time and in the right format (Weiss, 1972a, pp. 14–18).

The CEEM consists of a series of tasks to be accomplished by the change agent/evaluator: identify key decisions in the change episode; for each key decision, identify the decision makers; for each key decision, identify the time frame; for each key decision, identify the kinds and amounts of information needed by each decision maker; design and execute an evaluation plan to gather and analyze data, including existing data; communicate the right information to the right decision makers at the right time and in the right format.

A community planned change episode will illustrate the CEEM. In Sunnyvale, times were bad. Although Sunnyvale was in the fabled Sun Belt and a tourist mecca of sorts, national economic problems touched the lives of most citizens. Tourists came in smaller numbers, for shorter stays, and spent less than they used to. Unemployed persons from other parts of the country were attracted to Sunnyvale because they believed the Sun Belt was immune to economic hard times. But the worst blow to the economy came when the mine laid off workers, eventually operating at 27% of its capacity. Almost every business and family in this community of 35,000 was affected when 1700 of the 2300 mine employees were laid off.

Human services were stretched to their limits even before the recession hit Sunnyvale; funding had been reduced by 10% to 15% in each of the past three years as government reduced its commitment to human services. As the economy deteriorated, alcoholism, family violence, child neglect and sexual abuse, and other social problems became increasingly common and severe.

But as far as the community was concerned the most troublesome aspect of hard times in Sunnyvale was the emergence of the street people as a visible segment of downtown society. These people gathered in empty lots and in a city park near the railroad yard, living in their cars, tents, and hastily rigged lean-tos, scavenging for food outside food stores, and congregating on street corners. Although the street people were involved in few incidents with other townspeople, they became a focal point of citizen discontent. People talked about what should be done with the street people, labeling them as trouble-making outsiders and eyesores. Business owners downtown believed they hurt business. Human service professionals and religious leaders saw a need to provide at least a few basic services (emergency shelter, sanitary facilities, clothing, and food) as the cold winter approached.

The city council and county commissioners refused to address the plight of the street people, saying existing services and voluntary efforts would suffice, even though some voluntary services formally gave highest priority to permanent residents rather than transients.

Based on the interest of the executive director of a religious agency, two religious agencies, working together as a single service system, identified hot meals and emergency shelter for families and individuals as the most needed services. Clothing, counseling, and job referrals were seen as secondary priorities, to be provided if resources were available.

Individual citizens responded to media coverage of the street people with contributions of food and clothing, often stopping their cars next to the open lots and city park to offer the street people boxes of food and especially children's clothing. An individual offered a large warehouse downtown as a possible shelter. After overcoming resistance from local business operators to the location of the shelter, the city council approved the warehouse, with structural modifications, as a community emergency shelter. Labor unions contributed skilled construction workers to convert the warehouse. Church members volunteered as unskilled helpers. A local food bank, supplemented by Sunday food collections at churches and government surplus commodities, provided basic foods.

The two church-related welfare agencies sponsoring the project allocated a few administrative and service staff positions for an indeterminate period of time to establish the shelter and associated services. The executive director of the religious agency became the shelter manager. Other social service agencies agreed in a series of meetings to give priority to the needs of the street people as identified by the shelter project staff. Thus, with much cooperative activity, the shelter opened its doors.

The following sections describe and discuss each task of the CEEM. The Sunnyvale change episode illustrates activities associated with each task.

Identify Key Decisions

Evaluators have developed the notion of targeted, user-oriented evaluations (Suchman, 1972, p. 80; Tripodi, Fellin, & Epstein, 1978, pp. 16–19, 105; Weiss, 1972a, pp. 14–18; Weiss, 1972c, pp. 318–326). "The all-purpose evaluation is a myth" (Weiss, 1972b, p. 15; also pp. 10–12). In this model, therefore, the change agent/evaluator begins the evaluation process by identifying the decisions that key participants believe need to be made during the change episode. As noted, the content of the evaluation is derived from the factors hypothesized as potentially significant during the earlier phases of the change process.

The evaluator carefully reviews the entire change episode to identify these key decisions. As proposed here, evaluation is not limited to a measure taken before (or at the beginning of) the change episode and a second measure taken when the episode is complete. Although these before-and-after measures can be helpful for some decisions, most decisions draw on measures taken during each phase of the change process. At a minimum, a decision must be made near the end of each phase to move the emphasis of change effort to the next phase. Alternately the decision might be made to return to the tasks or activities of an earlier phase if it becomes apparent the earlier phase was incompletely accomplished or if new information reveals the earlier tasks were flawed. Another decision considered periodically is whether to continue the change effort. The problem being addressed might be resolved in other ways, the plan might become unworkable, or resources to support the change effort might be withdrawn.

Each phase of the change process directs evaluation efforts to different results and activities. Table 11-1 displays the product and process for each phase of the change process. For example, during the change opportunity identification and analysis phases, the change agent evaluates the content and quality of the identification and analysis statements before deciding to move on to the next phase, setting objectives. At the same time, to evaluate the

TABLE 11-1. Products and process for each phase of the change process

Phase	Product	Process
Change opportunity identification and analysis	Statement that describes and analyzes the opportunity—its nature, contributing factors, and epidemiology.	Consensus on statement and on desirability of moving on to the next phase by initiators, change agents, clients, and perhaps planners and implementers.
Objective setting	Statement of what is expected from change effort.	Consensus about expectations and anticipated outcomes, with most planners and implementers agreeing to move on to the next phase.
Action planning and resource planning	Blueprint for moving from current state to desired future state, including plan for acquisition and use of resources.	Consensus about methods to be used, especially among planners and implementers. Actors are ready to implement change. Resources are ready.
Implementation monitoring and evaluation	Reports of activities completed and short-term objectives achieved. Activities and products are tracked, judged, and adjusted.	Consensus about modifications based on experience. Sorting out what is done and achieved. Looking back to original change opportunity notions.

process, the change agent seeks specific indications that the key initiators and planners share a common understanding of the change opportunity and will participate in and support the next steps in the change process. Specific measures may vary from one key participant to the next. For one person, attendance at meetings may be a significant indicator; for another, verbal statements of support at the meeting; and, for a third, a written letter of support or even a financial contribution to the change effort.

Similar decisions are made at the end of each phase of the change process. The specific products may vary (statements of objectives, action plan, budget), but in each phase the change agent evaluates both formal documents and commitments to the change process before deciding to move on to the next step. Other decisions during a phase may also be evaluated. For example, the decisions that identify the participants at various points during the change effort may be evaluated to determine whether key participants have been involved.

The change agent also evaluates the implementation process and outcomes in order to refine implementation. During implementation, the best laid plans must be put to the test of reality. Are implementation activities proceeding as scheduled? Are implementers contributing as projected? Are key bench marks being attained? Are key activities falling behind schedule? Is the quality of the products acceptable? Are resources being made available and being used as planned? The management information system generates much of the raw data on which these judgments are based. For example, the data may indicate that activities are falling behind schedule or that fewer units of service are being delivered than was anticipated. In each case a decision might be made to adjust expectations or to devote additional resources to the effort.

In addition to monitoring schedules and tangible products of the implementation phase, the evaluator monitors the commitment of key implementers, using qualitative, perhaps highly selective, checks. When the systematic data of the information system are enriched with selective measures of commitment, the evaluator gains an appreciation of the status of the total implementation process that it would be impossible to gain using either source alone. Often this augmented appreciation allows the evaluator to prevent implementation problems before those problems would even have been identified using either source alone. For example, selective checks on commitment might indicate that a key community leader is losing interest. The influential person needs additional incentives to remain involved.

Perhaps the single most productive way to identify significant decisions that need to be made is to ask key participants. The change agent/evaluator also reviews documents from earlier phases of the change episode (statements of objectives, action plan, budget) for clues to which decisions are important. When documents suggest vital decisions, the change agent/evaluator verifies their importance with the probable decision makers before continuing the evaluation.

In Sunnyvale, before moving to the objective-setting tasks, the change agent/evaluator assessed the content and quality of the problem definition and analysis statements. Was there evidence of unmet needs of the street people? Were key participants essentially in agreement that the most pressing problems and needs were housing and food? Did key participants evidence a commitment to address these needs?

At various times later in the change episode, the evaluator needed to know whether key participants (the street people, the city council, labor unions, the two church groups, other human service agencies) agreed to the specific plan of action: using the warehouse as a shelter. Did the various parties commit resources to the plan? When implementation began, did each implementer participate as anticipated? Was the shelter opened on schedule? Were meals available? Did the street people come to the shelter? How many? What did they think of the shelter and its services? At times, adjustments needed to be made by implementers. For example, based on the characteristics of early users, partitions were installed in the shelter to provide privacy for families.

We will analyze two decisions made during the Sunnyvale change episode at each step in the evaluation process: to allow the warehouse to be used as an emergency shelter and to install additional partitions in the shelter to provide privacy for families.

Identify the Decision Makers

When a key decision is identified, the change agent/evaluator needs to analyze who will be involved in making the decision. In some cases the decision maker is formally designated by the action plan or by a participating group or organization. This formal designation frequently occurs in routine decision situations—for example, the production of units of service (casework hours). If the expected level of activity is not achieved as shown by information system displays, the administrator is the decision maker who must decide why this is so and what, if any, adjustments are needed to ensure that the change process proceeds as planned.

For other decisions, the decision makers may not be formally designated. Even with the most carefully structured implementation blueprints, the totally unexpected often occurs. Sometimes no clearly identified responsible party is visible or comes forward. The change agent may need to elicit a decision from the participant seen as the most appropriate one to make the decision based on considerations such as these: Who has the knowledge and experience needed to make the decision? Who has sanction or can obtain sanction to make the decision? Who is willing to make the decision? In essence the change agent designates, and even prods, the decision maker.

The evaluator also recognizes the possibility of multiple or joint decision makers. Perhaps no one participant can decide on a specific issue. It may be necessary to negotiate a decision among contesting parties. In these cases, the change agent/evaluator may facilitate positive resolution of differences or may bring multiple decision makers together so the decision can be made in a deliberate and timely manner.

Some decisions require active decision making by one or more parties and passive decision making by others. That is, at times key participants may contribute to a decision by not opposing the decision. An influential party may not need to sanction a decision by positive response but may be looked to by others to ensure that he or she does not oppose the decision. These passive decision makers are often key power brokers and should be identified by the change agent/evaluator and treated with the respect their stature and role demand. A small negative shake of the head in a community meeting by one of these people can devastate an otherwise viable change effort.

In Sunnyvale, initially no one wanted to assume responsibility for serving the street people. The change agent, who was executive director of one religious agency and subsequently the shelter manager, initially involved two religious agencies in the situation. It soon became apparent that for the shelter to be situated in the warehouse (the implementation plan), the city council and other implementers (labor unions, service agencies) would have to reach agreement. Thus the city council became a vital decision maker. Further, it became apparent that downtown business leaders and civic leaders were keys to convincing the city council to agree to the plan. In some instances, business leaders had to agree not to object to the plan before individual members of the city council were prepared to approve it.

Once the shelter opened, each religious group and agency assumed responsibility for a specific part of the services. Yet the decision to add partitions for privacy of the families did not fit neatly into anyone's responsibility. The construction crews used to renovate the warehouse had completed their work and departed. The change agent assumed responsibility for recalling the construction crews, based on client feedback about lack of privacy and the make-up of the consumer population. Table 11-2 identifies the decision makers.

Identify the Time Frame

The change agent/evaluator must next identify the time at which each decision can be or must be made in order to ensure that the decision maker will have the needed information in time to use it. Few things are more frustrating for both evaluator and decision makers than to receive important information after a decision has been made. If information arrives after a decision has been made, the decision makers might have to live with a decision that represents less than the best judgment possible or might have to reverse a decision made earlier. The evaluator must ask decision makers to identify a time frame for each key decision because decision makers may not have explicitly considered the timing. The evaluator's question to the decision maker—"By what date will you need this information?"—thus provides further structure to the change episode. The evaluator also needs to observe actual patterns of use by decision makers in order to adjust time frames for later decisions accordingly.

Once a time frame is established for making a key decision, the change agent/evaluator devises a timetable for developing the needed information. The evaluator realizes that, depending on the nature of the information to be produced, data availability, and other factors, the development of needed information might be a lengthy process. As with any time-frame consideration, the evaluator understands that unexpected and unplanned delays may occur. Therefore, the prudent evaluator builds in a safety zone—a little extra time—so that if a delay is encountered, the information can still be delivered on time to the decision maker. The evaluator exercises judgment in determining this slack factor in the evaluation timetable, weighing the costs of providing information too late against the benefits of getting the information to the decision maker in time to be used.

If multiple decision makers are involved with a particular decision, each

TABLE 11-2. Identification of decision makers

Key Decision	Decision Makers
1. Use warehouse as emergency shelter	A. Individual who offered use of building B. Downtown business leaders (passive) C. City council members
2. Install privacy partitions for families	Executive director of religious agency who managed the shelter

may require the information at a different time. Some may require more time to digest the information provided. Others may need to consider more complex information bases. The evaluator attempts to respond to the time frames of each decision maker.

In Sunnyvale, the decision by the city council to allow the warehouse to serve as the shelter for the street people had to be made before implementation could proceed. The decision of the religious groups to sponsor the project preceded even the city council decision. The point here is that although we did not specify time frames in the description of the Sunnyvale situation, the sequencing of the decisions was crucial. Each decision fed into subsequent decisions.

Figure 11-1 displays the major decision sequence. Many contributing decisions and actions are not included, among them the initial decision of local business owners to oppose the warehouse location for the shelter and their subsequent decision not to oppose this proposal. The decision by the local business leaders not to oppose the shelter needed to be made before a positive city council decision was possible. Table 11-3 identifies the time frames for the two key Sunnyvale decisions.

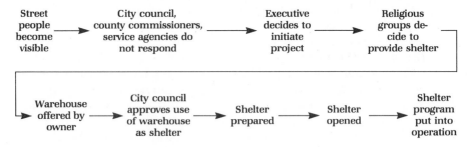

FIGURE 11-1. Sunnyvale decision sequence

TABLE 11-3. Identification of the time frame

Key Decision	Decision Makers	Time Frame*
1. Use warehouse as emergency shelter	A. Individual who offered use of building	First decision in sequence (by March 15th)
	B. Downtown business leaders	Middle decision in sequence (by March 30th)
	C. City council	Final decision in sequence (by April 15th)
2. Install privacy partitions for families	Executive director of religious agency who managed the shelter	After initial experiences with shelter residents (by May 30th)

*Time frame is defined here by sequencing of decisions. In practice, the change agent/evaluator would identify time frames specifically by date.

Identify the Kinds and Amounts of Information Needed

When multiple decision makers are involved with a given decision, the evaluator recognizes that each may need, want, and use different kinds and amounts of information. Or the same decision maker may need, want, and use different kinds and amounts of information for different decisions. The change agent/evaluator tailors the kinds and amounts of information to each decision to be made by each decision maker.

The best way to identify the kinds and amounts of information is simply to ask the decision makers involved. Whether or not the evaluator considers a particular kind of information relevant to a decision, if the decision maker sees a connection, the information should be provided. Another way is to observe how decision makers operate—what information they use in making decisions. Finally, the evaluator may unilaterally decide that the nature of the decision requires certain kinds of information.

A decision maker may need, want, and use more detailed information for some types of decisions than for others. For example, decisions that are perceived as more important (longer range, larger scope, less reversible) might require more information than those perceived as less important. Decisions that must be made quickly may have to be made using less information.

Yet given these differential characteristics of the decision situation, which influence the amounts of information developed and used, the change agent/evaluator understands that each decision maker has a unique pattern regarding amounts of information needed, requested, and used. For a given decision involving two decision makers, the evaluator may develop two sets of information. Decision maker A, who requires detailed information, might be provided extensive raw data and analysis, including charts, tables, and background documents. Decision maker B, who asks for and uses much less information, might be provided only summary documents. The evaluator asks each decision maker how much information is needed for this particular decision. Also the evaluator observes how much information is used by different decision makers. A decision maker's pattern of using information influences how much information is provided for future decisions.

The change agent/evaluator recognizes that a decision maker may request more information than that decision maker is likely to use. For example, a decision maker might ask for complex information, while the evaluator understands from the decision maker's earlier information-use pattern that the decision maker is unlikely to use the detailed information. In this situation the evaluator might provide a summary document with additional detailed materials appended.

In making the decision to approve the use of the warehouse as a shelter for the Sunnyvale street people, each city council member might have used different mixtures of information. Member A might have been most impressed by the media coverage of the plight of the children of the street people. Member B might have been most influenced by the sponsorship of the religious groups. Member C might have waited to see what his or her constituents thought of this issue, as determined by letters, calls, and comments of friends and constituents. Member D might have waited to hear the arguments presented at the council meeting or looked to see how the other members voted. Each council member might have used data on the problem supplied by the religious groups and perhaps council staff in a different way—one carefully reading over the statistics and comparing them, another glancing at the figures during the council meeting to see whether anything was important. In summary, each council member was influenced by different data, from different sources and based on different methods, to arrive at a decision, even though each also was presented much common data.

In making the decision to add the privacy partitions to the shelter, the change agent might have used primarily one source of information as the basis for the decision—feedback from the first residents of the shelter. Or the change agent might have consulted staff, toured the shelter at night to gain direct, observation-generated information, or used statistics that indicated that while most street people were single persons, most shelter residents were family members.

Table 11-4 identifies the information needed by each decision maker.

Design and Execute an Evaluation Plan

This step in the evaluation process is comprehensively described and discussed in the current research and evaluation literature. (See for example Babbie, 1983; Bloom & Fischer, 1982; Campbell & Stanley, 1963; Suchman, 1967; Tripodi, Fellin, & Epstein, 1978; Weiss, 1972b.) The choice of methodology is dictated by two factors: the intended use of the information to be generated and the realities of the change episode, including the intervention methodologies.

It is beyond the scope of this chapter to discuss in detail the wide variety of research designs available. Bloom and Fischer (1982, pp. 1-27, 233-387, 475-486) discuss experimental designs appropriate to social interventions. Others (Campbell, 1972, pp. 187-223; Campbell & Stanley, 1963; Perkins, 1983, pp. 314-327; Suchman, 1967, pp. 91-114; Tripodi, 1983, pp. 121-144) describe in detail a number of research designs that yield information potentially useful in human service evaluation. Evaluative research designs can be selected to produce specific kinds of information: *descriptive* (something happens or exists), *correlational* (something happens or exists in relation to something else), or *cause and effect* (something causes something else to happen or exist) (Epstein & Tripodi, 1977, pp. 5-32, 119-170). If a decision to make permanent or expand a pilot project depends on knowing that the project is popular with key political leaders or is well received by client groups, data developed from an experimental design may not be needed. If, however, the decision to make permanent or expand a pilot intervention depends on whether the intervention causes specific effects in a client population, then rigorous methodologies are indicated.

Between the most rigorous experimental designs and the superficial (testimonial) evidence often passing as evaluation research, a range of quasi-experimental designs are available that "can produce results that are sufficiently

TABLE 11-4. Identification of the kinds and amounts of information needed

Key Decision	Decision Maker	Time Frame	Kinds and Amounts of Information
1. Use warehouse as emergency shelter	A. Individual who offered use of building	First decision in sequence (by March 15th)	A. Perhaps media coverage of street people or the concern or involvement of religious agencies.
	B. Downtown business leaders	Middle decision in sequence (by March 30th	B. Perhaps above-noted information; needs-assessment data showing that street people tended to be long-term residents of Sunnyvale and that street people were not trouble makers.
	C. City council	Final decision in sequence (by April 15th)	C. Perhaps, for any council member, above-noted information; reaction of business leaders; constituent response.
2. Install privacy partitions for families	Executive director of religious agency who managed shelter	After initial experiences with shelter residents (by May 30th)	Possibly the fact that many initial shelter residents were families; observation of shelter operations; reports of staff (formal and informal); opinions of residents (formal and informal); an incident in the shelter (observed or reported).

convincing for many practical purposes" (Weiss, 1972b, p. 73). Rigor is essentially a question of degree, and rigorous and useful quasi-experimental approaches to evaluation are available.

A second factor to consider when making evaluation design decisions is the realities of the change episode. Evaluation is conducted in the real world, on a real intervention, and within a political context. At times it is not possible to conduct the best evaluation because resources are not adequate. In addition, the evaluator and others involved with the change effort must weigh the probable benefits against the costs. The political costs of a rigorous evaluation may be considered if the intervention or change episode is found to be ineffective, inefficient, or both. Finally, all the conditions needed for the best evaluation may not exist: baseline and other data may not be available, objectives may not have been specified or may be vague, the intervention may in reality be an unspecified series of interventions, and so forth. Rigorous attention to the details of the change process proposed in the previous chapters will minimize these difficulties.

The change agent/evaluator identifies the ideal evaluation design to accomplish the intended job and then begins a set of adjustments to bring the design in line with the realities of the situation. The evaluator recognizes that design modifications may be necessary and attempts to make these modifications in a way that maximizes the information benefits. The evaluator recognizes the utility of using existing sources of data. Although the fit of existing knowledge to what is being evaluated is seldom perfect, to ignore the work of other researchers or evaluators is inefficient at best. A rich variety of measures is available to measure human phenomena without, or at minimal risks of, validity problems related to the intrusiveness of the measures. Physical traces, archival materials, and observations of various types all contribute valuable data (Tripodi, 1983, pp. 50–60; Webb, Campbell, Schwartz, Sechrest, & Grove, 1981, pp. 1–196).

The evaluator recognizes that the evaluation plan may also need to be modified based on experience during the evaluation. Data promised to the evaluator may not exist, may be seriously flawed, or may be withheld. Time and other resources anticipated in the original evaluation plan may not materialize or may be withdrawn. The nature of the key decisions may change. New decision makers may be added to the change episode, or original decision makers may leave. Information needs may change.

In writing the evaluation plan, the change agent/evaluator may use a format such as that in Table 11-5.

The data needed for evaluation can be gathered and analyzed in several ways. First, targets or clients or both can be asked about their perceptions of progress. This method is probably the simplest and least expensive but obviously solicits a subjective viewpoint. Second, progress can be evaluated from the perspective of a third party. Often a family, organizational, or community member is in a position to evaluate changes. A costly variation of third-party evaluation is judgments made by an expert or panel of professionals. A third source of data is the change implementer. The advantage, again, is low cost. The disadvantage is subjectivity or, at least, the perception of subjectivity.

A fourth method is to collect hard, measurable data on target system behavior or status. Indicators of progress can be, for example, reduction in the number of parent/child arguments per week, reduction in the number of automobile deaths associated with alcohol in a community, achievement of a specified level of service units delivered, or similar measurable behaviors. The advantage is that these behaviors are usually strong and valid indicators that

TABLE 11-5. Evaluation plan

Key Decisions	Decision Makers	Time Frames	Kinds and Amounts of Information	Measures	Analysis
				What When How Who measures and records	What When How Who

something has changed for the targets or clients. As such, they are more meaningful than someone's perception or opinion that something has changed. The disadvantage is that the data are expensive and time consuming to collect.

Fifth, client satisfaction data are probably among the simplest and least expensive of all data to collect. Client views are also gaining in respectability as a valid and reliable source of program effectiveness (Giordano, 1977). Measuring client satisfaction simply requires the construction of a questionnaire that deals with the service-delivery process or outcomes. Clients give their opinions of services received or record how they or their situation has changed.

If an episode of organizational change involves provision of counseling services to street people, and the implementers opt for collection of data from all sources, the data base for evaluation purposes would include client perceptions of progress, worker perceptions of progress, third-party perceptions of progress, measurable data on behavioral change, and client satisfaction with services. Each of these measures could be cross-tabulated with a number of client and agency variables for comparative purposes. Depending on the decisions that need to be made during the change episode, these variables might include:

Client Variables
1. Age
2. Sex
3. Race
4. Census tract
5. Housing
6. Occupation
7. Socioeconomic status
8. Income

Agency Variables
1. Program
2. Worker
3. Progress achieved
4. Units of service
5. Cost per unit of service
6. Service location

Cross-tabulation of these data will yield a clear profile that permits comparison of progress and satisfaction of young clients to older, male to female, racial and ethnic groups to each other, and many other valuable comparisons. The value of such a data system is that it is simple and cost effective. It can yield a great deal of data that, viewed as a mosaic over time, can help significantly in increasing effectiveness (Webb, Campbell, Schwartz, Sechrest, & Grove, 1981, pp. 4–7).

The information system provides much of the data for evaluation, especially on the implementation phase. The format and content of the information system devised for monitoring remain the same during the evaluation activities. (For an example of an information system compatible with evaluation activities, see Kane, 1974.)

The Sunnyvale city council decision might have rested on multiple sets of data, each generated and analyzed using a specific design. Media coverage might have been collected and provided to council members by council staff or the change agent. Evidence of the concern and commitment of the religious groups could have been provided to council members in the form of phone calls by religious leaders, letters, and statements during council meetings. Evidence of popular support for the shelter project might have been generated in a mass meeting or by a phone or letter campaign in support of the project. Surveys of street people might have been used to establish a clear picture of their needs, their characteristics, and their probable contribution to Sunnyvale if they received this emergency assistance. Staff might have reviewed the experiences of similar communities with street people or emergency shelters as reported in research articles, conference presentations, and newsletters of professional organizations. Multiple methods probably would have been used to tap diverse sets of data.

The decision on privacy partitions might have been straightforward. It probably involved informal data collection and analysis of the problem, a limited scan for alternatives, and an exploration of the costs of the most likely option (the partitions).

Communicate the Information

The final task is to communicate useful information to the identified decision makers on time and in a useful format. This information includes that requested by decision makers and other information identified by the change agent as needed. The values and priorities of the potential users of evaluation information, the decision makers, are important factors considered by the evaluator in communicating evaluation findings (Weiss, 1972a, pp. 14–18; Weiss, 1978).

If evaluation findings are to be a basis for informed decisions, and therefore for improved social interventions, they must be used, but decision makers vary considerably in what they find useful. Some use large amounts of detailed information; others use limited summary information. Some respond readily to the spoken word, others to a written message, and still others to visual representation such as graphs and tables. The overriding reality is, however, that most decision makers use limited information in making choices. Even when a decision maker takes considerable time to digest a large quantity of information, the decision is based on a limited set of considerations.

For the evaluator, therefore, the key to effective communication with decision makers is knowing what kinds of information each decision maker considers significant. Perhaps the decision maker is sensitive to information on consumer satisfaction or the costs of service units or the effectiveness of the intervention. Alternately, the decision maker might value information on how experts rate the quality of the intervention or the popularity of a project with funding sources or the time it takes for an intervention to have an impact. What may be significant information for (and therefore used by) one decision maker may be useless to another.

Individualizing the communication of evaluation results can be done in several ways. The most obvious and time consuming involves the preparation of a unique report for each decision maker. Alternately, reports can be assembled using information modules, each of which contains a unique information set. Tailoring a report entails assembling the information modules deemed appropriate for each decision maker. A third option, which is the least costly, is distributing a relatively standard set of information to all decision makers but supplementing the information verbally to highlight key points or otherwise increase the decision maker's ability to understand the information.

In Sunnyvale, each city council member probably was influenced by a highly selective, small portion of the total information provided as the basis for the decision on warehouse use. Therefore, to communicate effectively, the change agent needed to use the right medium, message, and delivery time for each city council member. One council member might have been moved by a call from a friend, another by television scenes of children living in boxes in a vacant lot, and a third by the needs assessment data and the projections of the future contributions of the street people developed by a university research center. One council member might have made the decision early, based on an initial thorough briefing, while another might have been influenced by the last presentation made before the vote. One member might have been influenced by the comprehensive nature of the information presented, another by a single statistic (85% of street people have lived in Sunnyvale for over five years). The point is that each member's decision reflected the results of this (right) information in this (right) format at this (right) time.

Increasing the utilization of evaluation findings is a constant concern of evaluators. Weiss (1972c), Suchman (1972), and Coulton (1982, pp. 401–402) propose guidelines to improve the usefulness of evaluation; these guidelines summarize key points of the evaluation model proposed here.

1. Recognize the limits of the evaluation process. The evaluation cannot be all things to all persons. Be candid about the limits.
2. Specify the purpose and objectives of the evaluation. What do the various key participants expect from the evaluation?
3. Specify who will use the evaluation findings, for which decision, at which time.
4. Involve implementers collaboratively in the evaluation process. They are potential generators of evaluation data as well as users of the evaluation findings.
5. Stress positive as well as negative results. Few change episodes or interventions are totally without merit. Acknowledge strengths and provide alternatives if problems with implementation are identified. Stress means of improving the change effort.
6. Ensure effective communication to decision makers. Be prompt and timely with reports. Use individually tailored methods of presenting evaluation results. Be clear about the implications of evaluation findings.
7. Tie the evaluation process to ongoing organizational or community structures and processes. Involve key participants in the overall evaluation process, including the change agent, initiators, clients, targets, planners, and implementers. If possible tie compliance with proposed courses of action to existing reward systems.

Case Study

The Martin Luther King Community Mental Health Center served a largely rural population from a facility located in Centerville, a governmental and commercial center for the region. Although 25% of the center's client population lived in Centerville, another 25% lived more than 50 miles from the Centerville facility. Statistics indicated that this distant population was underserved.

King Center board members, the executive director, and staff members recognized this service delivery problem and proposed various solutions. Based on further staff analysis of the problem, they decided to open satellite clinics in two distant towns and to evaluate the effectiveness and efficiency of this response to the needs of the underserved population. Three-year funding for the satellite clinics was provided by a federal demonstration grant (40%), the state mental health agency (25%), local government and United Ways (20%), and client fees (15%).

Case Study Discussion Questions

1. Based on what you know about this response to a service delivery problem, as the project director/evaluator design an evaluation of this demonstra-

tion project using the CEEM. Include the following components:

a. Key decisions to be made

b. Decision makers for each decision

c. Time frame for each decision

d. Kinds and amounts of information needed by each decision maker

e. Design for the gathering and analysis of needed information: How is it to be gathered and analyzed? When? Who will gather and analyze the information? What kinds of needed information would probably indicate the choice of an experimental design? What kinds of needed information would be obtainable using less rigorous designs?

2. How would you communicate the results of the evaluation to key decision makers? What do you know about the information needs and preferences of the possible key decision makers? How can you learn more about the information needs and preferences of key decision makers?

3. List and discuss possible problems you might encounter in conducting an evaluation of this demonstration project. What can you do to prevent these problems from occurring or to minimize the impacts of these problems?

SUMMARY OF PHASE VIII

I. Definition

Evaluating the change episode involves the development and communication to key decision makers of information on which decisions can be made to improve the effectiveness and efficiency of the change episode. The change agent/evaluator designs the evaluation in response to the information needs and preferences of identified decision makers.

II. Information needed

A. What is the definition of the change opportunity?

B. What objectives were set for the change episode?

C. Who was to do what and at what time according to the action plan?

D. What resources were to be used during the change episode? For what purposes?

E. What key decisions are expected to be made during the change episode?

F. Who will make each key decision?

G. When will each decision be made?

H. What information is needed and preferred by each decision maker?

I. What is the best method for obtaining this information?

J. What is the best way to communicate this information so that decision makers can make decisions during the change episode?

III. Tasks to be accomplished

A. Review definition and analysis of the change opportunity, change episode objectives, action plan, and budget

B. Match these early documents against evaluation system

C. Identify key decisions in change episode

D. Identify decision makers for each decision

E. Identify time frame for each decision
F. Identify information needed for each decision
G. Design and conduct evaluation to provide the necessary information
  1. Collect data
  2. Analyze data
H. Communicate needed information to the right decision makers at the right time and in the right format
IV. Products to be developed
  A. Chart of items in III C-G above
  B. Evaluation design
  C. Reports of evaluation findings
V. Next steps: transition to Phase IX
  Decision makers and change agent/evaluator use information and judgments from evaluation in the reassessment and stabilization activities that follow.

SUMMARY OF MAJOR POINTS

1. The purpose of evaluation is to provide information for decisions that will make the change episode effective and efficient.
2. Evaluation is conducted during each phase of the change process. Evaluation makes judgments about the value or worth of the change effort or activities, performance or outcomes, adequacy of outcomes compared to total need, efficiency of the change episode, and explanations as to how and why an intervention works or does not work.
3. Although problems may develop as an evaluation is conducted, careful attention to designing and conducting a user-oriented evaluation will minimize disruptions of the evaluation process.
4. The Change Episode Evaluation Model (CEEM) is a structured approach to user-oriented evaluation. The steps in the CEEM are:
   a. Identify key decisions in the change episode
   b. For each decision, identify the decision makers
   c. For each decision, identify the time frame
   d. For each decision, identify the kinds and amounts of information needed by each decision maker
   e. Design and execute an evaluation plan to gather and analyze the information needed
   f. Communicate the right information to the right decision makers at the right time and in the right format
5. Focusing on the information needs and preferences of potential users of the evaluation increases the probability that the evaluation will produce useful and used information.

DISCUSSION OR SELF-STUDY QUESTIONS

1. How does evaluation relate to the other phases of the change process? What does evaluation contribute to the change effort?

2. How does each type of evaluation contribute to decisions during an episode of change?
3. As the change agent/evaluator, what can you do to increase the chances that problems will not arise in an evaluation and that your results will be used?

SUGGESTED READINGS

Babbie, E. *The practice of social research* (3rd ed.). Belmont, Calif.: Wadsworth, 1983.

Bloom, M., & Fischer, J. *Evaluating practice: Guidelines for the accountable professional.* Englewood Cliffs, N.J.: Prentice-Hall, 1982.

Campbell, D. T., & Stanley, J. T. *Experimental and quasi-experimental designs for research.* Chicago: Rand McNally, 1963.

Chommie, P. W., & Hudson, J. Evaluation of outcome and process. *Social Work,* 1974, *19,* 682–687.

Tripodi, T. *Evaluative research for social workers.* Englewood Cliffs, N.J.: Prentice-Hall, 1983.

Webb, E. J., Campbell, D. T., Schwartz, R. D., Sechrest, L., & Grove, J. B. *Nonreactive measures in the social sciences* (2nd ed.). Boston: Houghton Mifflin, 1981.

Weiss, C. H. *Evaluation research.* Englewood Cliffs, N.J.: Prentice-Hall, 1972.

CHAPTER
TWELVE

Reassessing and Stabilizing the Situation

OBJECTIVES

Studying the contents of this chapter should enable the reader to:

DEFINE THESE KEY CONCEPTS

Reassessment

Stabilization

DESCRIBE OR EXPLAIN

The process of unfreezing, instituting a change, and refreezing

The relationship between stabilization and change residue

Possibilities for stabilization of changes considering duration, scale, and scope

The technical and interpersonal tasks in reassessment and stabilization

Seven considerations in the process of reassessment and stabilization

Seven components of reassessment

Activities that have been contributing to stabilization throughout the change process

The process of phasing out change agent intervention

Four components of stabilization

Change agent roles in the reassessment and stabilization phase

$\mathbf{T}$he reassessment and stabilization phase is a time of transfer of responsibility. The change agent brings closure to the episode of change. The formal system of external help constructed specifically to carry out the change episode is withdrawn. Continuation of the policy, program, or project depends on the internal strength, integrity, and viability it has developed and on arrangements for ongoing provision of resources. Stabilization is the ultimate test of the success of the change effort if that effort was designed to continue beyond the end of the change episode.

The role of the change agent in a change episode is frequently an active and involved one. In addition, many people have worked together to support the change effort. Their presence may have stimulated enthusiasm and energy similar to a Hawthorne effect (that is, people react to being observed). Now the time has come to phase out this support system and let the change stand on its own. Will it survive and grow, return to an earlier state, or collapse? Participants address these questions in the reassessment and stabilization phase.

Lewin (1951) conceptualizes the process of change as one of unfreezing the system, intervening to create a change in status or functioning, and then refreezing in the new state. Reassessment and stabilization processes are integral to refreezing. They focus the change agent's and actors' attention and energy on progress and continuity for the change. They provide directed activity designed to facilitate autonomous functioning and planned withdrawal of external intervention.

As the change episode moves into the late states of the implementation phase, the change agent may be tempted to let the successful process run its course. The earlier anticipation of improvements is replaced by satisfaction that benefits from the change effort have become visible to participants and others. Change agents may be inclined to check to see that things are going well and then to terminate the episode.

The model of organizational and community change proposed here, however, requires that one final set of tasks be completed to maximize the continuing benefits of the change episode. The purpose of these final tasks, reassessment and selective stabilization, is to produce the desired change episode residue. The entire change episode has been intended to leave the organization or community improved in some specific ways. Although having a change episode well conceptualized and executed greatly increases the probability that organizational and community improvements will result, the reassessment and selective stabilization tasks ensure that the positive results of the episode are exploited to produce the greatest benefit and that negative results of the change episode are identified and their consequences minimized.

ANALYZING STABILIZATION OPTIONS

Assessing the positive results of the change episode, the change agent examines anticipated changes, intended changes, duration, and scope. Some changes will have been anticipated, others unanticipated; some intended, others not intended. Some will be permanent, some will be temporary, and others will require the collection of further information and the analysis of results of additional experiments. Some need to be extended or generalized in scope or scale; some are one-time improvements only; and some are to be made permanent in their present scale or scope. These possibilities are depicted graphically in Table 12-1.

The Martin Luther King Community Mental Health Center satellite clinic project, the case study for Chapter 11, will be used to illustrate these options. Two different possible outcomes would require different responses during the reassessment and stabilization phase.

If, during the first year of operation, evaluation showed the project to be a total failure, incapable of being modified to achieve its objectives, then the change agent and participants might decide to terminate the project. The reassessment and stabilization tasks might then include an orderly termination of the structure and transfer of responsibility to other interim providers.

Duration: Temporary → Changes cease to exist immediately
Scale and scope: One-time results only → Results terminate at close of change episode

However, positive and constructive use of the experience might result in preparations for a second attempt, based on what was learned from the failed

TABLE 12-1. Possibilities for stabilization of changes considering duration, scale, and scope

	At End of Change Episode	After Change Episode Terminates
Duration	Permanent Interim/experimental Temporary	Changes may be continued or made permanent Changes may persist, then cease or terminate Changes may cease or terminate immediately
Scale and scope	One-time results only Continuation of results at same level Expansion of results	Results may be expanded and generalized Results may be stabilized at existing level Results may terminate at end of change episode Results may be reversed and deteriorate

project. One component of the residue of the project would be the distribution of data on what did and did not work in the satellite-clinic model. Reports, journal articles, and presentations at conferences might focus on understanding how and why the project failed. Efforts in the project communities might focus on motivating local leaders to consider the project to be a learning experience, the basis for a new, effective center at a later date.

If, however, during the first year of operation, the evaluation showed that the satellite clinics were successful mechanisms for delivering services to previously underserved rural communities, then the change agent and participants might consider different stabilization tasks. Documented success might indicate that plans be initiated to do one or more of the following:

Initiate refinements in the model in the two project communities.

Duration: Interim/experimental → Changes continued
Scale and scope: Expansion → Results expanded and generalized

Seek permanent funding for the satellite centers before the third year of the project.

Duration: Permanent → Changes made permanent
Scale and scope: Continuation → Results stabilized

Establish satellite clinics in other small towns within the King Center catchment area.

Duration: Permanent → Changes made permanent
Scale and scope: Expansion → Results expanded and generalized

Implement specific innovations from the satellite clinics in the major facility of the King Center.

Duration: Interim/experimental → Changes continued
Scale and scope: Expansion → Results expanded and generalized

If the project was a state or national demonstration project, residue might include wide dissemination of the positive results in reports, articles in professional journals, or conference presentations. In the project communities, the residue might include an understanding by local leaders of the project's success and a willingness to support the satellite clinics and other human service efforts in the future.

Some successful projects, having achieved the results desired, might need to be dismantled, which precludes continuing outcomes. Dismantling takes place when no further results are desired or when a new mechanism begins to produce the outcomes. In this case, the change agent is careful to disengage the actors.

REQUIREMENTS FOR SUCCESSFUL REASSESSMENT AND STABILIZATION

In the reassessment process, *input from all participants* involved in the change effort is important. Their perspectives may vary on whether the change is meeting their expectations. They view the change from distinct vantage points, are involved with the process to different degrees, and have diverse interests in the outcome. A comprehensive and thorough review will elicit these multiple perspectives and allow their integration into the final reassessment.

The thrust of this input should be toward *reflection on the meaning of the change effort* not just the content. What is the significance of the new status quo? Have the benefits justified the costs? What were the dynamics of the change process? Reflection helps give meaning to events and prepares participants for the transition to stabilization.

The *timing* of reassessment is an important factor. Implementation, monitoring, and evaluation must be well enough along so that participants have developed ongoing relationships and structures. They also need to have experienced the initial results of interventions and have had the opportunity to make any modifications suggested. Yet the change must be new enough so that patterns of activity are not irreversible if reassessment identifies a need for additional adjustments.

Timing is a factor not only in reassessment but in stabilization as well. To be institutionalized, a change needs to have built up enough *momentum* to carry it onward after the withdrawal or changed role and responsibilities of the change agent. Channels of communication, lines of accountability, and patterns of behavior should be set. Sufficient time needs to have elapsed for the change process to operate without ongoing external attention and support.

Timing relates not only to momentum but to *readiness* for stabilization, which includes the phasing out of the activity of the change agent. Readiness implies that roles, relationships, and structures are clear and that the change process is capable of self-perpetuation. Such continuity requires identification of ongoing supports and reinforcement of a sense of self-sufficiency.

Another factor essential to stabilization is the *acceptance and approval of the change* by those organizations and individuals whose support is crucial. As objectives are met, as benefits become apparent, as processes become routine and require less energy, acceptance increases and stability is enhanced. Awareness of acceptance and approval allows the change agent to phase out active intervention.

Finally, the change agent must be receptive to the possibility of *ending a change effort* rather than stabilizing it. In some cases, change should be temporary. In other cases, reassessment reveals that the costs outweigh the benefits or that resources are insufficient for continuation. Although the change agent may find it difficult to terminate the change after investing so much time and energy, it is the appropriate resolution of these situations.

OVERVIEW OF TASKS

Reassessment and stabilization tasks are both technical and interpersonal. They strengthen the capability of the policy, program, or project to maintain its momentum and continue to meet its objectives. They also help the change agent relinquish responsibility for direction and terminate or redefine relationships.

The technical tasks entail summative evaluation and institutionalization. In reassessment, the change agent reviews the entire episode. Has the change created the intended result? Has it avoided or dealt with detrimental side effects and negative consequences? Planned and formal reassessment activities allow participants in the change effort to make judgments about the strengths and weaknesses of both process and outcomes. Using information from reassessment as feedback to guide the change effort, the change agent works for stabilization, or establishing permanency. Three activities contribute to the process of stabilization of the change: Strengthening integration with other systems promotes acceptance and interdependence. Routinization of procedures enables the new system to function more or less automatically. Development of an ongoing base of support helps assure the continuing availability of internal and external resources.

The interpersonal tasks are reciprocal and address needs of clients, targets, change agent, and other key actors. They entail confirmation of capabilities and accomplishments, transfer of responsibility and control, and formal transformation, closure, or termination. In reassessment, the judgments about strengths and weaknesses provide feedback not only to guide the change effort but also to guide the change agent in the selection of professional roles (for example, consultant, expert, or advocate). Planners and implementers can reflect on what they have learned that will be useful in future change episodes. They can feel satisfaction in the progress of the change effort. Interpersonal tasks in stabilization contain elements of both pleasure and pain. The change agent may experience some anxiety and may find full relinquishment of responsibility difficult. The termination of any relationship involves a sense of loss. However, successful stabilization also provides the change agent with a sense of accomplishment and a validation of skills. It permits energies to be redirected to new change opportunities.

Reassessment and stabilization activities allow planned and systematic closure to be brought to the cycle of a planned change effort. This phase establishes the conditions—positive or negative—for subsequent change activity. Successful institutionalization of the change and withdrawal of the change agent enhance receptivity to participation in a future change effort. The reassessment and stabilization phase has a direct effect on the change residue, which is the final component of an episode of change.

We discuss the specific tasks of this phase in the following sections, using the adult protective services program described here as an example. A caseworker in the Adult Protective Services (APS) Division of a county Department of Human Resources did a study of selected characteristics of her clients for a class she was taking. She identified a group of elderly whose problem could be classified as self-neglect. After writing the paper, she made a presentation to her colleagues in the division. They discussed the situation at a lunch seminar and decided that this category of clients should receive specialized services not presently being provided. They also believed that prevention education could help reduce the problem of self-neglect among the elderly.

Two workers, following the process for initiating change, developed a proposal to set up a unit within the division to work exclusively with cases of self-neglect. This unit of three workers would have caseloads, would carry out an active educational program with other professionals and with the community, and would also mount a program of preventive intervention with elderly groups.

Their proposal, which included a request for one new position and the reassignment of two workers, was approved. While recruitment was under way, however, a hiring freeze was instituted for the whole department, so the third position was never filled. Three months after the freeze, a 5% budget cut necessitated a policy of not replacing workers when vacancies occurred. One worker in the APS Division retired and was not replaced.

The APS Self-Neglect Unit managed to get under way but not with full implementation of the program. Some workers were unwilling to transfer self-neglect cases with whom they had developed ongoing relationships. Others complained about higher caseloads because of picking up non-self-neglect cases from the workers in the new unit. The shortage of staff put pressure on everyone. Travel funds were reduced because of the budget cut, curtailing the educational outreach program. Some intake workers complained of the extra work required to identify and separate self-neglect cases from others. Other workers simply did not cooperate.

The change agents engaged in an extensive reassessment process that included analysis of the impact on the existing service system as well as an exploration of possible resources. They regretfully concluded that the change effort ought to be ended at this point, although they believed the idea had been good and should be reinstituted when resources permitted. They decided to continue the educational effort among professionals by publishing an article on the problem of self-neglect and presenting a paper at the next statewide gerontology conference.

REASSESSMENT ACTIVITIES AND COMPONENTS

The change agent is responsible for facilitating or guiding the reassessment process. Participants may meet jointly or in separate groups. Their ideas, judgments, and perspectives need to be solicited in a climate of openness and candor. Although reassessment-type reflections are ongoing as the episode moves toward termination, formal reassessment sessions are often scheduled for half or full days. Reassessment activities may be held in conference or retreat centers, which take participants out of their daily setting and promote an objective analysis.

Reassessment is a critical, participatory, systematic overview of the entire change effort. It is comprehensive, integrative, and interpretive. There is substantial overlap between reassessment and evaluation. However, the thrust and purpose of these two phases are somewhat distinct. The purpose of the evaluation phase is to make judgments that provide the basis for correction and refinements. The purpose of the reassessment phase is to examine data and information that will support decisions about continuation or termination of the change and will facilitate closure of the change episode.

Reassessment considers the entire change effort from Phase I (identification of the change opportunity) through Phase VIII (evaluation). Data and information generated by monitoring and evaluation activities, plus the reflections of participants, are used to respond to the following questions:

1. To what extent has the change effort been responsive to the opportunity as initially defined and analyzed?
2. To what extent has the change effort met its objectives?
3. How functional have the design and structure proven to be?
4. What resources for continuity are available? Are they sufficient?
5. Is the implementation creating unexpected consequences or negative side effects?
6. Is the information generated by the monitoring system being used to keep the change effort moving and on course?
7. Has the evaluation process demonstrated that the change is making the intended difference?

In short, reassessment involves a brief reexamination of each of the earlier phases of the change process in light of the experiences of the nearly completed change episode.

Responsiveness to the Change Opportunity

Reexamining the initial definition and analysis of the change opportunity reminds participants of the reasons for undertaking the change effort. It allows assessment of the connection between the way in which the precipitating situation was conceptualized and the impact the change effort is having.

The questions to be raised are those raised in the identification and analysis phases of the process but with the benefit of experience.

1. Was the situation correctly defined as a need, problem, issue, or opportunity?
2. Were the correct people involved as participants?
3. Were the characteristics of the situation analyzed in sufficient detail, including complexity, intensity, incidence and prevalence, control, urgency, and duration?
4. Were factors supporting the existence of the problem correctly identified? Were barriers to resolution correctly identified? Were costs and consequences of nonresolution correctly identified?
5. Did the analysis turn out to provide an appropriate theoretical understanding of the situation, an appropriate use of research and practice findings, an accurate delineation of boundaries, an understanding of history and etiology, and an appropriate review of political and economic variables?
6. What changes, if any, should be made in the definition or analysis if the effort is to continue?

Reassessment may suggest some refinement of the original statement of the change opportunity if the intervention has contributed to an increased understanding of the dynamics of the situation. It may also raise the question of whether the change effort is addressing the substance of the opportunity identified or is tangential to it.

In the APS example, the need was originally conceptualized as identifying and serving elderly people who neglected some of their basic health and safety needs. Nothing indicates that the need was in any way incorrectly or incompletely identified, defined, or analyzed. However, appropriate people may not have been involved as participants. Other APS workers were less than supportive of the program. The need clearly did not have high enough visibility and strong enough support to allow for filling the third position and allocating the needed travel funds for the educational outreach program. Increased effort might have been put into identifying and involving secondary beneficiaries and enlisting a broad base of support.

Fulfilling Objectives

The activities of the change effort have been guided by a set of objectives. In the reassessment phase, the change agent and other participants review initial and ongoing progress toward these objectives. When delays, deviations, or other difficulties persist, adjustments may be necessary: modifying the activity, increasing resources, or changing the objective itself. Reassessment further looks at the significance of the objectives and their accomplishment. How do these objectives relate to the opportunity? What changes have occurred because of them?

A reexamination of efforts of the earlier phase of goal and objective setting includes discussion of these questions:

1. Were significant parties and interests involved in developing the list of all possible goals and directions that this process might take?
2. Where were the disagreements over directions? How were they handled?
3. Were conceptual frameworks developed in earlier phases continued in establishing goals and objectives?
4. Were data and information generated in earlier stages used? Did individuals or organizations influence the process toward a predetermined direction?
5. Were outcome objectives clear and attainable?
6. Were process objectives appropriate to achieve desired outcomes?
7. What modifications in objectives should be made if the change effort is to continue?

The APS worker had been enthusiastic about her discovery of the problem of self-neglect among the elderly. She appropriately involved the other APS workers in a discussion and generated their support. However, at that point, two workers developed the proposal. Possibly some breakdown occurred in securing total support for the program and commitment to the goals and objectives from other workers and the community. Key participants may have been ignored. Thus, the limited initial support expressed by colleagues quickly evaporated when pressures mounted in the division.

Functional Design and Structure

In the reassessment phase, the change agent and participants critique the strengths and weaknesses of the approach chosen (policy, program, or project). Is it effective and efficient in responding to the change opportunity? If it addresses only part of the problem, what further change efforts should be undertaken, and when? The answers to these questions require an assessment of priorities and resources.

The design elements include the nature of the service provided, the delivery system, and responsibilities within that system. A review of the appropriateness and clarity of the design may be coupled with a reexamination of structural issues. Do the subunits of the delivery system fit together well, and are formal and informal communication channels open and functional? Do the lines of accountability operate to assure clarity of roles and responsibilities?

Reexamination of earlier design and structure decisions includes a discussion of the following questions.

1. If a policy approach was selected:
   a. Was the target group appropriately defined?
   b. Were the provisions adequate?
   c. Was the implementation plan appropriate and workable?
   d. Was the financing plan sound?
2. If a program or service project approach was selected:
   a. Was the target group appropriately defined?
   b. Were outcomes clearly defined and appropriate?
   c. Were sound and reasonable standards established?
   d. Were definitions for services provided clear?
   e. Was the service delivery method appropriate?
   f. Were service tasks clearly defined?
   g. Did the structure work well in response to the need?
   h. Were job descriptions well constructed in response to the need?
3. If a support project approach was selected:
   a. Was the management plan well conceptualized?
   b. Was it followed?
   c. Did the project keep on schedule and on target?
4. What modifications in design and structure should be made if the change effort is to continue?

The Self-Neglect Unit may have suffered from some flaws in design and structure. Definitions of the target group may have been unclear, causing problems for intake workers. Other design components may have been vague enough to generate concern among the other APS workers about the value of the program, given dwindling resources. The structure may have prevented collaboration or limited communication, thus causing workers to be reluctant to let go of their cases. Possibly other workers viewed positions in the Self-Neglect Unit as elitist and felt that workers in that unit did not have to deal with some of the difficult and complex problems that they did. Any of these design flaws could have contributed to program failure.

Resources for Continuity

Reassessment includes an examination of resource planning and allocation. If initial funding came from external sources and is to be phased out, plans for local community or organizational assumption of support need to be made. Will the change effort continue at the same level of support? Will the program or intervention need additional resources or adapt to a reduction in resources? Has the resource plan been adequate to meet the demands of the intervention? Has the allocation of resources to this intervention had an impact on other systems in the organization or community, and, if so, what are the implications for the future? Reassessment activities should lead to some ongoing budget plan.

The change agent and participants need to consider these questions in reexamining resource planning:

1. Were resource needs accurately anticipated?
2. Were all possible contributors for each resource identified?
3. Were both monetary and nonmonetary contributions explored from all sources?
4. Did planners anticipate funding reductions and prepare for adjustments in the definition of the change opportunity, the objectives of the change episode, or the action plan?
5. What resources will be needed if the change effort is to continue?

It appears that those who prepared the APS proposal did not explore other resources for serving self-neglect cases. Support for the project was to come entirely from creating specialized caseloads for two workers, adding a new position, and providing funding to support educational activities. Were there groups or organizations in the community who may have helped in case finding and referral? Would they have helped remedy the symptoms of self-neglect? Would they have acted as volunteer visitors or telephoners? Might some groups have underwritten the cost of the educational and prevention program? Or, if no community support was available, could the program have been scaled down in order to achieve success with fewer resources? Overreliance on one funding and support source appears to have severely limited the options available to the APS Self-Neglect Unit.

Consequences of Implementation

The change agent and other participants review the implementation phase looking especially for unexpected negative consequences. According to Brager and Holloway (1978, p.230), if negative consequences are uncovered, the change agent may consider three possible courses of action. The first choice, if it is feasible, is to overcome and eliminate the problem. The second is to accept or adjust to the negative consequences. If the benefit and value of the change are judged to be higher than the difficulty caused by the consequence, acceptance or adjustment may be the best choice. The third option is to terminate the change effort. The change agent usually views this alternative as the last resort, because considerable time and energy have been invested in and considerable resources have been committed to the effort.

The change agent and participants should ask these questions about implementation during the reassessment phase:

1. Were expectations for compliance and performance met?
2. Did implementers demonstrate commitment and the capacity to carry out the change effort?
3. What barriers were experienced? Should they have been anticipated? Why weren't they?
4. Was the amount of communication appropriate to the needs of all participants? Was it timely?
5. Were overlaps between planners and implementers adequate?
6. Were interpersonal issues dealt with satisfactorily?
7. Was the support base adequately strengthened?

Implementation of the Self Neglect Unit failed to progress as planned. First, staff reductions created a need to modify the plan, but the change agents moved ahead without engaging in a process of rethinking the design. Compliance was further eroded by resistance from intake and referring workers. Communication with and involvement of important supporting actors was inadequate, and this led to a weakening of the support base. The change agents appear to have ignored warning signs of difficulty and to have adhered rigidly to an unfeasible plan during initial implementation.

Information from Monitoring

In reassessment, the management information system is reviewed to determine how well it is carrying out the monitoring function and to assure that appropriate corrective action is resulting. Those who use the data may return to the original plans to see what was expected and compare that with present functioning.

The change agent and participants should raise these questions about monitoring during the reassessment phase:

1. Were the anticipated uses of management information appropriate?
2. Were the correct participants identified as needing information?
3. Were data and information communicated appropriately to those who should have had them?
4. Was the information system correctly and carefully designed?
    a. Were staff and others persuaded to accept and use the system?
    b. Were costs correctly anticipated?
    c. Was information properly safeguarded?
    d. Were people trained to use the system?
    e. Was the utilization of data and information built into the system?
5. Was the system designed to support decision making? Was it used for decision making? Did it help to make sound decisions?

6. Did the system monitor progress toward achievement of objectives?
7. What additional data will be needed if the change effort is to continue? What data will no longer be needed?

Again, it is possible that the design of the monitoring or management-information system for the Self-Neglect Unit was flawed. It appears that only the two workers themselves (who were also the change agents) were involved in decision making. No regular reports of progress appear to have been circulated among other APS workers or among supervisors or managers. Needed corrections in the design and implementation of the program were not made, in spite of negative feedback from other workers. Budding structural problems between intake and the Self-Neglect Unit were not addressed. Reduction in travel funds was not seen as an early warning of the need to explore alternate resources. Any of these factors could have led to the eventual program failure.

Adequate Evaluation

The change agent and participants review the information developed during the evaluation process to see what kinds of conclusions can be drawn from the data collected. Summative evaluation provides the basis for reassessment and stabilization tasks and activities.

Reassessment of the adequacy of the evaluation enables the change agent and participants to have a shared sense of accomplishment. Charting progress from initiation to the present time reinforces awareness of strengths and weaknesses and identifies areas needing improvement. Judgments are made regarding the soundness of the change effort and future directions. These activities lay the groundwork for stabilization.

The change agent and participants should consider these questions about evaluation at this point:

1. Did the change episode deal with the problem, need, issue, or opportunity as initially defined?
2. Were outcome objectives met?
3. Did the evaluation system produce information useful for decision making? Was it used? Was it timely? Was it accurate?
4. Which decision makers used what types of information? Were information needs correctly anticipated?
5. What parts of the evaluation system should be eliminated, modified, or enhanced if the effort continues?

The Self-Neglect Unit never made it to the point where formal evaluation data could be used to assist in decision making about problem definition and analysis, objectives, design and structure, resource planning and allocation, or implementation. Before sufficient data were generated, the decision was made to discontinue the program. Had data been available on achievement of even limited outcomes, perhaps they could have been used to reduce the size

ope of the program while retaining some of its successful features. As it
n article on the experience was all that remained of a well-intended
;e effort.

STABILIZATION ACTIVITIES AND COMPONENTS

The change agent directs or oversees the stabilization process. The goal is to
establish permanency or institutionalization for the results of an intervention.
Lippitt, Watson, and Westley (1958) conceptualize the function of the change
agent at this point to be one of promoting the generalization and spread of the
change effort. They suggest that change agents ask themselves such questions
as these: "Does the change diffuse through the client system, or does it remain
a relatively isolated and minor phenomenon in one subpart? Is it necessary to
give the client system special support for a while in order to assure the
permanent penetration of change into the system's internal dynamics?"
(p. 217).

Stabilization prepares the intervention to be maintained. The goal is to
facilitate autonomy and continuity. It is also to phase out the direct involvement of the change agent and other temporary participants. Warren (1977b,
p. 54) reminds practitioners that resistance to change, both internal and
external, is a continuing problem. He advises: "Stabilization thus involves
arriving at a condition where the balance of forces working to preserve the
change is great enough to neutralize the forces working to destroy it."

Activities contributing toward stabilization of change have occurred
throughout the planned change process. Those to be involved in the change
effort have participated in the decision making. Many diverse people now
have an interest in preserving the new state. Goals and objectives and roles
and responsibilities have been specific and clear. The monitoring and evaluation systems have helped measure progress. The change agent has attended
to both technical and interpersonal aspects of the effort. Now, during the
stabilization phase, the change agent concentrates on strengthening and
reinforcing three aspects of the process: integration of the change effort with
other systems; routinization of procedures; and development of an ongoing
base of support. The change agent also makes plans to phase out or withdraw
from active intervention and involvement.

Integration with Other Systems

Change becomes less vulnerable to opposition and undermining when it is
well integrated with other systems in the organization or the community or
both. Mutually beneficial links, which have been established and developed
during earlier phases of the change effort, need to be checked and cultivated
as part of stabilization.

Essentially, ongoing, established institutions need to see that it is in their
interest for the change to continue. Integration and interdependence are
facilitated by exchange processes—identifying and meeting perceived needs

of other systems or subunits in return for their recognition and support (Blau, 1967; Levine & White, 1970). Links can include meeting needs currently unmet by other services, establishing mutual referral relationships, participating in community problem-solving efforts, and other activities that establish the value of this service to others. Visibility and publicity can also sometimes help establish positive relationships and integration with other systems.

Routinization of Procedures

Stabilization and permanency are enhanced by the routinization of procedures associated with the change. Initially, a change effort is disruptive, in part because it requires participants to develop new relationships and patterns of behavior. As new roles are learned, however, communication channels are established, and decision making parameters are defined. Procedures and interactions become familiar and predictable, and less open to challenge.

Routinization of procedures is important not only to participants in the change process but also to surrounding systems. A changed state often leads to uncertainty about links, about resources, and about access. With routinization, the changed state produces a set of consistent expectations. These, in turn, help create new stability.

To facilitate routinization of procedures, the change agent ensures that patterns of interaction and decision making are clearly defined and communicated and are functional. The actors ensure that policies related to access, benefits, eligibility, and other conditions are in writing, understood, accepted, and working. Flow charts and policy handbooks are useful tools in this process. These charts, handbooks, and other documents need to be circulated both among the actors and among those who interact with them.

Development of Ongoing Support

Support for the change must be both internal and external. Internal support comes from the implementers and other interdependent components of the organization. External support comes from primary and secondary beneficiaries and from others who philosophically agree with the change. It is necessary to assure needed resources, including political support and legitimation. In the reassessment and stabilization phase, support systems must be strengthened.

Support depends on recognition and approval. Workers who have learned new skills and planned or implemented the change should receive acknowledgement and reward for their participation, effort, and the results achieved. A change demands extra energy and commitment. It places stress on participants and those who interact with the change effort. Recognition and reward mechanisms may be monetary or they may be tangible items or events. Merit pay, personalized certificates, publicity, or a reception or dinner for those who have worked for the change are specific means of expressing appreciation.

External support may be secured by gaining the endorsement of influential community or organizational leaders. It is most often secured by establishing reciprocal and mutually beneficial transactions with other units or organizations. Successful collaboration on an activity can build support. Providing opportunities for observation of the program and publicizing its outcomes can also contribute to building external support.

Phasing Out Change Agent Intervention

The crux of the stabilization phase is the planned withdrawal of the change agent from active involvement. Termination or change of any relationship is likely to be accompanied by some negative emotions: anxiety, a sense of loss, uncertainty, emptiness. Both the change agent and the implementers are subject to these feelings; either or both may try to prolong the relationship.

The change agent, as a professional, should anticipate the difficulties and pitfalls of termination and plan ways to work through them. The implementers may need reassurance of their capability to function independently. Affirmations of skills and resources and identification of sources of help if problems are encountered may strengthen the transition. The change agent's firmness about the intent to withdraw—including setting a timetable—is also helpful.

Sometimes change agents have trouble letting go. Then the implementers may wish to prod a bit. Giving a recognition dinner and presenting an award is one approach. Asking the change agent to train an implementer in how to carry out some of the change agent's roles and responsibilities is another. Both the change agent and the implementers should watch for signs of readiness for termination and should avoid encouraging unnecessary or prolonged dependency.

CHANGE AGENT'S ROLES

The change agent assumes several important roles in the reassessment and stabilization phase. One is as *critic* and *reviewer* of the entire change effort; this role includes making self-criticisms. The change agent asks probing questions about the process, outcomes, and impacts. To get a comprehensive perspective, the change agent needs to have all systems—initiator, client, target, planning, and implementing—contribute to this assessment. Some participants will want to give only optimistic and positive input. The change agent needs to encourage and probe for negative assessments as well.

A second role is *facilitator* or *enabler*. The change agent helps strengthen integration with other systems and routinization of procedures. In this way, the change agent assists the implementers to use their resources and to establish patterns of behavior that will support stabilization. Activities directed toward integration and establishing links may call for the use of a *mediator* role as well.

The *advocate* role is useful in strengthening the ongoing base of support for the change. The change agent speaks on behalf of the intervention. Advocacy is particularly important in securing financial and political support. The change agent may need to learn marketing skills: how to design a product or service to meet a real need, how to describe the benefits and advantages of the change, and how to persuade an audience to respond favorably.

The change agent also plays an *interpreter* role by having various participants reflect on the change episode and its significance. They can then understand what the change effort means to those who have participated, to those who benefit, and to the change agent. Interpretation helps bring closure and facilitates termination.

The final role the change agent plays has no adequate name, but it involves *bringing closure*, allowing the change to stand independently. A saying used by some parent education groups describes the goal of the change agent at the end of an episode of change: "There are two gifts we can give our children: roots and wings." After the change agent has helped the effort become rooted, it is time to let it try its wings.

Case Study

Four years ago, a group from a rural Western community contacted the Department of Family and Community Medicine at the medical school 50 miles away. The group consisted of the minister of the community church, a rancher, the school principal, and the school nurse. Their request was for a volunteer doctor or medical student to come to the community one day a week. They had furnished a room of the church as a clinic and wanted to provide maternal and infant health care in the community.

The Department of Family and Community Medicine assigned a physician and a health educator to respond to the request. They met with the leaders and agreed to provide volunteers on one condition. The community agreed to set up a planning committee to assess the full range of community health needs and to determine an adequate way to meet them.

The committee included the original four leaders, four additional community representatives, and the two medical school faculty members. They met, discussed community needs, and explored options for meeting them. They decided that a full-time, basic medical clinic was needed. The medical school faculty provided information about government funding. Most members of the committee opposed this approach. They did not wish to be dependent on outside sources or controlled by external regulations. They finally overcame their reluctance when it became clear that no other option was available. A complete plan for development of a clinic was prepared, involving all the appropriate participants.

After local fund raising events earned the community a share of block grant matching money, a modern, well-equipped clinic was built. The clinic committee advertised extensively for a doctor to practice in the community. They were unsuccessful, however, in attracting a physician to relocate. They then turned to a federal program designed to provide medical personnel to underserved areas. The clinic was able to bring in a young physician whose salary was partially subsidized by that government program. A dentist who practiced in the city 50 miles away came once a week to see patients. The school nurse was provided with additional training as a nurse practitioner and worked full time in the clinic. The committee reconstituted itself as a governing board prior to the opening of the clinic.

The volume of patients from the community and surrounding areas has been high. One development that the board did not anticipate was the number of patients seeking services for emotional problems. The clinic staff had neither the time nor the training to meet those needs. The board negotiated with the Department of Psychology and the School of Social Work at the university to see whether interns might provide counseling services.

A health fair and fiesta marked the clinic's first anniversary. The Medical School faculty members submitted letters of resignation from the board but indicated their willingness to be available for consultation. The board chair decided to make them members of a technical advisory committee, along with a lawyer, a representative of the county Health Department, and faculty members fom the School of Nursing, the School of Pharmacy, and the School of Social Work.

Case Study Discussion Questions

1. What duration, scale, and scope were expected for the change? What would you predict the duration, scale, and scope will actually be?
2. In the reassessment and stabilization activities, how will these requirements be met: securing input from all participants, reflecting on the meaning of the change effort, assessing timing, assessing momentum, assessing readiness, securing acceptance and approval of the change, and deciding whether to end the change effort?
3. What might be modified, eliminated, or increased in the second and succeeding years of the clinic relative to problem or need identification and analysis, goals and objectives, design and structure, resource planning, implementation, monitoring and evaluation?
4. Plan activities for integration with other systems, routinization of procedures, and development of ongoing support.

SUMMARY OF PHASE IX

I. Definition

Reassessment is the critical review of the process and outcomes of all phases of the change process. *Stabilization* is the strengthening of supports and relationships to assure the maintenance of the change after the withdrawal of the change agent and other temporary participants. Reassessment and stabilization include reflection on the meaning of the change effort.

II. Information needed
   A. What duration, scale, and scope were expected for the change? What are the current options? What results are likely?
   B. What factors should be considered in the reassessment and stabilization phase?
      1. How can critical input be secured from all of the participants involved in the change?
      2. How can these participants be helped to reflect on the meaning of the change?
      3. Is reassessment taking place at a time when changes are well established yet not rigid?
      4. Is there sufficient momentum to carry the change forward?
      5. Is there readiness for termination of the change effort?
      6. Are acceptance and approval by interacting systems sufficient to overcome negative forces?
      7. Should this change effort be ended rather than stabilized?
   C. What are the key questions to ask in reassessment?
      1. To what extent has the change effort been responsive to the problem as initially defined and analyzed?
      2. To what extent has the change effort met its goals and objectives?
      3. How functional have the design and structure proven to be?
      4. What resources for continuity are available? Are they sufficient?
      5. Is the implementation creating unexpected consequences or negative side effects?
      6. Is the information generated by the monitoring system being used to keep the change effort moving and on course?
      7. Has the evaluation process demonstrated that the change is making the intended difference?
   D. What needs to be done to stabilize the change?
      1. Is the change effort being integrated with other systems?
      2. Are procedures becoming routine?
      3. Is an ongoing base of support being developed?
      4. Is change agent intervention being phased out?
   E. What are the change agent's roles in reassessment and stabilization?
      1. Is the change agent a critic and reviewer?
      2. Is the change agent a facilitator, enabler, and mediator?
      3. Is the change agent an advocate?
      4. Is the change agent an interpreter?
      5. Is the change agent bringing closure?
III. Tasks to be accomplished
   A. Involve all participants or their representatives in the reassessment process
   B. Respond to the seven basic reassessment questions
   C. Carry out any essential modifications suggested by the responses to the questions
   D. Strengthen integration with other systems, routinization of procedures, and the ongoing base of support

      E. Formally terminate the change process
IV. Products to be developed
    A plan for continuation without temporary participants and supports.

SUMMARY OF MAJOR POINTS

1. Reassessment activities critique the change process to see how well it has achieved its purposes.
2. The change agent and participants need to consider options for the duration of the change and its scale and scope.
3. Stabilization activities promote maintenance of the change and allow withdrawal of the change agent.
4. Stabilization affects change residue, thereby having an impact on future change efforts.
5. Reassessment and stabilization require input from all participants, reflection on the meaning of the change, appropriate timing, sufficient momentum, readiness for termination, acceptance and approval of the change by those whose support is crucial, and a decision to end rather than stabilize the change when appropriate.
6. Reassessment critiques the outcomes of each phase of the change effort in relation to its purpose.
7. Stabilization works toward integration with other systems, routinization of procedures, strengthening an ongoing base of support, and phasing out change agent intervention.
8. Change agent roles in this phase include critic and reviewer; facilitator, enabler, and mediator; advocate; and interpreter. The change agent also brings closure to the change episode.

DISCUSSION OR SELF-STUDY QUESTIONS

1. Give examples of some factors that might impede progress toward termination by the implementers and by the change agent.
2. If the reassessment reveals serious discrepancies between intent and performance, should work on stabilization proceed or not? Defend your position. Give examples.
3. What techniques might a change agent and implementers use to facilitate integration with subsystems and external systems?

SUGGESTED READINGS

Lippitt, R., Watson, J., & Westley, B. *The dynamics of planned change.* New York: Harcourt Brace Jovanovich, 1958.

Warren, R. L. *Social change and human purpose: Toward understanding and action.* Chicago: Rand McNally, 1977.

REFERENCES

Abels, P., & Murphy, M. J. *Administration in the human services.* Englewood Cliffs, N.J.: Prentice-Hall, 1981.

Accreditation Council for Services for Mentally Retarded and Other Developmentally Disabled Persons. *Standards for services for developmentally disabled individuals.* Washington, D.C.: Accreditation Council for Services for Mentally Retarded and Other Developmentally Disabled Persons, 1980.

Alexander, C. A. What does a representative represent? *Social Work,* 1976, *21,* 5–9.

Alexander, C. A., & McCann, C. The concept of representativeness. *Social Work,* 1956, *1,* 48–52.

Alinsky, S. *Rules for radicals.* New York: Vintage, 1972.

Altschuler, A. A. *Community control.* New York: Pegasus, 1970.

Anderson, W. H. *Financing modern government.* Boston: Houghton Mifflin, 1973.

Armentrout, E. H. (Ed.). *Techniques for needs assessment.* Atlanta, Ga.: The Research Group, 1976.

Arnstein, S. R. A ladder of citizen participation. *Journal of the American Institute of Planners,* 1969, *31,* 216–224.

Aronson, S. H., & Sherwood, C. C. Researcher versus practitioner: Problems in social action research. In C. H. Weiss (Ed.), *Evaluating action programs.* Boston: Allyn & Bacon, 1972.

Babbie, E. *The practice of social research* (3rd ed.). Belmont, Calif.: Wadsworth, 1983.

Banfield, E. Politics, planning and the public interest. In F. M. Cox, J. L. Erlich, J. Rothman, & J. Tropman (Eds.), *Strategies of community organization: A book of readings* (1st ed.). Itasca, Ill.: Peacock, 1970.

Banner, D. K., Doctors, S. I., & Gordon, A. C. *The politics of social program evaluation.* Cambridge, Mass.: Ballinger, 1975.

Bardach, E. *The implementation game: What happens after a bill becomes a law.* Cambridge, Mass.: MIT Press, 1979.

Barker, R. L., & Briggs, T. L. *Differential uses of social work manpower.* New York: National Association of Social Workers, 1968.

Blau, P. M. *Exchange and power in social life.* New York: Wiley, 1964.

Blau, P. M., & Scott, W. R. *Formal organizations.* San Francisco: Chandler, 1962.

Bloom, M., & Fischer, J. *Evaluating practice: Guidelines for the accountable professional.* Englewood Cliffs, N.J.: Prentice-Hall, 1982.

Boston College Graduate School of Social Work. *National social services definition project.* Springfield, Va.: National Technical Information Service, 1978.

Bowers, G. E., & Bowers, M. R. The elusive unit of service. *Human Service Monograph Series, Project SHARE,* 1976, *1.*

Brager, G., & Holloway, S. *Changing human service organizations: Politics and practice.* New York: Free Press, 1978.

Brager, G., & Specht, H. *Community organizing.* New York: Columbia University Press, 1973.

Braybrooke, D., & Lindblom, C. *A Strategy of Decision.* New York: The Free Press, 1963.

Brody, R., & Krailo, H. An approach to reviewing the effectiveness of programs. *Social Work,* 1978, 23, 226–236.

Bryan, W. L. Preventing burnout in the public interest community. *Grantsmanship Center News,* 1981, 9, 14–27, 66–75.

Buck, M. F., Ealy, C. M., Haworth, C. T., Stanley, R. C., McClellan, V. J., & Vinson, W. L. *Developing contract work statements.* Columbus, Ohio: The Ohio State University Research Foundation, 1973.

Burian, W. A., *Service management by objectives.* Kalamazoo, Mich.: Specialty Program in Alcohol and Drug Abuse, Western Michigan University, 1977.

Burkhead, J. The budget and democratic government. In F. J. Lyden & E. G. Miller (Eds.), *Planning, programming and budgeting* (2nd ed.). Chicago: Rand McNally, 1972.

Burns, T., & Stalker, G. M. *The management of innovations.* London: Tavistock, 1961.

Burton, L. E., Smith, H. H., & Nichols, A. W. *Public health and community medicine,* 3rd ed., Baltimore: Williams and Wilkins, 1980.

Campbell, D. T. Reforms as experiments. In C. H. Weiss (Ed.) *Evaluating action programs.* Boston: Allyn & Bacon, 1972.

Campbell, D. T., & Stanley, J. T. *Experimental and quasi-experimental designs for research.* Washington, D.C.: American Educational Research Association, 1963.

Chommie, P. W., & Hudson, J. Evaluation of outcome and process. *Social Work,* 1974, 19, 682–687.

Cobb, R. W., & Elder, C. D. *Participation in American politics.* Baltimore: Johns Hopkins University Press, 1972.

Cohen, N. E. (Ed.). *Social work and social prolems.* New York: National Association of Social Workers, 1964.

Coleman, J. *Equality of educational opportunity.* Washington, D.C.: U.S. Government Printing Office, 1966.

Coleman, J. S. *Community conflict.* New York: Free Press, 1957.

Compton, B. R., & Galaway, B. (Eds.). *Social work processes* (Rev. ed.). Homewood, Ill.: Dorsey Press, 1979.

Cotter, B. *Planning and implementing social service information systems.* Washington, D.C.: Project SHARE, U.S. Department of Health and Human Services, 1981.

Coulton, C. J. Quality assurance for social service programs: Lessons from health care. *Social Work,* 1982, 27, 397–402.

Cox, F. M. Alternative conceptions of community: Implications for community organization practice. In F. M. Cox, J. L. Erlich, J. Rothman, & J. Tropman (Eds.), *Strategies of community organization: A book of readings* (3rd ed.). Itasca, Ill.: Peacock, 1979.

Cox, F. M., Erlich, J. L., Rothman, J., & Tropman, J. (Eds.). *Strategies of community organization: A book of readings* (3rd ed.). Itasca, Ill.: Peacock, 1979.

Daley, J. M. *Participation in comprehensive health planning.* Unpublished doctoral dissertation, Tulane University, 1971.

Daley, J. M. Practice by objectives. In B. Ross & S. Khinduka (Eds.), *Social work in practice.* New York: National Association of Social Workers, 1976.

Daley, J. M. Setting objectives in the human service agency. In K. Dea (Ed.), *Perspectives for the future: Social work practice in the '80's.* New York: National Association of Social Workers, 1980.

Daley, J. M. *Creative grantsmanship: An approach to proposal development.* Unpublished manuscript, 1982. (Available from Arizona State University, School of Social Work Tempe, AZ 85287.)

Daley, J. M., & Kettner, P. M. Social services and income maintenance. In A. K. Karnig & J. S. Hall (Eds.), *The impact of the new federalism on Arizona.* Tempe, AZ: Arizona State University, 1982.

Daley, J. M., & Kettner, P. M. Social services and income maintenance. In A. K. Karnig & J. S. Hall (Eds.), *The impact of the new federalism on Arizona.* Tempe, Az.: Arizona State University, 1982.

Davidoff, P. Advocacy and pluralism in planning. *Journal of the American Institute of Planners,* 1965, 31, 321–333.

Davidoff, P., & Reiner, T. A choice theory of planning. In A. Faludi (Ed.), *A reader in planning theory.* New York: Pergamon Press, 1973.

Delbecq, A., Vandeven, A., & Gustafson, D. *Group techniques for program planning.* Glenview, Ill.: Scott, Foresman, 1975.

Devore, W., & Schlessinger, E. G. *Ethnic-sensitive social work practice*. St. Louis: C. V. Mosby, 1981.

Drucker, P. *The practice of management*. New York: Harper & Row, 1954.

Drucker, P. *Managing for results*. New York: Harper & Row, 1964.

Drucker, P. *Management: Tasks, responsibilities, practices*. New York: Harper & Row, 1974.

Edwards, G., & Sharkansky, I. *The policy predicament: Making and implementing policy*. San Francisco: W. H. Freeman, 1978.

Enthoven, A., & Smith, K. *How much is enough: Shaping the defense program, 1961–69*. New York: Harper & Row, 1971.

Epstein, I., & Tripodi, T. *Research techniques for program planning, monitoring, and evaluation*. New York: Columbia University Press, 1977.

Etzioni, A. *Social problems*. Englewood Cliffs, N.J.: Prentice-Hall, 1976.

Federal Electric Corporation. *A programmed introduction to PERT*. New York: Wiley, 1963.

Filley, A. C., House, R. J., & Kerr, S. *Managerial process and organizational behavior*. Glenview, Ill.: Scott, Foresman, 1976.

Fischer, J. Is casework effective? A review. *Social Work*, 1973, *18*, 5–20.

Fisher, R. *International conflict for beginners*. New York: Harper & Row, 1969.

Fisher, R., & Ury, W. *Getting to yes: Negotiating agreement without giving in*. Boston: Houghton Mifflin, 1981.

Freeman, H., & Sherwood, C. *Social research and social policy*. Englewood Cliffs, N.J.: Prentice-Hall, 1970.

Freire, P. *Pedagogy of the oppressed*. New York: Herder & Herder, 1972.

Friedmann, J. *Retracking America, a theory of transactive planning*. Garden City, N.Y.: Doubleday/Anchor, 1973.

Gamson, W. A. *A strategy of social protest*. Homewood, Ill.: Dorsey Press, 1975.

Gates, B. L. *Social program administration: The implementation of social policy*. Englewood Cliffs, N.J.: Prentice-Hall, 1980.

George, C. S., Jr. *The history of management thought*. Englewood Cliffs, N.J.: Prentice-Hall, 1968.

Gil, D. G. *Unravelling social policy*. Cambridge, Mass.: Schenkman, 1973.

Gilbert, N., & Specht, H. *Dimensions of social welfare policy*. Englewood Cliffs, N.J.: Prentice-Hall, 1974.

Gillespie, D., & Marten, S. Assessing service accessibility. *Administration in Social Work*, 1978, *2*, 183–197.

Giordano, P. C. The client's perspective in agency evaluation. *Social Work*, 1977, *22*, 34–39.

Goodman, R. *After the planners*. New York: Simon & Schuster, 1971.

Grosser, C. F. *New directions in community organization*. New York: Praeger, 1976.

Gruber, M. L. (Ed.). *Management systems in the human services*. Philadelphia: Temple University Press, 1981.

Hall, M. *Developing skills in proposal writing* (2nd ed.). Portland, Ore.: Continuing Education Publications, 1977.

Hamilton, G. *Theory and practice of social case work*. New York: Columbia University Press, 1940.

Hasenfeld, Y. *Human service organizations*. Englewood Cliffs, N.J.: Prentice-Hall, 1983.

Hickey, A. Inequality and service access: The utilization of medical services. *Journal of Social Service Research*, 1979, *2*, 267–283.

Huenefeld, J. *The community activist's handbook*. Boston: Beacon, 1970.

Illich, I. *Celebration of awareness: A call for institutional revolution*. Garden City, N.Y.: Doubleday, 1970.

Joint Commission on Mental Illness and Health. *Action for mental health*. New York: Basic Books, 1961.

Jones, J. *Bad blood: The Tuskegee syphilis experiment*. New York: Free Press, 1981.

Kadushin, A. *Child welfare services*. New York: Macmillan, 1974.

Kahn, A. J. *Theory and practice of social planning*. New York: Russell Sage Foundation, 1969.

Kahn, S. *How people get power*. New York: McGraw-Hill, 1970.

Kahn, S. *Organizing*. New York: McGraw-Hill, 1982.

Kane, R. S. Look to the record. *Social Work*, 1974, *19*, 412–419.

Kettner, P. M. Developing a practice co-planning model. *Public Welfare*, 1973, *31*, 32–35.

Kettner, P. M. A framework for comparing practice models. *Social Service Review*, 1975, *49*, 629–642.

King, W. R., & Clelland, D. I. The design of management information systems: An information analysis approach. In M. L. Gruber (Ed.), *Management systems in the human services.* Philadelphia: Temple University Press, 1981.

Kiresuk, T. J., & Garwick, G. Basic goal attainment. In B. R. Compton & B. Galaway (Eds.), *Social work processes* (Rev. ed.). Homewood, Ill.: Dorsey Press, 1979.

Kiritz, N. J. *Program planning and proposal writing* (expanded version). Los Angeles: The Grantsmanship Center, n.d.

Klein, A. F. *Social work through group process.* Albany, N.Y.: School of Social Welfare, State University of New York, 1970.

Kramer, R. M., & Specht, H. (Eds.). *Readings in community organization practice* (2nd ed.). Englewood Cliffs, N.J.: Prentice-Hall, 1975.

Kramer, R. M., & Specht, H. (Eds.). *Readings in community organization practice* (3rd ed.). Englewood Cliffs, N.J.: Prentice-Hall, 1983.

Kreitner, R. *Management* (2nd ed.). Boston: Houghton Mifflin, 1983.

Kurzig, C. M. *Foundation fundamentals: A guide for grantseekers.* New York: The Foundation Center, 1980.

Lauffer, A. *Getting the resources you need.* Beverly Hills, Calif.: Sage, 1982.

Levine, S., & White, P. E. Exchange as a conceptual framework for the study of interorganizational relationships. In H. A. Schatz (Ed.), *Social work administration: A resource book.* New York: Council on Social Work Education, 1970.

Levy, C. Ideological pathways to policy and practice. *Administration in social work,* 1983, *7,* 51–60.

Lewin, K. Frontiers in group dynamics. *Human Relations,* 1947, *1,* 5–41.

Lewin, K. *Field theory in social science.* New York: Harper & Row, 1951.

Lewis, J. A., & Lewis, M. D. *Management of human service programs.* Monterey, Calif.: Brooks/Cole, 1983.

Lindblom, C. E. The science of muddling through. In F. M. Cox, J. L. Erlich, J. Rothman, & J. Tropman (Eds.), *Strategies of community organization: A book of readings* (1st ed.). Itasca, Ill.: Peacock, 1970.

Lippitt, R., Watson, J., & Westley, B. *The dynamics of planned change.* New York: Harcourt Brace Jovanovich, 1958.

Lloyd, G. A., & Daley, J. M. Community control of health and welfare programs. In *The social welfare forum.* (Official proceedings for the 98th annual National Conference on Social Welfare, May, 1971.) New York: Columbia University Press, 1971.

Lohmann, R. A. Financial management and social administration. In F. D. Perlmutter & S. Slavin (Eds.), *Leadership in social administration.* Philadelphia: Temple University Press, 1980.

Lourie, N. V. Poverty. In N. E. Cohen (Ed.), *Social work and social problems.* New York: National Association of Social Workers, 1964.

Lowi, T. J. *The politics of disorder.* New York: Norton, 1971.

Lyden, F. J., & Miller, E. G. (Eds.). *Planning, programming and budgeting* (2nd ed.). Chicago: Rand McNally, 1972.

MacMahon, B., & Pugh, T. *Epidemiology: Principles and methods.* Boston: Little, Brown & Co., 1970.

Mager, R. F. *Preparing instructional objectives.* Belmont, Calif.: Fearon, 1962.

Mager, R. F., & Pipe, P. *Analyzing performance problems: Or, you really oughta wanna.* Belmont, Calif.: Fearon, 1970.

Majone, G., & Wildavsky, A. Implementation as evolution. In J. L. Pressman & A. Wildavsky (Eds.), *Implementation* (2nd ed.). Berkeley: University of California Press, 1979.

Mali, P. *Managing by objectives.* New York: Wiley, 1972.

Marris, P., & Rein, M. *Dilemmas of social reform* (2nd ed.). Chicago: Aldine-Atherton, 1973.

Maslow, A. H. A theory of motivation. *Psychological Review,* 1943, *50,* 370–396.

Matthies, L. H., & Waalkes, A. K. *Essentials of project management.* Colorado Springs, Colo.: Systemation, Inc., 1974.

Mayer, R., Moroney, R., & Morris, R. *Centrally planned change.* Urbana: University of Illinois Press, 1974.

McLaughlin, M. Implementation as mutual adaptation. In W. Williams & R. Elmore (Eds.), *Social program implementation*. New York: Academic Press, 1976.

Meenaghan, T., & Washington, R. *Social policy and social welfare: Structure and applications*. New York: Free Press, 1980.

Meier, E. G. Child neglect. In N. E. Cohen (Ed.), *Social work and social problems*. New York: National Association of Social Workers, 1964.

Meld, M. B. The politics of evaluation of social programs. *Social Work*, 1974, *19*, 448–455.

Miles, R. E. *Theories of management: Implications for organizational behavior and development*. New York: McGraw-Hill, 1975.

Millar, A., Hatry, H., & Koss, M. *Monitoring the outcomes of social services*. Vol. 1, *Preliminary suggestions*. Washington, D.C.: The Urban Institute, 1977. (a)

Millar, A., Hatry, H., & Koss, M. *Monitoring the outcomes of social services*. Vol. 2, *A review of past research and test activities*. Washington, D.C.: The Urban Institute, 1977. (b)

Millar, R., & Millar, A. (Eds.). *Developing client outcome monitoring systems*. Washington, D.C.: The Urban Institute, 1981.

Miller, D. *Handbook of research design and social measurement*. New York: David McKay, 1977.

Miringoff, M. L. *Management in human service organizations*. New York: Macmillan, 1980.

Moe, E. O. Consulting with a community system: A case study. In R. L. Warren (Ed.), *Perspectives on the American community*. Chicago: Rand McNally, 1966.

Montero, D., & Levine, G. (Eds.). *Journal of social issues*, 1977, *33*, No. 4.

Moroney, R. M. *The planning process: Approaches, concepts and definitions*. Unpublished manuscript, 1976. (Available from Arizona State University, School of Social Work, Tempe, AZ 85287.)

Moroney, R. M. Needs assessment for human services. In W. F. Anderson, B. J. Frieden, & M. Murphy (Eds.), *Managing human services*. Washington, D.C.: International City Managers Association, 1977.

Moroney, R. M., & Grubb, C. T. Research and evaluation: Contributions to social work practice. In N. Gilbert & H. Specht (Eds.), *Handbook of the social services*. Englewood Cliffs, N.J.: Prentice-Hall, 1981.

Morris, J. A., & Ozawa, M. N. Benefit-cost analysis and the social service agency. In M. L. Gruber (Ed.), *Management systems in the human services*. Philadelphia: Temple University Press, 1981.

Morrisey, G. L. *Management by objectives and results*. Reading, Mass.: Addison-Wesley, 1970.

Morse, J. J., & Lorsch, J. W. Beyond theory Y. *Harvard Business Review*, 1970, *48*, 61–68.

Mosher, F. C. *Democracy and the public service*. New York: Oxford University Press, 1968.

Mott, B. J. *Anatomy of a coordinating council*. Pittsburgh: University of Pittsburgh Press, 1968.

Nader, R., & Ross, D. *Action for a change*. New York: Grossman, 1971.

National Association of Social Workers. *Compilation of public social policy statements*. New York: Author, 1983.

National Commission on Excellence in Education. *A nation at risk: The imperative for educational reform*. Washington, D.C.: U.S. Government Printing Office, 1983.

Newman, E., & Turem, J. The crisis of accountability. *Social Work*, 1974, *15*, 5–17.

Northwood, L. K. Deterioration of the inner city. In N. E. Cohen (Ed.), *Social work and social problems*. New York: National Association of Social Workers, 1964.

Office of Economic Opportunity. *New Jersey graduated work incentive experiment*. Washington, D.C.: U.S. Government Printing Office, 1970.

Oppenheimer, M., & Lakey, G. *A manual for direct action*. Chicago: Quadrangle, 1964.

Parloff, M. B. *Psychotherapy and research: An anaclytic depression*. Unpublished manuscript, 1980. (Available from National Institute of Mental Health, 5600 Fishers Lane, Rockville, MD 20857.)

Patti, R. J. *Social welfare administration*. Englewood Cliffs, N.J.: Prentice-Hall, 1983.

Perkins, D. N. T. Evaluating social interventions: A conceptual schema. In R. M. Kramer & H. Specht (Eds.), *Readings in community organization practice* (3rd ed.). Englewood Cliffs, N.J.: Prentice-Hall, 1983.

Perlman, R., & Gurin, A. *Community organization and social planning*. New York: Wiley, 1972.

Pilisuk, M., & Pilisuk, P. *How we lost the war on poverty.* New Brunswick, N.J.: Transaction Books, 1973.

Pincus, A., & Minahan, A. *Social work practice: Model and method.* Itasca, Ill.: Peacock, 1973.

Pressman, J. L., & Wildavsky, A. (Eds.). *Implementation* (2nd ed.). Berkeley: University of California Press, 1979.

Project SHARE. *The Project SHARE collection, 1976-79.* Rockville, Md.: Author, n.d.

Pyhrr, P. A. Zero-base budgeting. *Harvard Business Review,* 1970, *48,* 111-121.

Raia, A. P. *Managing by objectives.* Glenview, Ill.: Scott, Foresman, 1974.

Reddin, W. J. *Effective management by objectives: The 3-D method of MBO.* New York: McGraw-Hill, 1971.

Reid, W. J. Target problems, time limits, task structure. *Journal of Education for Social Work,* 1972, *8,* 58-68.

Reid, W. J. Developments in the use of organized data. *Social Work,* 1974, *19,* 585-593.

Reid, W. J., & Hanrahan, P. Recent evaluations of social work: Grounds for optimism. *Social Work,* 1982, *27,* 328-340.

Rein, M. *Social policy: Issues of choice and change.* New York: Random House, 1970.

Rein, M., & Peattie, L. Knowledge for policy. *Social Service Review,* 1981, *55,* 525-543.

Resnick, H., & Patti, R. J. (Eds.). *Change from within.* Philadelphia: Temple University Press, 1980.

Rivlin, A. *Systematic thinking for social action.* Washington, D.C.: The Brookings Institute, 1971.

Robbins, S. P. *The administrative process.* Englewood Cliffs, N.J.: Prentice-Hall, 1980.

Rosenberg, M. L., & Brody, R. *Systems serving people: A breakthrough in service delivery.* Cleveland, Ohio: School of Applied Social Sciences, Case Western Reserve University, 1974. (a)

Rosenberg, M. L., & Brody, R. The threat or challenge of accountability. *Social Work,* 1974, *19,* 344-350. (b)

Rossi, P. H., Freeman, H. E., & Wright, S. R. *Evaluation: A systematic approach.* Beverly Hills, Calif.: Sage, 1979.

Rothman, J. *Planning and organizing for social change.* New York: Columbia University Press, 1974.

Rothman, J. Three models of community organization practice, their mixing and phasing. In F. M. Cox, J. L. Erlich, J. Rothman, & J. Tropman (Eds.), *Strategies of community organization* (3rd ed.). Itasca, Ill.: Peacock, 1979.

Rothman, J., Erlich, J. L., & Teresa, J. G. *Promoting innovation and change in organizations and communities.* New York: Wiley, 1976.

Rutledge, P. J. Can local government afford not to pay the price? *Public Management,* 1975, *57,* 3-17.

Skidmore, R. *Social work administration.* Englewood Cliffs, N.J.: Prentice-Hall, 1983.

Slavin, S. (Ed.). *Social administration: The management of the social services.* New York: Haworth Press, 1978.

Stein, H., & Sarnoff, I. Model for analyzing social problems. In N. E. Cohen (Ed.), *Social work and social problems.* New York: National Association of Social Workers, 1964.

Suchman, E. A. *Evaluative research.* New York: Russell Sage Foundation, 1967.

Suchman, E. A. Action for what? A critique of evaluative research. In C. H. Weiss (Ed.), *Evaluating action programs.* Boston: Allyn & Bacon, 1972.

Tenbrunsel, T. W. *The fund raising resource manual.* Englewood Cliffs, N.J.: Prentice-Hall, 1982.

Tripodi, T. *Evaluative research for social workers.* Englewood Cliffs, N.J.: Prentice-Hall, 1983.

Tripodi, T., Fellin, P., & Epstein, I. *Differential social program evaluation.* Itasca, Ill.: Peacock, 1978.

Tropman, J. E., Johnson, J. R., & Tropman, E. J. *The essentials of committee management.* Chicago: Nelson-Hall, 1979.

Tropp, E. Expectation, performance and accountability. *Social Work,* 1974, *19,* 139-148.

Turem, J. S., & Born, C. E. Doing more with less. *Social Work,* 1983, *28,* 206-210.

Turnbull, A. B., III. *Government budgeting and PPBS: A programmed introduction.* Reading, Mass.: Addison-Wesley, 1970.

United Way of America. *UWASIS II: A taxonomy of social goals and human services programs.* Alexandria, Va.: Author, 1976.

Voth, D. E. Problems in evaluating community development. *Journal of the Community Development Society,* 1975, *11,* 147-162.

Wallace, W. *The logic of science in sociology.* Chicago: Aldine-Atherton, 1971.

Warheit, G. J., Bell, R. A., & Schwab, J. J. *Planning for change: Needs assessment approaches.* Washington, D.C.: National Institute of Mental Health, 1977.

Warner, M. B. Minorities and human rights. In W. F. Anderson, B. J. Frieden, & M. J. Murphy (Eds.), *Managing human services.* Washington, D.C.: International City Managers Association, 1977.

Warren, R. L. (Ed.). *Perspectives on the American community.* Chicago: Rand McNally, 1966.

Warren, R. L. The Model Cities program: An assessment. In *The social welfare forum* (Official proceedings for the 98th annual National Conference on Social Welfare, May, 1971). New York: Columbia University Press, 1971. (a)

Warren, R. L. *Truth, love, and social change.* Chicago: Rand McNally, 1971. (b)

Warren, R. L. *New perspectives on the American community.* Chicago: Rand McNally, 1977. (a)

Warren, R. L. *Social change and human purpose: Toward understanding and action.* Chicago: Rand McNally, 1977. (b)

Warren, R. L. *The community in America* (3rd ed.). Chicago: Rand McNally, 1978.

Warren, R. L., Rose, S. M., & Bergunder, A. F. *The structure of urban reform.* Lexington, Mass.: Lexington Books, 1974.

Wasserman, H. Early careers of professional social workers in a public child welfare agency. *Social Work,* 1970, *15*, 93–101.

Webb, E. J., Campbell, D. T., Schwartz, R. D., Sechrest, L., & Grove, J. B. *Nonreactive measures in the social sciences* (2nd ed.). Boston: Houghton Mifflin, 1981.

Weiner, M. E. *Human services management: Analysis and application.* Homewood, Ill.: Dorsey Press, 1982.

Weiss, C. H. Evaluating educational and social action programs: A treeful of owls. In C. H. Weiss (Ed.), *Evaluating action programs.* Boston: Allyn & Bacon, 1972. (a)

Weiss, C. H. *Evaluation research.* Englewood Cliffs, N.J.: Prentice-Hall, 1972. (b)

Weiss, C. H. Utilization of evaluation. In C. H. Weiss (Ed.), *Evaluating action programs.* Boston: Allyn & Bacon, 1972. (c)

Weiss, C. H. Alternative models of program evaluation. *Social Work,* 1974, *19*, 675–681.

Weissman, H. H. *Community councils and community control.* Pittsburgh: University of Pittsburgh Press, 1970.

Whittington, C. Organizational research and social work. In S. Slavin (Ed.), *Social administration: The management of the social services.* New York: Haworth Press, 1978.

Wholey, J. S., Scanlon, J. W., Duffy, H. G., Fukumoto, J. S., & Vogt, L. M. *Federal evaluation policy.* Washington, D.C.: The Urban Institute, 1970.

Williams, W. Implementation analysis and assessmant. In W. Williams & R. Elmore (Eds.), *Social program implementation.* New York: Academic Press, 1976.

Williams, W. *The implementation perspective: A guide for managing social service delivery programs.* Berkeley: University of California Press, 1980.

Williams, W., & Elmore, R. (Eds.). *Social program implementation.* New York: Academic Press, 1976.

Wrong, D. *Max Weber.* Englewood Cliffs, N.J.: Prentice-Hall, 1970.

Zweig, F., & Morris, R. The social planning design guide: Process and proposal. *Social Work,* 1966, *11*, 13–21.

AUTHOR INDEX

SUBJECT INDEX